AFRICAN URBAN EXPERIENCES IN COLONIAL ZIMBABWE

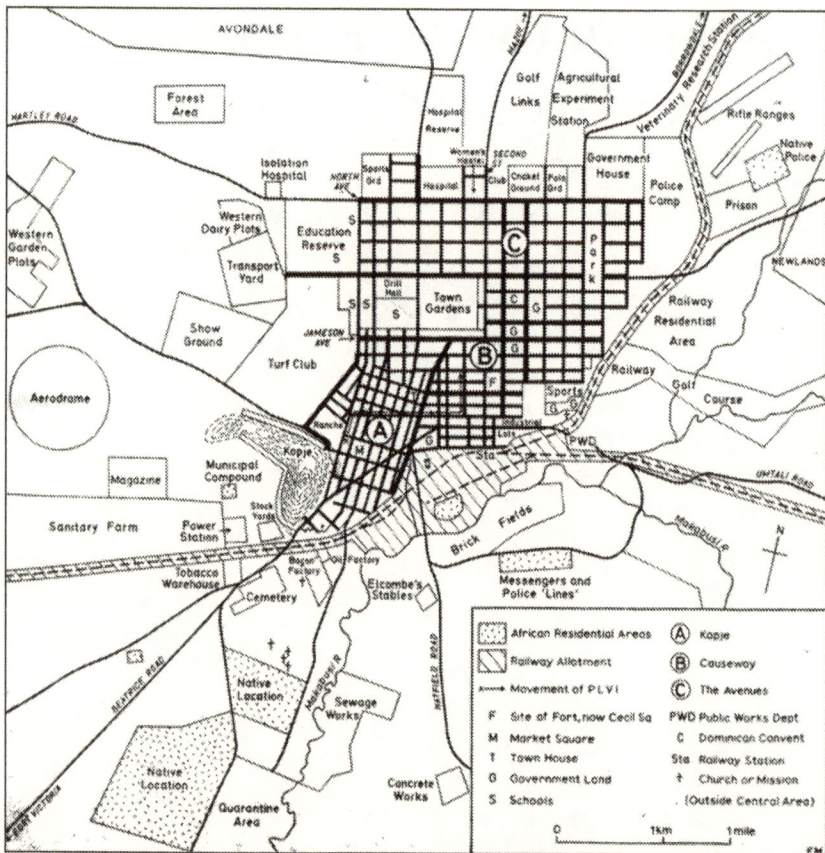

Map of Salisbury, c.1930

Source: A. J. Christopher, 'Early settlement and the cadastral framework', in G. Kay, and M. Smout (eds.), Salisbury (London, Hodder and Stoughton, 1977), 15.

AFRICAN URBAN EXPERIENCES IN COLONIAL ZIMBABWE

A Social History of Harare before 1925

TSUNEO YOSHIKUNI

Weaver Press
P O Box A1922
Avondale
Harare
Zimbabwe
2007

Layout and typesetting by Frances Marks
Cover design: Baynham Goredema
Cover photograph: National Archives of Zimbabwe
Printed and bound in Zimbabwe by Sable Press

ISBN-10 1-77922-054-5
ISBN-13 978-1-77922-054-7

Contents

List of Figures   *vi*
Preface   *1*

PART ONE
SEGREGATIONIST LANDSCAPES & AFRICAN SETTLEMENTS

1
The rise of bourgeois Salisbury & the state control of African housing: 9
The origins of the location, 1892-1908

2
'We, the "People in Location"':   38
Municipal ghetto & community action, 1907-1923

3
Straddling town & countryside: 66
The rise of black suburbia

PART TWO
THE EMERGENCE OF MIGRANT WORKERS AS A 'CLASS'

4
Migrants and labour protest: 99
A strike movement after World War I

5
Migrant workers' worlds: 122
The birth of mutual aid associations after World War I

Figures   142

List of Figures

1   European population by birthplace, Salisbury, 1897, 1911   142
2   Plan of Salisbury location, 1940   143
3   Ratio of location population to total African population, Salisbury,   144
    1904-1940
4   Employer-rented housing units in Salisbury location, June 1930   145
5   African population pyramids, Salisbury, 1911, 1969   146
6   Ethnic/regional composition of Africans, Salisbury, 1897, 1911   147
7   Prosecutions under the Kaffir Beer Ordinance, Salisbury and   148
    Bulawayo, 1912-36
8   Annual profits of canteen, Salisbury location, 1913-30   149
9   Men, women and children in Salisbury location, 1914-47   150
10 Sketch of Salisbury location, by superintendent, 1920   151
11 Ethnic/regional composition of Africans, Salisbury and Bulawayo, 1921   152
12 Population in Salisbury location, June 1930   153
13 Major private locations outside Salisbury commonage, 1914-29   154
14 Rental structure of Salisbury location, 1930   155
15 African industrial protest (and criminal cases of 'refusing to obey'),   156
    November 1918 to December 1921
16 African Christians by ethnicity, Salisbury, 1911   158
17 Salisbury population by race, 1897-1969   159
18 African population by nationality, Salisbury, 1897-69   160
19 African employees by occupation, Salisbury, 1904, 1911   161
20 African employees by industrial sector, Salisbury and its suburbs, 1936-69 162

Salisbury, as viewed from Kopje

Around 1895/6 – Early Salisbury was made of two townlets, the Kopje and
the Causeway. The substantial building in the right is Market Hall
(Chinhoyi St, between Bank St and Bute St.)

1910 – The Kopje and the Causeway began to be linked, as the Manica
(Robert Mugabe) Road area developed.

The 1930s – The Salisbury township was now evenly and rather densely occupied,
though still having a few vacant stands.

Source: National Archives of Zimbabwe, Harare, Photographic Collection

Preface

At the centre of Zimbabwe's modern history lies the question of what ensued after the 'encounter' between African pre-colonial societies and colonial capitalism, and how African people, traditionally agriculturalists in their way of life and culture, were changed and changed themselves in that process. This great transformation can be explored in many ways, but the present study seeks to do so by examining one particular African experience, or, to be more precise, one particular set of African experiences, which took place in the country's capital town, Salisbury (now Harare), up to the middle of the 1920s.

This book originates from my doctoral thesis, 'Black Migrants in a White City: A Social History of African Harare, 1890-1925', presented to the History Department of the University of Zimbabwe, in 1989. Despite the admirable development of Zimbabwean historiography since the late 1980s, no similar study has appeared on the early history of Zimbabwe's first African township. I offer this book in the hope that it will be more accessible to a wider audience than my thesis, and that it will stimulate further research.

The old, historic nomenclature of place names is retained throughout the study, though this rule is occasionally bent. Although technically a British colony for the greater part of the 20th century, I refer to Rhodesia (or Southern Rhodesia) as a country and a nation, prefiguring its emergence as the nation of Zimbabwe in 1980.

This book is a social history of one of the oldest parts of Zimbabwe's capital city. The city is now called Harare; but before 1982, that name – and 'Salisbury municipal location' before World War II – adorned the old township, which is now called Mbare. When and how did this township come into being? Chapter 1 investigates this question. The conventional account is that the location was first introduced in Salisbury around 1900; the motive force behind it were the sanitation crises that threatened the early town, or a segregationist inclination among the European citizens. The opening of the location resulted in a massive removal of urban Africans from the town centre. It will be shown, however, that the location, together with its attendant residential restrictions for Africans, was started as early as 1892, even before the formal proclamation of Rhodesia as a British crown colony, when Salisbury was but a rough frontier settlement. It was re-established in 1907-08, as the colony and Salisbury emerged from a series of crises beginning in the late 1890s. In 1892 the idea of establishing a segregated location for urban Africans was imported from Cape Colony in what is now South Africa, on the model developed in the mining boom town of Kimberley. By 1907-08 its institutionalisation was consequential upon a movement of settler citizens arising over such 'urban problems' as African 'free' residents in town, the so-called Black Peril, and the urban decay of the Kopje area – rather than upon the threat of epidemics, or a formal policy of territorial segregation. The underlying logic of state intervention into African housing common in both 1892 and 1907-08 was to eliminate African free residence from the town, so making it easier, in combination with the labour contract (town pass) system, to identify 'delinquent servants' and 'loafers'. Although there were specific, targeted relocations of Africans to the new location, no massive removals of Africans occurred at the time: the location at its start was a small housing estate, which was to develop only gradually. Whatever the racialist discourse insisted about the necessity of separating whites from Africans, a reality of the urban political economy hardly budged: the major form of African housing in the early years was not public housing in the location, but the living-in system in which workers were accommodated in the so-called white town, in the servant's quarters or compounds of white employers.

Chapter 2 traces this gradual development of the municipal location after 1907, both as a colonial institution and as an African settlement. It deals with the events that marked the formative years of the location, such as tougher housing restrictions in town, and the demolition of 'private locations' on the commonage; the establishment of a church reserve next to the location (1909); the employment of a European full-time superintendent (1913), coupled with dispensing with African headman; and the introduction of the so-called Durban system, a municipal monopoly of African beer, which provided the local authority with a key financial source for its otherwise costly African administration (1913-20). The growing amount of public housing not only curtailed Africans' already limited freedoms, but also helped collectivise African grievances over living issues, as it concentrated more and more people in one place. This made the location a focal site of African urban social movements. Such social movements reached a peak in the years immediately after World War I, including a storm of protest by women against the local authority's usurping of the production and sale of African beer. Initially, before the war, people's protests frequently took the form of staying away from the location to settle outside the town. In the post-war years, however, the protest was much more location-based, with mobilisation occurring among the people living in the location, and over issues directly relevant to the life of the location. This was a clear sign of the birth of an African urban *community* in the official housing estate.

Chapter 3 highlights the urban periphery. Stricter regulations and controls in the town gave a great impetus to the exodus of town-based Africans to peri-urban farms, where they stayed as tenants and created their 'own' settlements. The longevity of this strategy and of these settlements were such that they merit the appellation 'suburbs'. These African suburbs were to feature in Salisbury's landscape up to around 1950. We will examine their localities, magnitude and nature, and the responses of the authorities such as the establishment in 1922 of the No. 2 location for married Africans. The life histories of a few prominent Salisbury residents are presented. Apart from a small group of beer-makers and the like, residents were typically mission-educated men who worked in town on the long-term basis, with their incomes often supplemented by their wives' involvement in market gardening. Notwithstanding their long association of wage labour and urban life, these families were often in the process of becoming 'progressive farmers', investing urban incomes into peasant production at rural homes. That the town's periphery was a focus of African accumulation gives us a clue to understanding the origins and logic of African 'modernist' politics in Mashonaland, such as the Rhodesia Native Association launched by suburban dwellers in Salisbury in 1919. The pattern of African settlements reveals the bipolar nature of the early African Salisbury, where the inner town (as represented by the municipal location) was typically inhabited by urbanites, proletarians, the marginal, and 'foreign men', whereas the outer suburbs tended to be populated by indigenous mission-educated, better-paid workers, rural accumulators, and their families.

If the first three chapters (Part 1) are primarily concerned with the creation and development of African urban settlements, and a minority of long-term African urban dwellers, the remaining two chapters (Part 2) address the growth of the social and cultural world of migrant workers, who constituted a vast majority of Salisbury's African population. They highlight the growing intensification – and the dramatic flowering immediately after World War I – of collective activities among black workers in Salisbury (and other urban centres). This social, cultural phenomenon reflected, so it will be argued, a change which historians have documented at the level of political economy across central Africa in which the migrant labour system, set in motion with the advent of colonialism, began to develop into a fully-fledged institution.

Chapter 4 details a national wave of African industrial protest after World War I, perhaps the first of its kind in the country's history. With the railway and municipal workers at the forefront, it was even reminiscent, though on a smaller scale, of the post-World War II labour militancy. Yet, strike behav-

3

iour displayed a number of features unique to the industrial relations under the migrant labour system. These features included a threat of going back home, a demand to be immediately discharged (i.e. released from labour contract obligations), attempts to make the leadership anonymous, and the militant strategy of going to gaol together.

Simultaneous with the wave of industrial action were the birth and proliferation of burial associations and dance societies, which are the subject of Chapter 5. Associations such as the Tete Burial Society No. 1, the Senna Burial Society, Chinyao, the Atonga Club, the Northern Rhodesia Burial Society were the ancestors, so to speak, of the 'tribal' clubs, or the burial and benefit societies which were big part of the life of the post-World War II Harare township. As an integral part of their continual comings and goings, migrant workers had created mutual-aid 'communities' in urban areas since the early days of colonialism. These communities, invariably consisting of brothers, uncles, compatriots, and friends, made the migrants' industrial lives safer, more pleasant, and more meaningful. The formalised post-war associations grew directly from this tradition, though much stimulated and influenced by the particular circumstances of the day, such as high prices, the Spanish influenza epidemic, and the aftermath of the experience of the colony's involvement in World War I.

Despite their apparent differences, the two post-war processes of industrial protest and mutual aid grew from the same root, i.e. a struggle to defend the integrity of the migrant workers' world. Indeed, they developed simultaneously in the post-war years, and dramatically converged in the case of the Tonga municipal workers in Salisbury; in August 1918 these workers staged a work stoppage and, a few weeks later, registered their Northern Rhodesia Burial Association with the government.

As Anderson and Rathbone have pointed out in *Africa's Urban Past*, with earlier African historiography having been primarily concerned with peasant societies and agrarian change, urban Africa was only 'discovered' by historians, especially those in South Africa, in the late 1970s, and this was closely associated with the rise of social history.[1] Setting out to do my research on Harare in 1983, I studied this intellectual trend carefully. Paying special attention to something social between economy and politics, the new urban history school seemed to provide a cynosure for going beyond the limited horizons of the 'political economy school' of the 1970s, whose analytical tools and methods (as to proletarianisation, labour compounds, class history, etc.) I found were frequently too rigid and reductionist to really grasp urban realities. The new social history school would redefine culture as a resource with which people interacted with their environment, a reorientation which I then considered, and still do, to be indispensable to writing people's history, or history 'from the bottom up'. The school's call for a holistic history was also impressive to me, as I was similarly concerned with how best to do justice to the complexities of the city (production vs consumption, work vs recreation, labour movement vs community action, family and social reproduction, etc.) and to present the city as a focal point of African social change.

For all this, however, I began to be concerned that the discovery of urban Africa might have been made at the expense of brushing aside rural Africa, so cherished as a research subject by earlier generations of historians. It appeared to me that with its grammar of history apparently constructed on the west European model of urbanisation/industrialisation (and modernisation), much of southern African urban historiography was marred by a tendency to examine the African town only in its urban/industrial context, so ignoring the interconnections between town and countryside. By interconnections I mean not only continuities, but also dichotomies.

As I said at the beginning, the Africans were 'traditionally agriculturalists in their way of life and culture'. The city did not emerge in this part of Africa for two millennia following the arrival of agriculture (perhaps with a few exceptions such as Great Zimbabwe several centuries before). Even after nearly half a century of the colonial rule, by which time a large number of people had experienced wage labour and city life, practically all Southern Rhodesian Africans discharged their tax obligation in rural areas: out of the total of 1,185,002 African taxpayers in the country in 1938, a mere 0.3%, (4,048) paid taxes on mines and in the towns.[2] Given these facts, and without going into a discussion on the nature and history of African precolonial/agrarian social formations, it is clear to me that it is impossible to try to understand the meanings of African urban experiences in the single dimension of urbanisation/industrialisation. This realisation must prompt us to ponder how the countryside penetrated, or perhaps enclosed, urban processes.[3] As a matter of fact, I had to constantly remind myself of this point in analyzing African urbanism. I hail from an East Asian country where urbanism has had its place from antiquity, to such an extent that it has now embraced the entire society. My mental frames of reference had to be prised open, to see the rural idioms behind the urban evidence in Harare. It may be wise and profitable for readers to do the same when reading the following pages.

TY
March 2006

Notes

[1] D. M. Anderson and R. Rathbone (eds), *Africa's Urban Past* (Oxford, 2000), 11.

[2] S.R., *Report of the Secretary for Native Affairs and Chief Native Commissioner for the Year 1938*, 2.

[3] The question of urban-rural continuum is discussed in T. Yoshikuni, 'Notes on the influence of town-country relations on African urban history, before 1957', in B. Raftopoulos and T. Yoshikuni (eds), *Sites of Struggle: Essays in Zimbabwe's Urban History* (Harare, 1999), 113-28; idem, 'Linking urban history with precolonial and rural history: From the Zimbabwean experience', *Azania*, 36-37 (2001-02), 157-71.

PART ONE

SEGREGATIONIST LANDSCAPES & AFRICAN SETTLEMENTS

1

The rise of bourgeois Salisbury & state control of African housing: the origins of the location, 1892-1908

In October 1907, the town council of Salisbury opened a new 'native location' outside the boundary of the township (the town proper). Shortly after this the central government, acting in concert, declared that beginning in May 1908, all Africans in Salisbury, except those already sleeping on employers' premises, must reside in the location. Thus, African 'free' residence in town became illegal. The dislocation and relocation of budding African urban communities followed. A segregated official ghetto, which was later to develop into the Harare African township, came into being.

This chapter investigates the origins of the Salisbury municipal location, and the housing restrictions which developed along with it. Key questions to be raised are: How or why did the whole issue of African urban 'living' (as against work) become highly problematic among the Europeans in Salisbury? How did the local authority come to intervene in the provision and control of African housing? What were the consequences of this public intervention on urban structure, as well as the life of urban Africans? These questions are of vital importance, because through them we go directly to the heart of the urban question in southern Africa: segregated public housing estates, compounds and servants' quarters, the machinery of controlling Africans, poor housing conditions, police raids, transport problems, neighbourhoods, community organisations, urban politics, etc.

The early location developed in two distinct phases. It first came into being in 1892, when Salisbury was just a frontier settlement of the British South Africa (BSA) Company, which was based in the then Cape Colony to the south. As Salisbury was built as the northern beachhead of the BSA Company in order to colonise the interior, the location, together with the urban 'pass' system, was imported from Kimberley, in an attempt to regulate the movement of African labourers. At this stage the whole affair was more or less temporal, or even ephemeral; thus the location was more permanently re-defined, and, indeed, re-established in 1907-08, by the local authority. The new location was built characteristically in reaction to some of the 'urban problems' generated in the process of Salisbury's transformation into a modern, bourgeois town.

The chapter starts with a section presenting an overall picture of Salisbury town and its society in the years after the South African War (1899-1902). This will serve as a backdrop for our discussion on the main theme of the chapter, as well as the remaining parts of the book which are more specifically concerned with the experiences of urban Africans. Narrowing focus, the second section will discuss the issues and circumstances which gave rise to a segregationist mood and impulse – such as European prostitution, the presence of African tenants in town, the decline of the Kopje area, and the citizens' movements against this decline – and the eventual opening of a new location in 1907-08. The following sections will take our inquiries further back into the past, to 1892, and investigate the origins and development of the location system in a more diachronic way.

It will be argued that although moments existed when sanitary concerns and/or racialist values (as manifested in the so-called Black Peril scare – mythologised fears in the white community of black male sexual assault) led to fervent upholding of the white city principle, in its early days Salisbury was never actually geographically divided on this basis. Contrary to what has been suggested by a number of urban segregation studies, the large majority of Africans were in reality accommodated and supervised on their employers' premises located throughout the town, with the public location housing only a small population. What the twentieth-century segregationist impulse did achieve was the banning of African free residence in the white city. Such banning ensured, in conjunction with the policy of requiring the Africans to carry labour-contract papers, a higher degree of control over urban Africans and the strengthening of the idea that Salisbury was a white city; Africans continued to live in town, albeit as dependents of their white employers.

Salisbury: Growth & tensions after the South African War

In 1908, eighteen years after its founding, the capital of Southern Rhodesia was still more like a hamlet than a town; in the derisive words of a contemporary, 'the most scattered little townlet in the world'.[1] Theoretically, it was very big: 'With a good pair of field glasses one may see the library, drill hall and other buildings from the town. They are right out in the veld, surrounded by weeds and rank foliage.'[2] Reflecting a high hope, on the part of the promoters of the trans-Limpopo colonisation, for the discovery of a legendary gold reef in Mashonaland, the Salisbury township was originally generously laid out for the occupation of no less than 25,000 inhabitants,[3] with an encircling commonage of more than 20,000 acres. However, no fabulous mines were found, and Salisbury was left undeveloped. In 1909 the town was inhabited by a mere two thousand settlers, and dotted with 420 houses, shops, and buildings.[4] Many of the building stands in the township, which the BSA Company and real estate developers had 'locked up' for speculative purposes, remained unoccupied. A retarded and bucolic settlement, indeed. Yet this belied the pivotal role which the town was beginning to play in the development of capitalism in the colony as a whole. By 1908 the economy was experiencing the first major expansive phase in its history, owing especially to the re-structuring of the gold-mining industry, the shift of government policy towards 'practical colonisation', the extension of roads and railways which linked the land-locked colony to world markets, and the commencement of land settlement and settler agriculture.[5] Salisbury, concentrating banks, mercantile houses, workshops, transport facilities, and postal and other administrative services, acted as a focal point for organising development works and production activities of the mines and farms in its hinterlands. The development of the primary industries in areas like Hartley, Gatooma, Mazoe, Lomagundi and Marandellas in turn stimulated business in the town.

By around 1908 the economic doldrums following the South African War were over. Salisbury's prosperity was so remarkable that the value of building work for the municipal year of 1910-11 hit a record figure of £260,536, 'a value not surpassed until 1927 and, allowing for inflation, probably not matched until the late 1930s'.[6] The booming economy rapidly absorbed both European immigrants and African migrants, with the result that the population had more than doubled between 1907 and 1911, with the European population reaching 3,479, the African 6,400, the Asian and Coloured 339.[7] Optimism was in the air. The Mayor was confident enough to declare in 1910: 'before long we shall find ourselves no longer citizens of a small town struggling to maintain efficient public services over a widely scattered area, but able, by means of our natural growth, to provide efficiently for all public requirement'.[8] In effect, it was during these years that Salisbury went though a 'municipal revolution', involving a wide range of civic improvements, perhaps the most outstanding of which was the introduction in 1913 of long-awaited piped water and electricity supplies.

One striking change in the town's landscape was the development of the south-eastern section, near the railway station, as a business centre. Stimulated by the mining and agricultural developments, 'some light industries, the repair of agricultural implements and mining machinery, harness-making, and maize-milling' were established there.[9] The town's leading stores and firms, formerly located in the Kopje area, moved to the same region, especially in the top of Manica Road.[10] It was obvious to everybody in Salisbury that trade and activity was shifting from the Market Square and Pioneer Street to the Railway Station and Manica Road.

Prior to this period, and notwithstanding its small population, the town was divided into two quarters: the Kopje ('little hill' in Afrikaans) in the west and the Causeway in the east. The division dated back to the very inception of the town, when, according to an observer writing in 1895:

> The great body of its non-official residents took up their abode on a portion known to fame as the Kopje, while the officials and those who catered to the wants of that important class, selected the Causeway ... . [The] two portions of what is theoretically one and the same town lie a good quarter of a mile apart and ... at the Kopje are the principal business establishments, while at the Causeway are the Government offices, official residences, the English and Roman Catholic Churches and the admirable and influential Salisbury Club.[11]

The Kopje was home to 'the storekeeper and artisan', whereas the Causeway became the base for 'the official and financial man'. This spatial division of the colonists both at work and at home entailed a bitter sectional competition for scarce urban facilities and services. As the same observer wrote: 'The two ends have been ever since playing the monotonous game of "pull devil, pull baker" to the infinite harm and loss of Salisbury city itself ... . Causeway and Kopje have become political terms in their little way, and the thing is so notorious that a Bulawayian orator is said to have recently adjured his fellow citizens not to be as Salisbury, a house perpetually divided against itself.'[12]

The same opposition was still found in 1908, when erection of a central post office was proposed jointly by the town council and the chamber of commerce. They insisted that it should be at a centrally located place, that is, a site not away from the Kopje, whereas the administration favoured a place on the eastern side.[13]

In retrospect, however, this was one of the final episodes of the old feud. The *fin de siecle* installation of a railway station on the Causeway side had decisively tipped the balance in favour of the east. By the first years of the 1910s a group of large enterprises, including the Standard Bank, the Meikles Store, the Bechuanaland Trading Association, the Government Post Office and the Magistrates' Court, flocked to the First Street and Manica Road intersection. In contrast to the tin shanties of the old Rhodesian type, many of the premises there were substantial two-storey buildings with elaborate frontages. They were monuments to the commencement of a modern, competitive business era.[14]

Two important points should be noted. First, the primordial anarchy among the rulers of Salisbury was coming to an end. It was apparently increasingly replaced by a closer co-operation between commerce, finance and government. Secondly, the strategy of capital investment was switching not only spatially from one area to another, but also temporally from short- to long-term. The town's key enterprises, having access to the benefits of an expanding urban infrastructure, began to commit themselves more to the future of the colony. To turn to residential patterns, change was less clear-cut, but we can find a trend parallel to these business developments. With the development of a common business centre came that of the first residential suburb. Wealthier residents, old and new, began to take up residence in the hitherto sparsely populated northern part of the township (later known as the Avenues). At that time the most prized residential sites were those nearest the town centre. So, the point of growth was the north-eastern section, the Greenwood area, which was almost contiguous to the government buildings and adjacent to the emerging business centre. Greenwood was becoming an exclusively middle- and upper-class suburb. The inhabitants there comprised both bureaucrats and private citizens (company managers, merchants, professionals, mine engineers, clerks, and others), and relatively large numbers of British nationals.[15]

Yet for all its conspicuousness, the making and ascendancy of a bourgeois Salisbury represented only part of the story. It should not be overlooked that around 1908, with the South African economy still in a depression, the northern colony attracted no less attention from workers, artisans, and jobless men in South Africa than from international financiers and investors. An ironical result was that a so-called 'Poor White' problem reached a critical level in these prosperous years. Since the number of unemployed whites had increased greatly, to quote a 1908 newspaper expose:

> ... a casual is now looked upon askance, and instead of the tolerant good-natured welcome to sit down and take a meal, he is usually met with frowns and told to clear. Along the railway these men are to be met with in numbers that would astonish the town dweller. Jumping aboard at out of the way sidings and dropping off before more populated centres are reached, they travel up and down the line, a pest and a nuisance. Others remain in towns, where they become a thorn in the side of the police, and a godsend to the "boys" as liquor procurers. Others, again, reside on the veld and develop into white kafirs, sinking to a lower degree of degradation than the native with whom he becomes an intimate.[16]

This tide of the unemployed ebbed towards 1910, but the inflow of relatively low-income workers and artisans dominated (especially, carpenters, bricklayers, and others associated with the building trade), while the middle-class arrivals were numerically insignificant.[17] Unlettered colonists arrived in such numbers that the 1911 national census recorded a rise from 1904 in the proportions of illiterate Europeans and uneducated children.[18] A considerable number of the new immigrants were non-British. The German/Austro-Hungarian, Polish and Russian immigrants typically entered the colony at the time of the South African War, and were followed by those from Macedonia, Greece and Italy. Their ranks swelled, and by 1911, thirteen per cent of Salisbury's white population had been born on the European continent (Figure 1).[19] Also revealing was a distorted sex ratio. Not least because of the notoriously primitive living conditions and high cost of living in the up-country colony, roughly one-third of married men who entered the country left behind their wives and children, usually in South Africa or Britain. Significantly, this tendency was more pronounced in 1911 than in 1904.[20] In a similar way, although the sex ratio of Salisbury's European population became more balanced in the long term, the trend was reversed in the post-depression years. In 1911 males in Salisbury outnumbered females by 2,297 to 1,182, a ratio of 19:10.[21] This was roughly equivalent to that of Johannesburg fifteen years before, when it was a rowdy mining camp.[22]

All in all, the situation in the late 1900s appears to have been quite complex. The rapid *embourgeoisement* of the dominant groups was compounded by the continued, and even growing, presence of a large 'floating population'. The settler community remained very much the world of male workers who migrated to secure a better chance in life in the northern colony. Only in the following decade, from the eve of World War I to the early 1920s, did European workers bring in their wives and children and strike deeper roots in the colony, a process accompanied, as in South Africa, by workers' collective struggle to secure better access to power and wealth.[23]

On this historical canvas we must now sketch in a picture of the African migrant workers. By this time the system of labour migration was rapidly developing in central Africa owing to the imposition of taxes, and processes of labour recruitment. African rural households were selective and discretionary in supplying labour to the capitalist sector. They sent, if necessary, only their junior and male members to the labour market. Thus, 95 per cent of Salisbury's 6,400 Africans in 1911 were males, of whom about 85 per cent were between 10 and 29 years of age, practically all of them being in employment.[24] About half of the Africans in Salisbury came from the northern and Portuguese regions. These long-distance migrants generally remained in town for twelve months or more. The rest were predominantly the Shona-speaking peoples who came from within the colony, usually taking up much shorter periods of service.[25]

Industry relied heavily on cheap, unskilled African labour, while using European labour only for skilled, managerial work. Broadly reflecting this structure of the labour process, the town's aggregate racial complexion was very dark. The African population was nearly twice as big as the European, one of the highest ratios in urban southern African. Demographically at least, then, Salisbury was more like a city of black peasants than a city of white settlers. It filled with the colonised, rather than the coloniser.

The peace of white Salisbury was not troubled yet by African urban riots and trade unions, but it was certainly disturbed by the large agglomerations of African rural migrants, whose culture was highly incongruous with that of the dominant groups, and whose behaviour patterns were not particularly amenable to the rhythm of the capitalist mode of production. The resulting dissonances and conflicts produced a wide range of racial problems, further accentuating the disorganised social order of Salisbury. At the workplace there were endless complaints, on the part of the European employers (with their increasing emphasis on efficiency and stabilisation) of the irregular or unexpected behaviour of African servants.[26] At the living place tensions also arose over issues and problems concerning African use of urban services and the environment. Many aspects of daily life (spatially located at sidewalks, streets, sanitary lanes, parks, shops, unoccupied tenements and vacant plots) became 'battlefields', giving rise to remarkably diverse institutions to regulate relations between the coloniser and colonised. Checking African 'passes' by the police,[27] a night curfew, banning of Africans using sidewalks,[28] rigorous traffic controls over 'native scorchers' (African cyclists)[29] and 'ricksha boys', and regulating a new 'etiquette of race relations' (removing the hat before any Europeans, taking off shoes at government offices, etc.) were but a few examples of this.

At the heart of this growing network of control institutions was the system of servants' quarters and compounds, under which African workers were confined to a relatively well-structured world built around the organisation of production. Domestic servants, for example, constituted more than one third of the Africans employed in the town.[30] The day's work for a typical 'house boy' would start at cock-crow with drawing water from a well and boiling it for the use of his employer. It would end only at night after having removed the remains of supper from the table and straightening the kitchen. The servant then retired to and slept in a 'kia' in the backyard. He received rations as well as accommodation from the boss. Insofar as this routine was repeated every day, the worker's 'urban interaction' was extremely marginal. He lived at his workplace under the employer's supervision.[31]

Residential hierarchy, the decline of the Kopje & citizen pressure for segregation in the 1900s

Salisbury's rapidly increasing and highly mobile workforce in the late 1900s was not evenly distributed. Large numbers of European workers made their ways to obsolescent tenements, boarding houses and hotels in the Kopje area, a few going outside the township and living 'in huts to avoid the high rents' in town.[32] Absorbing labour and losing capital, parts of the Kopje area showed signs of urban decay. Among such signs was the fact that its southern end, mainly along Pioneer Street, had become a red-light zone. Bespeaking the town's distorted social structure, there existed in 1909 nine brothels (eight of which were owned by the prostitutes themselves) containing twenty or thirty European females.[33]

African workers flocked to the Kopje area. Premises in the old business quarter were in many instances both the workplace and the sleeping place for a multitude of Africans. Congregations of Africans aroused anxiety among European residents, especially when the former were out in streets as anonymous consumers and pedestrians, coming to and from 'kaffir-truck shops', 'native eating houses', 'kias', the pass office, and the location, all of which were clustered in and near that locality.

Of all the interracial issues at the time nothing elicited more hostile European reaction than that of African workers renting rooms on their own account, which implied immobility and permanence, and thus an African stake in town. For European neighbours it even conjured up the image of anarchy and danger. African tenancy was most commonly found in the Kopje, where an old back room would be let at the monthly rent of 15s. or £1.[34] It started around 1904, when the depression caused so extensive a settler exodus that landlords came to accept African tenants.[35] Accommodation of this kind was perhaps irrelevant to ordinary migrant workers, but not all the town Africans were such labourers. From the earliest days there were a small number of town-based Africans in Salisbury. To such people 'vacant rooms' in town meant the possibility of separating 'life' from 'work' and creating a living space free from the scrutiny of their masters or a location inspector. The following is a 1907 police report on one of the African-rented premises:

> The premises comprise three rooms and are occupied by three families. Room No. 1 is occupied by a Native named Said and Badi his reputed wife. Room No. 2 is occupied by a Hottentot woman named Lena Jacobs a reputed prostitute. She states that the room ... is rented by a coloured man named Blackbird ... Room No. 3 is occupied by a coloured man named September, his wife (a Hottentot) and their two children. September is a driver in the employ of Mr. Jas. Lawson.[36]

This report and other evidence reveal that the African tenants consisted of drivers, policemen, and other workers with relatively high incomes. It also suggests that they were long-time urban dwellers, often of South African origin, living with their families, female partners, or friends.[37]

To take a town-wide view, then, it is clear that the growth of Salisbury was generating a hierarchy of urban space. The scale of residential prestige declined in a diagonal way, from the homogenous north-east, with its elegant, colonial-style cottages and bungalows, down towards the polyglot south-west, where a motley collection of 'houses of ill fame', boarding houses, Indian shops, a Jewish synagogue, a 'native location', and the dwellings and stores of 'pioneers' were to be found.

Such structuring of space in turn influenced the 'ideologies' of peoples living in particular localities. In the Kopje, European property-owners and old citizens were embittered over a decline of their neighbourhood, where property values were depressed, when appreciating in other places,[38] and where living conditions deteriorated – or so it was believed – when improving elsewhere. 'Unfortunately', grumbled one citizen in 1909, 'several of us have invested our little lot and built our homes here, and have not the means to migrate to Greenwood or Hillside, nor the wherewithal to purchase vehicles to carry us to and fro, as several of our more fortunate colleagues.'[39] With this kind of ambience went a belief that the norms and values of the south end were dangerously at variance with those of the 'respectable' Salisbury. One citizen witnessed a 'horrifying' case:

> Some time ago, I saw one of the women from Pioneer Street going down Manica Road in a rickshaw. Quite a dozen "boys" were at the time standing at the corner of Victoria Street, and as the woman passed she called out to them and waved her hand in salutation. Needless to say, there was a chorus of ribald laughter from the natives, and we can well imagine the evil effect on their minds.[40]

Residents reacted. Pressure mounted in the Kopje to curb 'deviant' behaviour and to stop 'noxious' facilities. They demanded a tougher control, or a wholesale removal, of brothels, 'kaffir-truck shops', African 'free' residents, and other what they considered social evils. It should be remembered that since the earliest days the commercial Kopje dominated the town council (which increasingly came under the control of local entrepreneurs rather than agents of international capital). They could still command substantial power and influence, and the area retained influential businessmen and high-status families. Moreover, it had symbolic and sentimental value for the colonists. Not surprisingly, the grievances and demands of Kopje citizens resonated easily with the contemporary public concern for civic improvements and came to the fore in local politics.

The ethos of the movement against prostitutes was well articulated by a Kopje homeowner and former Mayor, Edward Coxwell. A leading member of the town council, he addressed a meeting in 1909, which was reported as follows: 'outside his official position he had taken this matter up on personal grounds in as much as he was fighting for his home and its surroundings, a home which he acquired 15 years ago, and which was situated on a site which he considered was second to none in Salisbury. He built his home long before any of these women came to Pioneer Street... . Perhaps in the olden days there was not the same urgent necessity for their removal as was the case now that they had women and children in their midst'.[41] Earlier, in November 1907, the council had resolved to tackle this issue. The following year a joint committee was formed by the council and ratepayers, and a petition by 75 prominent citizens was sent to the central government, asking for total suppression of the trade.[42]

Thereafter, the police supervision of brothels was tightened – but not as much as citizens wished. The colonial administration was not particularly enthusiastic about taking drastic steps; the government, being alive to the industries' heavy reliance on single male workers, and the colony's urgent necessity of attracting settlers, held that the movement was too parochial. They viewed the commercialisation of sex as a 'necessary evil' and reminded the town council, in early 1909, of 'the nature of the population, which contains an excessive of unmarried males'. This reply, published in the press, invited stronger public indignation. The movement, now joined by clergymen, became something of a moral crusade concerning, it was claimed, the whole foundations of the British Empire, as well as the purification of Salisbury itself. The council and ratepayers appealed for the intervention of the High Commissioner, Lord Selborne, with whom they had an interview in November 1909; in the same month residents in Victoria Street successfully expelled a brothel-keeper through a petition to the council; the following year the Mayor brought the matter in person to the directors of the BSA Company in London, and in 1911 a further petition, signed by 259 citizens, was sent to them.[43]

One could continue this story, but the point is that after around 1907 middle-and upper-class residents became quite sensitive to, and belligerent about, problems concerning their immediate living environment. In their efforts to transform the town in accordance with their values and aspirations, they fully mobilised the powers of the local authority.

This was the same kind of process and dynamic that underlay, closer to our contemporary concerns, the growing impulse for relocation of African tenants: it developed around a 'neighbourhood issue' and occurred at almost the same time and in the same areas, and had a similar leadership.[44]

It was in early 1905 that the problem of Africans entering into the real estate market first drew attention from the town council. The location inspector, John Smith, reported: 'the huts in the Town Native Location are gradually becoming unoccupied. There are eleven huts now without tenants. This has been going on within the last two months and is due to the fact that the natives are renting houses within the township. Not only is this a loss of revenue to the Municipality but is also a source of danger to the township in many ways'.[45] Citizen action over this issue started in February 1906, when a group of Kopje residents lodged a petition with the council. The petitioners complained bitterly of 'the disgraceful nuisance' emanating from a stand in Pioneer Street, and of 'a continual stream of boys going to and fro, making the neighbourhood more like a native reserve'.[46] But the town was in the depths of a depression, and inactivity carried the day.

The situation changed in 1907. No sooner had the town council undertaken a new location scheme that year than a stream of citizens' letters reached them, exposing African town dwellers to official scrutiny. A Second Street resident evoked the sacrosanct white city principle, which, he said, he and his fellow settlers had taken for granted. His reaction was emotional and violent: 'I counted a dozen Kaffirs there on the 15th. The smell from the said Krall [sic] is now so bad that I cannot have my family in Town, and unless you move the Kaffirs I shall have to leave the house altogether.

18

My next move will be to pull the house down. The Town is not meant to contain Kaffir Kralls.'[47] Another citizen living in Forbes Avenue reacted in a more genteel and moralistic manner. He alleged that immorality was rampant, and set it against the values of family-centred life, a pattern of censure commonly found in the citizen movements of the time:

> Adjoining my house is a property ... in which are Hottentots and native women who use the house as a brothel ... it is impossible for my wife or daughters to come to the front at all, and as the house adjoins at the back, there is no place for them to be without seeing and hearing that which ought neither be seen nor heard by respectable people.[48]

Protest took the most organised form in the Kopje, as one might expect. Once again, in January 1908, shopkeepers and residents in the area approached the council with a petition. This time the issue was conceived as a community crisis, and demanded the control of 'kaffir-truck shops' and better policing of the locality. The plea started by pointing to 'the annoyance and discomfort, fraught even with danger, that is occasioned us by natives being allowed to occupy dwelling houses in the midst of white inhabitants'. It continued:

> Most of the houses are apparently Kafir stores, but as the rooms and outhouses seem to be occupied by native women, the nature of the business conducted at these premises is not far to seek.... . In view of the increase of crime of the most serious nature as instanced at the last Session of the High Court, we would urge, firstly, that some discretion be exercised in the granting of Trading Licenses, secondly, that no native be allowed to hire premises in the precincts of the town ... and thirdly that the town be more adequately policed, especially at night.[49]

To these voices authority responded with alacrity. They promptly blacklisted 'irregular' residents. There being no law to stop Africans hiring rooms, the town council, in co-operation with the police, approached landlords directly and pressurised them into evicting African tenants.[50] The municipal leaders also advised the Southern Rhodesia Constabulary not to allow 'police boys' to live outside the police compound.[51] The administrator, for his part, passed regulations under the Native Urban Locations Ordinance (No. 4 of 1906) prohibiting African 'free' residence in Salisbury from 1 May 1908, and by the end of April 1908 the town police reported: 'all natives in the Township and on the Commonage, occupying premises, not used by their masters, have been warned they will have to remove to the Location on the 1st May'.[52]

We have so far seen the re-establishment of the location in 1907-08 primarily in the light of the urban decay of the Kopje area and growing citizen pressure for segregation. The underlying logic of state intervention in the form of the location system may have become clear at this point. Our preceding discussion renders little support to the 'sanitation theory' often conveniently used by colonial officials to explain and justify their segregationist policy, and put forward by academics like Gann and Duignan, who argued that 'Fear of the African's unsanitary habits and the danger of diseases led to segregation in Rhodesian towns'.[53] According to Gann and Duignan:

> In the early days of Salisbury ... there was no segregation..... In the 1900s, however, disease struck the shanty-towns and convinced the white citizens that something must be done. They hastily cleared the infected area and shifted the Africans into a 'location'.[54]

Neither serious epidemic panic nor massive removals occurred in Salisbury at any point of the first decade of the century. The location policy of 1907-08 in fact focused on clearing the town, in particular, the Kopje area, of the African 'free' residents. At the citizen level, therefore, the policy meant a solution to a 'community crisis'. An editorial of the *Rhodesia Herald* was fully aware of what was at stake, when it praised the municipality in March 1908:

> One advantage [of having a location] is the benefit which will accrue to the town by the stopping of the system of letting houses to the natives. *The Kopje section of the town will feel this benefit more perhaps than the Causeway, with its more recent buildings.* After May 1 small native locations in town will cease to exist and their occupiers will be moved to the municipal location.[55] (my italics)

The scope of relocation was thus well defined:

> In older colonial towns, with large native populations such as this, natives employed as domestic servants and in other occupations are also compelled to live in the location, a system which has been found to work admirably. However, it is not the intention of the Council to go to this length at present.[56]

Racial ostracism took on a meaning at the institutional level as well. According to the same editorial, another advantage of the location system lay in that:

> A more adequate control over the natives will also be possible. The meanderings of the many natives who frequent the town and whose methods of obtaining a livelihood are doubtful in the extreme will be curtailed, and the enforcement of the law that all natives must either be in the location or at their employer's residence, after nine o'clock in the evening, unless allowed out by a special pass, should put an effective stop to the number of petty thefts which have recently been on the increase.[57]

Housing controls were conceptualised as a means, along with a pass and night curfew system, to control the behaviour of the African worker. If housing, a key issue in people's lives, was confined solely to the employer-controlled servants' quarters and a municipality-supervised location, the town would deprive misbehaving servants of sanctuary and thus perfect its matrix of social control.

Town location in urban frontier, 1892-1898

The history of urban racial policy and practices in Southern Rhodesia prior to the mid-twentieth century has conventionally been understood as an evolutionary process heading towards the more pervasive and unrelentingly segregationist measures of the 'Two Pyramids'. A corollary to this linear notion was the interpolation of a laissez-faire era in the start. It was argued, for instance, that African habitation in towns initially drew little official attention, a position which only changed when the impact of African urban concentrations began to be felt. Accordingly, the origins of urban locations were placed in the first phase of urban growth – around the beginning of the century.[58]

However, this evolutionary view has two weaknesses. First, in the early days racial 'separation', or the dual structure of society, was so obvious a reality (posing both problems and opportunities for the colonisers) that little need existed for the rulers to enshrine 'separation' as an ideology or policy. But this should not be misconstrued as an index for a laissez-faire spirit or an attitude of indifference. Rather, in some ways, European public opinion and urban administration in the early days were characterised by a low level of tolerance and a high level of authoritarianism. Secondly, it is essential to bear in mind the 'urban frontier' character of early Salisbury.[59] Salisbury was not a town in the ordinary sense: it was an overnight creation, embodying the whole configuration of forces systematically introduced by the Chartered Company for the purpose of the trans-Limpopo colonisation. It was a beachhead to hold out the interior for future capitalist development. Urban institutions, including African labour-control measures, were transplanted from the industrialising South Africa from the very beginning. Consequently, the inception of Salisbury town and its 'native location' antedated industrialisation and African urban concentrations.

The transformation of Fort Salisbury into a small town was rapid. During the several months after the rainy season of 1890-91 a township was laid out; stands were sold; a sanitary board (which was elevated to a town council in 1897) was organised; sanitation services were commenced; a magistracy came into being, and bank, postal and telegraph systems were established.

Among the problems which this embryonic urban settlement confronted was one of total chaos in the relations between white employers and black workers. This chaos was coupled with an acute labour shortage. There were 'a large number of native servants' desertions',[60] as well as incidents of colonists' failure to pay the promised wages to their servants.[61] Some local Africans did come to offer services, but, as agriculturalists, they were far from committed to wage labour: the indigenous peoples rather displayed 'a considerable aptitude for production and barter' in agricultural produce.[62] For their part, black workers, many of whom at the time had been recruited south of the Limpopo, and who constituted the core of the town's labour force, were no less mobile than the European colonists. When no news of a second Rand was forthcoming, and a route to the Indian Ocean was opened up, many of them abandoned Salisbury to try their luck in Manicaland.[63]

The BSA Company government did have some measures to prevent desertion and to regulate industrial relations. Since the laws of the Cape Colony had been in operation, contract-breaking was a crime under the Cape masters and servants laws. Indeed, one of the major tasks undertaken by the newly-established magistracy was to punish African deserters.[64] However, without any institutions for the registration of labour contracts and the identification of servants, arrests of contract-breakers were not easily secured.

In reaction to this difficulty, officials and local leaders decided at a sanitary board meeting in February 1892 to introduce a town pass system, modelled on 'the same lines as that in Kimberly',[65] then a logistics base for the Company's venture in the north. By the end of the month, L.S. Jameson, the administrator, had opened a registry office and proclaimed the Native Rules and Regulations.[66] The Regulations made the registration of labour contracts obligatory. Such registration was to be made every month at the registry office, which issued certificates of service contracts to workers; job-seekers had to obtain permits to that effect from the same office. All Africans, while staying in town, would be obliged to carry either a certificate of service contract or a permit for seeking work. Failure to do so would render them liable for penal sanctions. These documents, in effect, were passes. Nor was an African to be in town outside his employer's premises or the location between 9 p.m. and daylight without a special permit from his employer. Within a few weeks over 500 Africans registered themselves as servants, and by May the police began prosecuting pass offenders.[67]

Concurrently, a 'native location' was launched by the sanitary board. A few months earlier the board had been given, among other powers, one to organise 'native locations'.[68] One must note that the night curfew provision of the town pass system presupposed the existence of a location. In March 1892 a location was opened at a site about one kilometre south of the Kopje (next to the present Wesleyan chapel and Mupedzanhamo on Remembrance Drive). It contained eleven huts by the end of the month. A European sanitary inspector was appointed as superintendent and 'a Colonial native named Kleinboy' as headman. The location was set up at little cost to the authorities: inhabitants, mostly South African blacks, cleared the grass and erected their huts by themselves. The location regulations were 'read and made clear to the residents', who were to pay a monthly rent of 5s. for a plot.[69]

The location regulations, apparently borrowed verbatim from those of the city of Kimberley,[70] placed much emphasis on preventing the entry of unemployed persons. The area was to be supervised by a European superintendent who would keep a register of residence, and to whom every resident must satisfy 'of the manner in which he obtains his livelihood'. 'Strangers' were liable to prosecution, and officials were empowered to enter huts for inspection. In addition, no open-air dancing or assemblies were allowed in the location without official approval, and no shop or trading station was permitted within the precincts. These rules underlined the dormitory character of the place.[71]

In the meantime, efforts were made to force the Africans to sleep only in authorised places. Several workers who had settled 'independently' on the commonage were warned by the location superintendent that 'they will not be allowed to continue this practice'.[72] However, some others, like 'Colonial boys' occupying stands or huts within the town, and Zulu workers living 'on a portion of pound', were exempted from this policy, presumably in order not to cause their dissatisfaction and accelerate the exodus of more skilled workers.[73]

In such ways, a miniature version of the Kimberley system was set up. Its immediate aim was apparently to bind black servants to particular employers in a situation almost devoid of a free African labour market. Yet the system's logic itself had wider meanings, as William Worger recently summarised in his study of 'The rule of law in early Kimberly'. It was designed to ensure 'a regular and disciplined movement of the worker from first entry to the urban area, to the Registry Office, to an employer, to a location (while employed but not living on an employer's premises, or unemployed but with a pass permitting the worker to look for employment), to another employer, and then back out of the town once the period of contracted labor had been completed'.[74]

The historical significance of the 1892 system, then, lay in the fact that it inaugurated north of the Limpopo, in the earliest stage of colonialism, key concepts and basic components of the highly elaborate labour-control machinery developed in the first of the mining-boom towns in southern Africa. It was subsequently reproduced in Bulawayo and other major towns[75] and became a basis for urban African administration in the colony for decades to come. Given this historical background, there is no wonder that the 1907-08 location policy bore some similarity with that of 1892: in both cases the public authorities stepped in to control those Africans who spilt over from the private housing arrangements.

Yet having made this point, it is at once necessary to place a caveat. It is quite questionable whether, for most of the 1890s, the system was really an effective and smoothly-functioning one. The whole situation was at that time extremely fluid and uncertain. The period was characterised by a good deal of groping in the darkness. Autochthonous polities were not conquered yet. Salisbury remained a bush settlement, occupied by a mere 4-600 colonists; their mentality was invariably 'get-rich-and-get-out-quick', while the BSA Company magnates and their associates were said to be indulging in 'a six months' gamble in land and quartz reefs'.[76]

In short, it was a speculative era. Neither the interests of capital nor the limited resources of government necessitated or permitted a well-developed (and costly) apparatus for control.[77] Pass controls, for example, were proverbially ineffective. In Umtali in 1894 the introduction of a town pass law was opposed by European employers themselves, on the grounds of the poor law-enforcement ability of the state, but possibly also because the employers, operating on a short-term, speculative basis, were loath to bear the responsibility of paying a monthly registration fee.[78] This attitude was not confined to Umtali alone. In Salisbury a similar opinion was heard in the same year: 'Employers of native labour very justly argue what is the use of their paying for native passes when absolutely nothing is done to protect them against the boys bolting whenever they choose. That the boys do so with impunity is notorious, since there is seldom a policeman available to go after them.'[79]

In much the same way, the Salisbury sanitary board was feeble and incompetent. Their hands were full providing only the barest sanitary services for the town, resulting in charges of 'open neglect of more or less every municipal and sanitary regulation'.[80] The board could not afford at times to employ an African headman, much less a European superintendent, for the supervision of the location. This entailed such a degree of autonomy on the part of the location community that the management would find it difficult to collect rents or to evict unauthorised inhabitants.[81] At the turn of the century the location was, therefore, in the opinion of the Mashonaland constabulary, a refuge for loafers and thieves:

> ... there are a number of natives residing in the town location who have no work and who make no effort to get employment. This is accounted for by the fact that 'passes' are obtained by natives from the Inspector of Locations authorising them to reside in the location, and whether a native has employment or not, he can always obtain a pass ... there are two well-known thieves ... who know so long as they do not come into town or are not caught outside the limits of the location, they are not liable to be arrested by the police.[82]

Clearly, there was a colossal gap between theory and reality in urban administration, as in many other fields of the Southern Rhodesia colonisation.

Town location in the years of urban growth, 1898-1908

A change of tide was felt towards the end of the 1890s, after which the colonial society inched towards stable capitalist production and a politico-social

24

order compatible with it. In Salisbury this transformation was especially marked in two distinct periods, one covering the years from 1899 to 1902, and the other from 1907 to 1911. Some of the 'urban problems' for the latter period were found, in their rudimentary forms, in the former. One of these was prostitution. It first became a public concern in the last years of the 1890s, when the South African War disrupted and dispersed the booming trade of prostitution on the Rand. [83] In 1900 citizens in Bulawayo and Salisbury petitioned for suppression of the vice, and immorality legislation was passed.[84] Almost simultaneously, the African servant question arrested public attention.[85] In Salisbury this culminated in the town council's decision in 1902 to set up a segregated location, which was a prelude to the 1907-08 location scheme. We will now examine how this last development took place.

In the wake of the African risings of 1896-97, anxieties were frequently expressed by European employers over alleged misconduct of African servants. 'One is daily hearing the same complaints', one employer wrote to a local newspaper in 1900. '"My boy has run away," or "My boy has stolen something and gone" – "My boy is useless and the biggest rogue I ever met," and so on'.[86] 'Every one must have noticed', another employer bemoaned, 'the increasing independence and haughtiness in the manner of the blacks'.[87] Others even claimed that the Europeans were 'at the mercy of natives who enter domestic service' and were confronted with 'the predatory habits of the houseboy', 'the oppression of servants', and 'a perfected species of trades' unionism'.[88] These complaints invariably called for a more effective pass system, and for concerted action by the employers to curb the servants' wrongdoings as well as prevent high wage rates.

Obviously, this phenomenon had something to do with the growing employing class's offensive in relation to African labour. As the new century dawned, these urban complaints were echoed by more vociferous cries on the part of the mine-owners and the farmers for cheap, efficient African labour. The outcome was a formidable set of labour-coercive institutions, such as higher African taxes, a labour bureau, the consolidated masters and servants laws, new town pass legislation, and a national identification system. At the same time, urban administration as it related to the Africans was progressively strengthened and toughened. In Salisbury the police prosecution against pass offenders dramatically increased after around 1900,[89] and, significantly, African wage rates showed a tendency to drop in these years.[90]

On the other hand, the very nervous, anxious, and even pathological tone which nuanced the European responses to the servant question strongly hints that other forces were at work besides capital's onslaught on African labour. This is not the place to explicate this interesting theme, and here I only suggest two things. First, such malaise arose from problems of social instability and disorder in a nascent colonial town: the volatile mixture of different cultures; inability to control the urban environments (water, darkness, dust, infectious disease, etc.); frustrations over the poor performance of the public authorities; and a profound sense of drift felt among immigrants. Secondly, the dominant racial group – white immigrants from South Africa or Western Europe – had a marked tendency to point to supposed threats from the 'alien elements' (as in the case of public agitation against the 'Asiatic invasion' or the 'anti-Greek movement').[91] They were indeed often quick to lay the entire onus for the disordered state of society on the latter.

It was in this general mood, underpinned by an odd seesaw of ambitions and frustrations, strength and weakness, that the monotonous grumbles about the servants gave way to a far more critical phenomenon, i.e. public hysteria over the Social Pest or the Black Peril. Through such mass convulsions against real or imaginary dangers of the blacks, social tensions accumulated in primitive towns were violently released, the values of white solidarity were ritualistically re-affirmed, and race controls were in the end fortified. This chain of events exerted significant effects on the racialist ordering of society.

From late 1901 to mid-1902 both Salisbury and Bulawayo experienced a few instances of African male assaults on European women. In line with the current style in southern Africa the press gave sensational coverage to them.[92] Yet it was the Bulawayo 'outrage' which took place in October 1902 that triggered off a nationwide Black Peril scare, the first of its kind in the colony's history. In that case the accused 'was lassoed and dragged out of the dock, along the floor of the Court room, and into the street, to the amazement of the Magistrate'. 'The crowd became suddenly enraged, and the cries of "lynch him" and "hang him" filled the air'. 'The police tried to interfere, but were powerless. The crowd knocked the boy about, until a lot more police came up, when the rope was cut… . Practically all Bulawayo was present.'[93] When the prisoner was transferred to Salisbury, he was again mobbed at the railway station. In the legislative council a motion was promptly proposed for the infliction of the death penalty on Africans for rape or attempted rape of European women, and legislation to that effect was promulgated the following year.[94]

The uproar reached the Salisbury town house as well. At a council meeting held in November 1902, Mayor Dudley G. Bates proposed a drastic plan for a large, segregated location. Bates told his colleagues that it was high time that a stop be put to 'this state of things' – 'a social evil which would spread, if some very drastic measures were not adopted'. In his view, 'the native … was, in the first place, lazy; in the second place, he was dirty; and he was a born thief and liar'. Given this, and also the fact that 'the black population was considerably larger than the white', it was absolutely necessary, for the security of the whites, to remove all 3,000 town Africans, or at least 2,000 in consideration of the convenience of employers, to a location or locations situated outside the town. To quote a local newspaper, the mayor 'always thought there should be class legislation in Rhodesia, and the more distinctive they made it, the better for themselves and the black man (hear, hear.) The gulf between the two races, he hoped, would always exist.'[95]

Still another bone of contention was the issue of latrine facilities for Africans. It will be remembered that in the earlier speculative years, most firms and households failed to provide sanitary conveniences for their servants. For the sake of such employers the sanitary board built a few 'native latrines' at street corners, facilities which were totally inadequate for the needs of the African population. In 1895 the administrator attempted to stop this 'extraordinary' practice by passing the Townships Sanitary Regulations (No. 109 of 1895), which required every employer in Salisbury to provide latrines for servants. But the regulations proved a dead letter.[96] Obviously, the very curse on the early town, the sparsity of population and the preponderance of the natural over the built environment, proved a boon to the employers' parsimony on worker housing and sanitation. However, the more Salisbury progressed towards something of an urban agglomeration, the more frequently it was haunted by fears of epidemic disease, such as typhoid and smallpox. Time after time medical officials warned of the danger of the lack of sanitary conveniences for the majority of population, especially at a time when the town depended on wells for its water supply and was suffering from the excessive dust in the streets. Heated debates followed at the town house, but with no result. The municipal leaders always arrived at the conclusion that the cost of erecting 'native latrines' was too much for ratepayers. In 1902 this was estimated at between £7 and £15 for every household or firm.[97]

The Gordian knot should be cut, argued Bates. Proposed removals would straightaway relieve the latrine problem. In view of both 'the social evil' and 'the want of adequate sanitary provision', 'expenditure was necessary to establish a location or locations'. But how could a small town like Salisbury finance such a scheme, which would cost around £11,500? Bates's answer was to lay the onus on the central government. Since the administration was responsible for much of the control of the Africans, 'a very large portion of the expense of forming the locations should fall upon the Government, unless the Council participated in the revenue derived from passes'.[98]

The town council adopted the proposal. It advised the administrator to make a law 'giving the Council power to order natives out of the town in the evening'.[99] Shortly afterward, the council's position was endorsed by the 1903 Enteric Fever Commission which, comprising medical officials and municipal leaders, investigated the outbreak of typhoid fever in Salisbury in early 1903. In their report the commission pointed out a grave 'danger of living together with a large Native community' who, they believed, were suffering 'from mild forms of typhoid', and recommended that the African workers be confined to a segregated location.[100]

This was not the first time that local leaders had upheld the cause of total segregation. Ten years before, in 1892-93, the sanitary board had toyed with an idea of removing 'all coloured people', including the Asians, to 'separate portions of the town'. This was partly in response to a trickle of Asian immigrants. But in the event the action proved not so much a practical policy as the partisan expression of an ideal.[101] It was at once plain to everybody in Salisbury that the council's 1902 position had a similar utopian strand; as the press put it mildly, 'its feasibility or otherwise has yet to be determined'. Yet in spite of, or possibly because of, this weakness, Bates's proposal was greatly acclaimed as a 'timely action' being 'in the best interests of the Municipality'.[102] In those times of developing racial animosities, elements of emotion and fantasy often represented a virtue, rather than a sin.

The uniqueness of the 1902 decision was then not the idea of total segregation itself, but the fact that the idea was justified in terms of emerging 'urban problems' like the Black Peril, the public health problem, etc. In this respect the decision marked a new era. And it was perfectly in line with a trend in the subcontinent which was just undergoing the process of capitalist, industrial urbanisation. In contemporary South Africa segregated locations were increasingly viewed as a panacea for all sorts of urban racial problems, and when the bubonic plague attacked port towns in 1901, serious attempts were made at ousting African workers from inner cities.[103] The Salisbury councillors were conversant with these developments down south: upon adopting Bates's proposal the council sent letters to municipalities in the Cape Colony, asking for information on urban locations.[104]

However, the central state responded in a more sober and down-to-earth way. In their view, housing controls should be tightened by insisting on the principle that, as the attorney general put it, 'Natives who do not live on their master's premises should live in a location.'[105] But as for the control of the Africans sleeping on their employers' premises, the administration threw cold water on the council by pointing out that in regard to such people, 'the Council possesses the necessary power to frame bye-laws providing for proper sanitary arrangements and the prevention of overcrowding'.[106] The caution was reinforced as the colony's economy slipped into the doldrums. The public bodies were forced to tighten their purse strings, and the tremendous wave of capital's clamour for cheap labour and the settlers' frenzy over the Black Peril rapidly subsided.

Events thus headed towards the territorial government's giving new energy to the location system. In September 1904 the administration set out to streamline the location laws.[107] Hitherto, the powers to organise locations had been in the hands of local authorities, so that location policy differed from one place to another. Moreover, the municipal control of locations rested on a dubious legal basis, since locations were normally physically situated outside the actual jurisdiction of the municipalities. Nor did any statutory law exist to stop Africans asserting their freedom of residence.[108]

28

To iron out all these problems, a bill, drafted on the model of a Cape law, the Native Reserve Locations Act (No. 40 of 1902),[109] was adopted in the legislature in 1905, and sanctioned, after some modifications had been made, by the Imperial government in 1906. It was entered onto the Statute Book as the Native Urban Locations Ordinance (No. 4 of 1906).

The Ordinance enabled the administrator to take the initiative in organising urban locations and to define such locations as special areas under the day-to-day control of local authorities. It also spelled out where urban Africans were to sleep. Section 3 declared that they must reside in a municipal location. This sweeping rule was, however, watered down by section 4, which exempted both the 'native whilst in bona fide employment as a domestic or other servant, who may reside on the premises of an employer', and the African who received special permits to live within town. The combined result was that it was a crime for the African to reside outside the location or his master's premises.[110]

This development coincided with the Salisbury citizens' fresh interest in the African housing question. The rise of a bourgeois Salisbury in the early years of the twentieth century had highlighted the urban decay of the Kopje area, as well as the growing belligerence of the upper- and middle-class citizens with the anarchic social order of the pioneering days. Around the end of 1904 Africans began to move into rooms in town, especially in the Kopje, making location huts vacant. The presence of such 'free' African dwellers, along with crowds of African shoppers and passers-by, in the midst of the 'White city' greatly discomforted European citizens, in particular the wealthier ones, who asked the authorities to enforce both stricter segregation and better controls. Those people became vocal in 1907 and early 1908, when the town council took steps to establish a new location. The new Native Urban Locations Ordinance (No. 4 of 1906) came in precisely as a measure to provide a legal basis for these segregationist moves in Salisbury.

In 1907-08, it was only too obvious to both citizens and municipal officials, who must be relocated without delay. It was this specificity that was absent in the 1902 proposal, where attack was directed against Africans as a whole – and therefore, in effect, against nobody. As the issue became more specific and more definite, the prescription became more concrete and more real.

Yet we can broadly speak of the new scheme as the resuscitation of the 1902 one. To be sure, the new location was earmarked for those to be evicted, and it started as a small housing estate, with fifty Kaytor huts (made of circular, corrugated iron walls and thatched roofs), a brick barracks of four rooms, a well, communal latrines, and a refuse depot.[111] But at the same time it was projected as a decisive step towards comprehensive residential segregation, as envisaged in 1902. Because of this consideration, the site for a new location was carefully selected. The place of the old 1892 location was abandoned, because it 'was considered too near the Kopje'.[112] An area of about fifty acres was freshly demarcated. It was further away from the town centre, screened off by a railway line and trees, downstream and leeward of European habitation, 'capable of indefinite expansion to the South',[113] and adjacent to the cemetery, the slaughter poles, and the sanitation works. This was the core area around which the latter-day Harare African township was to develop (Figure 2).

Elements of continuity were still more apparent in that the 1907-08 scheme was tied to the latrine problem. Economic upturn and urban growth after 1907 prompted the council at last to insist on the Townships Sanitary Regulations of 1895. Cheap tin latrines were invented; the town house announced that sharing of one latrine by a group of employers would be permitted; and the cost-conscious ratepayers were told that 'the initial cost of a latrine, about £3, might save a heavy doctor's bill in the case of an epidemic'.[114] In April 1908 the option was given to householders and firms either to send their servants to the new location, or to erect latrines on their own premises. Most employers reluctantly complied with the regulation and built latrines, rather than sending their servants to the location and paying rents for them.[115]

This is an important point, for it implies that from the viewpoint of capital the advantages of the servants' quarters or the compounds generally outweighed those of utilising the location. Two major reasons for this disparity may be identified. One was that many employers believed that the servants' quarter/compound system, the product of the migrant labour economy, was the most effective method for the supervision of short-term contract workers. Besides, certain categories of employment, such as at households, boarding houses and hotels, required early morning and night services, and in such cases employers always stuck to a living-in system.[116]

More than that, employers' lack of enthusiasm for sending their workers to live in the location was due to a gap between the costs of public and private housing, as the former regularly exceeded the latter. Whereas a high-rental policy was adopted for the location, expenditure on worker housing on private premises was generally kept to an absolute minimum. Private housing as a rule consisted of ultra-cheap, dilapidated shelters, like overcrowded iron-sheet hovels, and paraffin-tin shacks built by occupiers themselves.[117] The municipal authority, for their part, rarely invoked the public health and overcrowding laws against such structures – at least until Salisbury entered another phase of centralisation and growth in the boom years of the mid-1920s.[118] Even as late as 1934, by which time higher land prices and stricter housing regulations had pushed up the cost of worker housing in town, the commissioner of police believed: 'This [total separation] would be ideal if it were practical – I am afraid that there would be much opposition on the part of Europeans, it would mean that wages would have to be raised in order that the employee could rent premises in a location and pay for the extra cost of living which would result.'[119]

All of which explains the primacy of the servants' quarters and compounds in African housing in the early years. It is clear that the central administration, the major agent of capital in general, was not much impressed by the 1902 municipal proposal seeking massive African removals. As Figure 3 indicates, there was no rush on the part of employers to send servants to the location at any time before World War II, at which time the location contained a relatively small population (roughly one-tenth of the African population of Salisbury in 1920).[120] And throughout the same period it was African residents, rather than employers, who usually paid the rental charges for accommodation in the location (Figure 4).

The settler attitude at this time demonstrated profound ambiguity. To dream, as citizens, of an official location removing 'racial problems' from their doorsteps was one thing, but to place, as employers, their own African employees into the location and to pay high rents for them was quite another.[121]

Conclusion

Just as the early history of the Salisbury town had two turning points, that of the African location therein also went through two phases. In 1892, when the Salisbury settlement was an urban frontier with an umbilical cord still tied to mineral-fevered South Africa, a location concept and housing restrictions, together with urban pass controls, were transplanted from Kimberley, and the system thus created set a pattern for the colony's urban African administration in subsequent years. Yet, like the whole settlement itself, the 1892 system was in practice little more than an interim arrangement, apparently with its immediate aim being to bind black contract workers to white masters. A real 'urban' location policy began to evolve only after the turn of the century, when the Salisbury settlement became 'urban' and felt the first batch of 'urban racial problems'.

In a rather schematic way, Salisbury's urban growth involved two mutually-related developments: one towards an administrative and commercial centre serving a nascent export-oriented capitalist economy, and the other towards a place of habitation where people's daily lives took place. This dual transformation, encompassing the production process as well as the consumption process, the workplace as well as living space, affected populations and neighbourhoods in complex ways. It spawned crosscurrents of conflict in both the workplaces and living spaces.

Gradually after around 1900, but dramatically after 1907, European colonists, especially of the upper and middle classes, made Salisbury a permanent or semi-permanent habitat, in which they enjoyed better access to new urban resources and opportunities. This change was accompanied by a higher degree of commitment to the values of family, and of concern over daily living conditions. The rulers of the town increasingly distanced themselves from the rough social order of 'old Salisbury' and resisted the decay of the Kopje area, a process which was exemplified by the citizen movement against the Pioneer Street brothels.

Meanwhile, the development and concentration of production necessitated the presence of an army of African rural migrants. This immediately posed a problem for locating these workers in the 'right place'. The arrangement which emerged in this respect, as a result of a complex combination of dogmatism and pragmatism, was one ubiquitous in southern African towns. African workers came to be shielded in the relatively well-regulated servants' quarter/compound system; African entry into the town proper was severely restricted. The practice of Africans hiring rooms for themselves and living independently in town clashed with this principle. It was this conflict (which constituted an important element of the Kopje crisis), coupled with the growing European concern over civic and neighbourhood affairs, that led to municipal intervention in African housing. Thus in 1907 a location was opened for the resettlement of 'free' dwellers, and the following year the administration made African 'free' residence illegal.

Obviously, this state intervention in African housing had tremendous implications for the social geography of Salisbury: it was, above all, through the control of housing that the public authorities were to play a vital role in regulating people's lives. But this should not lead us to exaggerate the nature and the degree of state involvement in the early days. The municipalisation of African housing was rather limited in scale, since the location came into being basically as a supplement to, rather than a substitute for, the servants' quarter/compound system, which well represented the logic of capital in the then developing migrant labour economy.

Notes

1 *Rhodesia Herald*, 21 Mar, 1906.
2 *Ibid.*
3 *Ibid.* 18 Sept. 1895.
4 *Ibid.* 13 Oct. 1909.
5 For a detailed account of this development, see Ian Phimister, *An Economic and Social History of Zimbabwe, 1890-1948* (Harlow, 1988), 45-64.
6 P. Jackson, *Historic Buildings of Harare, 1890-1940* (Harare, 1986), 8.
7 C/5/7/3, Natives of Central and South African Origin: C/5/11/1, Europeans or White Population in the District of Salisbury.
8 *Mayor's Minutes*, 1909-10, 1.
9 G.H. Tanser, 'The Birth and Growth of Salisbury, Rhodesia', in H.L. Watts (ed.), *Focus on Cities* (Durban, 1970), 153.
10 *Rhodesia Herald*, 17 Apr., 11 Aug. 1908.
11 *Rhodesia Herald*, 8 Feb. 1895.
12 *Ibid.*
13 LG/93/9, Council and Comm. Meetings, 12, 26, 28 Aug. 1908, 2 Oct. 1908, 19 May 1909; LG/38, Secr., Salisbury Chamber of Commerce to Town Clerk, 3, 19 Aug. 1908; *Ibid.*, Petition to Adm. adopted on 21 Sept. 1908.

14 *Rhodesia Herald*, 28 June 1910.
15 Based on my analysis of the householder's returns of the 1911 census, C/5/2/12-16. Among the new residents in the eastern and north-eastern section of the town was G. H. Huggins, then a young doctor who was to hold the premiership from 1933 to 1956. He entered the colony in 1911. 'As a bachelor he lived in a semi-detached cottage in Gordon Avenue where he got by on £1 a month, taking his meals in the Salisbury Club where most of the local worthies joined as members. Later on Huggins rented 'Fourways', the ex-treasurer's house in North Avenue, opposite the administrator's residence in one of the best parts of town': L. H. Gann and M. Gelfand, *Huggins of Rhodesia* (London, 1964), 57.
16 *Rhodesia Herald*, 10 Feb. 1908.
17 S.R., *Report of the Director of Census ... 1911* (Sess. Paps., A7, 1912), 22.
18 *Ibid*. 9.
19 C/5/11/1, Salisbury Township and Commonage.
20 S.R., *Report of the Director of Census... 1911*, 11.
21 C/5/11/1, Salisbury Township and Commonage.
22 C. van Onselen, *Studies in the Social and Economic History of the Witwatersrand 1886-1914, I New Babylon* (Johannesburg, 1982), 104.
23 The 1921 census showed a balanced sex ratio for the Europeans in Salisbury, with 2,372 males, as against 2,207 females: C/6/4/1, Salisbury Town. For the European labour movements, see D.J. Murray, *The Governmental System in Southern Rhodesia* (London, 1970), Ch. 7; E. Lee, 'The trade union movement in Rhodesia, 1910-1924', *Rhodesian Journal of Economics*, VIII (1974), 215-37; I. Phimister, 'White miners in historical perspective: Southern Rhodesia, 1890-1953', *Journal of Southern African Studies*, III (1976-7), 187-206.
24 C/5/7/3, Natives of Central and South African Origin. See also Figures 5 and 6.
25 '[It] is estimated that in the year 1910 86,103 [indigenous] males between the ages of 14 and 40 worked for an average period of four months': S.R., *Report of the Native Affairs Committee of Enquiry, 1910-11* (Sess. Paps, 1911), 30.
26 See the section, Town Location in the Years of Urban Growth, 1898-1908.
27 Pass controls also played an important role in regulating the African labour market in favour of the European employers.
28 See the Gov. Notice No. 198 of 1905.
29 At the beginning of the century, even African cycling invited strong public hostility, and the town council discussed a bye-law prohibiting Africans from riding bicycles: *Rhodesia Herald*, 20, 31 Dec. 1901.
30 See Tables A.8, A.9.
31 For the duties performed by domestics in the early days, see among others G. Page, *Jill's Rhodesian Philosophy or the Dam Farm* (London, 1910); S. Macdonald, *Sally in Rhodesia* (Sydney, 1927).
32 *Rhodesia Herald*, 12 Jan. 1910.
33 A/3/28/60, Town Clerk to High Commissioner, South Africa, 30 Apr. 1909.
34 LG/38, Sgt. T. Delahay to Sub-Insp., S.R. Constabulary, 19 Feb. 1908.
35 LG/52/6/1, J. Smith, Insp. of Location, to Town Clerk, 25 Jan. 1905.
36 LG/38, P. Curran to Sub-Insp., S.R. Constabulary, 29 Nov. 1907.
37 See among others LG/47/16, Town Clerk to Chief Insp., S.R. Constabulary, 25 July 1907; *Rhodesia Herald*, 10 Sept. 1909.
38 Tanser writes (G. H. Tanser, *A Sequence of Time: The Story of Salisbury, Rhodesia, 1900 to 1914* (Salisbury, 1974), 155): The lowering of property values in the Kopje area, and the rise in Manica Road, was shown by the prices obtained for properties put up for sale in a deceased estate. Two stands, with five small shops, in Pioneer Street, were sold for £100, while an empty stand in Manica Road, near Second Street, fetched £635. The stand opposite the Magistrate's Court (later Broadcasting House) also empty, was sold for £1,000.'
39 *Rhodesia Herald*, 27 Feb. 1909.
40 *Ibid*., 13 Mar. 1909.
41 A/3/28/60, Annexure No. 5, in Town Clerk to Adm., 25 Mar. 1909.
42 LG/93/9, Council and Comm. Meetings, 27 Nov., 16 Dec. 1907, 2 Nov. 1908, 18 Jan.

43 1909.
This paragraph is based on *Ibid.*, 10 Feb., 10 Mar., 5, 22 Nov. 1909, 28 Sept. 1910; LG/47/17, Town Clerk to Secr., Adm., 25 Mar. 1909; *Ibid.*, Town Clerk to Resident Commissioner, 30 Apr. 1909; LG/47/18, Town Clerk to Secr., B.S.A. Co., 23 Nov. 1911; LG/38, Petition to Town Council, Oct. 1909, Chief Insp., S.R. Constabulary, to Town Clerk, 12 Nov. 1909; A/3/28/60, correspondence; *Rhodesia Herald*, 11, 22 Mar. 1909, 30 Sept. 1910, 22 July, 24 Sept. 1911, 21 May 1912; Tanser, *A Sequence of Time*, Ch. 16. The quotations, from *Rhodesia Herald*, 11 Mar. 1909.

44 E. Coxwell took the lead in this affair, too: LG/93/8, Council meeting, 13 Feb. 1907. However, one should not be insensitive to differences between the two issues.

45 LG/52/6/1, J. Smith, Insp. of Location to Town Clerk, 25 Jan. 1905.

46 LG/38, Petition to Town Council, 2 Feb. 1906.

47 *Ibid.*, R. Phillips to Town Clerk, 17 July 1907.

48 *Ibid.*, D. Smith to Town Clerk, 27 Nov. 1907.

49 *Ibid.*, Petition to Mayor and Councillors, 27 Jan. 1908. According to the police, however, the petitioners' claim, 'the increase of crime of the most serious nature', was not substantiated: LG/38, Chief Insp., S.R. Constabulary, to Town Clerk, 21 Feb. 1908.

50 LG/47/16, Town Clerk to French South Africa Development Co., 25 July 1907; LG/38, Town Clerk to Sub-Insp., S.R. Constabulary, 28 Nov. 1907; *Ibid.*, Sgt. Delahay to Sub-Insp., S.R. Constabulary, 19 Feb. 1908.

51 LG/47/16, Town Clerk to Chief Insp., S.R. Constabulary, 25 July 1907.

52 LG/38, Chief Insp., S.R. Constabulary to Town Clerk, 29 Apr. 1908.

53 L. H. Gann and P. Duignan, *White Settlers in Tropical Africa* (Harmondsworth, 1962), 83-4. Murray also ascribes the evolution of urban administration to hygienic anxieties (Murray, *The Governmental System*, 315). The 'sanitation syndrome' thesis advanced by M.W. Swanson weakens considerably in the face of the Salisbury evidence: Swanson, 'The sanitation syndrome: Bubonic plague and urban native policy in the Cape Colony, 1900-1909', *Jour. Afr. Hist.* XVIII (1977), 387-410.

54 Gann and Duignan, 'Changing patterns of a white elite: Rhodesian and other settlers', in Gann and Duignan (eds), *Colonialism in Africa, 1870-1960, II* (London, 1970), 138-9.

55 *Rhodesia Herald*, 23 Mar. 1908. For a similar comment, see *Ibid.* 26 July 1907.

56 *Rhodesia Herald*, 23 Mar. 1908.

57 *Ibid.*

58 See for example S.R., *Report of the Urban African Affairs Commission 1958* (Sess. Paps, 1958), 29, 32; P. Duignan, 'Native Policy in Southern Rhodesia, 1890-1923' (Stanford Univ., Ph.D. thesis, 1961), 219-20; L. H. Gann, *A History of Southern Rhodesia, Early Days to 1934* (London, 1965), 192-3; I. R. N. Cormack, *Towards Self-Reliance* (Gweru, 1983), 78-9. D. Patel also suggests that the Salisbury location was started at the beginning of the century: D. H. Patel and R. J. Adams, *Chirambahuyo* (Gwelo, 1981), 5.

59 The urban frontier thesis, which seems highly relevant to the colonisation of the interior of southern Africa, has been postulated, in the context of the American West, by R. C. Wade: *idem*, *The Urban Frontier: The Rise of Western Cities, 1790-1830* (Cambridge, Massachusetts, 1959).

60 *Mash. Her. Zamb. Times*, 6 Feb. 1892.

61 See D/3/5/1, cases 1, 15, 20 of 1891.

62 *Mash. Her. Zamb. Times*, 23 Jan. 1892.

63 LG/47/1, O. H. Ogilvie to Board of Management, 7 Apr. 1892.

64 The masters and servants law offences constituted one of the most common African crimes in the earliest days: see for example D/3/5/1.

65 LO/5/2/17, H.M. Hole, Actg Secr., Salisbury, to Actg Secr., Cape Town, 22 Feb. 1892.

66 *Mash. Her. Zamb. Times*, 27 Feb. 1892: Rhodesia, *High Commissioner's and Administrator's Proclamations: British South Africa Co's and Government Notices, July, 1891 to September, 1894* ([Salisbury], n.d.), 12.

67 *Mash. Her. Zamb. Times*, 12 Mar. 1892; D/4/7/1, case 96 of 1892.

68 *Mash. Her. Zamb. Times*, 9 Jan. 1892.

69 This paragraph is based on LG/47/1, Ogilvie to Board of Management, 17 Mar., 7 Apr.

1892; Draft Location Regulations, in LO/5/2/18, H. Currey, Actg. Secr. B.S.A. Co., to Imperial Secr., Cape Town, 19 Apr. 1892.
70 For the location regulations in Kimberley, see W. Worger, 'Workers as criminals: The rule of law in early Kimberly, 1870-1885', in F. Cooper (ed.), *Struggle for the City: Migrant Labor, Capital, and the State in Urban Africa* (Beverly Hills, 1983), 70-1.
71 Draft Locations Regulations, in LO/5/2/18, H. Currey, Actg. Secr. B.S.A. Co., to Imperial Secr., Cape Town, 19 Apr. 1892.
72 LG/47/1, Ogilvie to Board of Management, 17 Mar. 1892.
73 *Ibid.* [2?] Mar., 7 Apr. 1892; *Mash. Her. Zamb. Times,* 5 Mar. 1892.
74 Worger, 'Workers as criminals', 70-1. The following passage in an editorial of the *Bulawayo Chronicle* (8 Feb. 1895) gives us an idea, though in the Bulawayo context, of how the role of the location was conceived by the early colonisers: 'The Sanitary Board has done well to adopt such laws in the early stage of the town's existence. It should not in the future be so difficult to trace natives for crimes committed as it has been in the past, for the register kept by the Superintendent gives all the information requisite for identification, and it will be easy to discover which native is missing if the delinquent had decamped.... . Section 12 is of great importance as it orders that every native shall satisfy the Superintendent as to the manner in which he obtains his livelihood, which gives an additional security to his employer and also to the police, showing the "boy" is not loafing around the town.'
75 *Ibid.* 12 Oct. 1894, 8, 15 Feb. 1895; CT/1/10/32, P.S. Inskipp, Secr. to Adm., to Secr., Cape Town, 4 July 1895. The Imperial Power initially questioned the legality of some of the administrative arrangements made by the Chartered Company, including pass controls under the Native Rules and Regulations, and the formation of the sanitary board and its 'native location': LO/5/2/17, H. Bower, Imperial Secr., Cape Town, to Secr., B.S.A. Co., 7 Apr. 1892; LO/5/2/18, Bower to Secr., B.S.A. Co., 26 Apr. 1892. These *ultra vires* arrangements were regularised only after the destruction of Lobengula's power. A Salisbury sanitary board was formally organised in 1894 under the Towns Management Ordinance (No. 2 of 1894) and the following year new location regulations, which were the same as the Bulawayo counterparts, were made. The Native Rules and Regulations of 1892 were re-enacted as the Registration of Natives Regulations of 1895, which were later consolidated into the Natives Registration Ordinance (No. 16 of 1901).
76 *Rhodesia Herald,* 16 Mar. 1894.
77 Yet another factor which hampered or mitigated the full enforcement of the control system was the need, on the part of the colonists, to attract, or at least not to scare away, African labour. In 1894, for example, the sanitary board successfully persuaded the government to relax pass law restrictions on African peasants seeking work in town: LG/93/2, Sanitary Board meetings, 3, 7 Oct. 1894. In the same vein, the acting administrator proposed, shortly after this, a plan to build a camp to provide food and shelter for 'Mashonas coming in to seek work': LG/88, F. Rhodes, Actg Adm., to Secr., Sanitary Board, 12 Dec. 1894.
78 *Umtali Advertiser,* 25 Dec. 1894.
79 *Rhodesia Herald,* 12 Jan. 1894.
80 *Ibid.* 15 Dec. 1893.
81 *Ibid.* 19 Feb., 13 Apr. 1896, 19 Jan. 1898; LG/93/4, Report by Commonage and Market Comm., 8 June 1898.
82 LG/38, Mashonaland Constabulary Office to Town Clerk, 5 Feb. 1901.
83 For a detailed account of 'prostitutes and proletarians' on the Rand, see van Onselen, *Studies in the Social and Economic History of the Witwatersrand, 1,* chapter 3.
84 S.R., *Debates [in the Legislative Council ...],* I, 26 Mar. 1900, 48, 51; *Rhodesia Herald,* 19 Jan. 1898, 20 Dec. 1900, 18 Jan., 8, 9 Apr. 1901.
85 It is worth noting that the periods both witnessed nationwide Black Peril cases, which occurred first in around 1902-3, and then in 1909-11.
86 *Rhodesia Herald,* 17 Oct. 1900.
87 *Ibid.* 18 Oct. 1900.
88 *Ibid.* 12 Oct. 1900, 19 July 1901.
89 See reports on crimes in Salisbury, in D/4/7/1; LO/4/1/3, 5, 10, 13, 16, 20.
90 In the domestic employment in Salisbury 'Colonial boys' drew a monthly wage of £5,

Shangaans, £2, and Shonas, £1 15s. in 1897, but three years later they received £3, £1 10s., and 15s. respectively: BSA Co., *Reports on the Company's proceedings ... 1896-1897*, 151; *idem*, *Reports on the Administration ... 1898-1900*, 315.

91 Especially before the mid-1900s (i.e. before the imposition of immigration restrictions and the local control of issuing general dealer's licences) there were frequent public agitations against the presence of Asians in major towns. See among others *Rhodesia Herald*, 23 Oct. 1895, 6 May 1898, 4, 9, 10, 30 Jan. 1899, 7 Feb. 1900. As for the anti-Greek movement (led by British mechanics), see *Ibid*. 11, 19 Feb. 1901.

92 *Rhodesia Herald*, 12, 20 Feb., 30 Oct, 18 Nov., 1901; 26, 27 Feb., 6, 17, 19, 20, 21, 26 Mar., 22 Apr., 21 June, 1902.

93 *Ibid*. 24 October. 1902; *Bulawayo Chronicle*, 25 Oct. 1902.

94 *Debates*, I, 11 Nov. 1902, 113-15: The Criminal Law Amendment Ordinance (No. 2 of 1903).

95 *Rhodesia Herald*, 27 Nov. 1902.

96 LG/93/6, Council meeting, 19 Feb. 1901.

97 *Rhodesia Herald*, 27 Nov. 1902.

98 *Ibid*.

99 *Ibid*. 18 Dec. 1902. See also LG/47/11, Town Clerk to Chief Secr. to Adm., 18 and 29 Dec. 1902.

100 Report of Enteric Fever Comm., in *Mayor's Minutes*, 1902-3.

101 *Rhodesia Herald*, 7, 14 Jan., 20 May 1893.

102 *Ibid*. 28 Nov. 1902.

103 See Swanson, 'The sanitation syndrome'; C. Saunders, 'The creation of Ndabeni: Urban segregation and African resistance', in C. Saunders (ed.), *Studies in the History of Cape Town*, *I* (Cape Town, 1979), 132-66.

104 LG/93/6, Council meeting, 5 Dec.1902

105 EC/4/4/8, Memo. by Attorney General, 9 Feb. 1903.

106 A/2/2/31, Chief Secr., Adm., to Town Clerk, 24 Feb. 1903.

107 EC/4/4/13, Minute No. 1287, 8 Sept. 1904.

108 But the Bulawayo town council had municipal bye-laws (the Gov. Notice No. 165 of 1899) to prohibit 'free' African residence.

109 *Debates*, I, 26 Apr. 1905, 4, 5. See also *Ibid*. 14 May 1906, 4; A/2/4/3, Milton, Adm., to High Commissioner, 10 Apr., 12 May 1905.

110 Up to that time there was no law to prohibit the Africans from living 'independently': LG/47/14, Town Clerk to Chief Insp., S.R. Constabulary, 5 Jan. 1905; Town Clerk to Sanitary Insp., 9 Feb 1905; Town Clerk to Insp. of Location, 9 Feb. 1905.

111 Overseer of Works' report, in *Mayor's Minutes*, 1906-7.

112 *Rhodesia Herald*, 20 Mar. 1907.

113 LG/38, M.O.H. to Town Clerk, 9 Apr. 1907.

114 *Rhodesia Herald*, 13 April. 1908.

115 *Mayor's Minutes*, 1907-8, 9.

116 Later in the 1950s this issue, the advantages and disadvantages of 'segregation', were examined in detail by municipal officials: H. R. Martin and G. H. Hartley, 'The Housing of Natives within the Areas of Local Authorities' (City of Salisbury, 1955), 6-15.

117 To take the railway compound for example, it was reported in 1908: 'there are 42 huts, 22 of which are made of iron V shaped, and the remainder are of old scrap tin and the like. These are very unsanitary, and the whole of the native quarters are in a very dirty state. All refuse and rubbish is thrown just outside the huts, and allowed to accumulate all over the place.' Only two latrines were provided, one of which was 'not made of iron but only of grass', with no roof. See LG/52/25, Report ... by Sanitary Insp., 18 May 1911; *Ibid*. Sanitary Insp. to Commonage Comm., 6 Oct. 1915; LG/51/1, R. Rae to Actg Town Clerk, 31 Dec. 1928; M.O.H.'s reports in the *Mayor's Minutes*, 1930-1, 1931-2, 1934-5.

118 See M.O.H.'s reports in the *Mayor's Minutes* in the late 1920s.

119 S1542/V4, Comm. of Police to C.N.C., 27 Feb. 1934.

120 But Figure 3 also shows the relatively rapid expansion of the location population in the 1930s. Note that at that time there was a growing practice on the part of employers, especially

in commerce and industry, of taking on Africans without providing accommodation for them.

121 In July 1913 the municipality wrote to 22 firms, employing 600 to 650 Africans between them, advising them to use the location, but the plea largely fell on deaf ears: LG/47/21, Town Clerk to Anglo-African Trading Co., 11 July 1913; LG/52/6/1, H.S. Winter to Town Clerk, 10 July 1913; *Ibid*. Ranger's report for July 1913. It may be added that the municipality itself, while championing the cause of the location and segregation, housed their own labourers in a separate compound outside the location. It follows, therefore, that there was something more to the urban location than a mere labour compound meeting the immediate needs of the employing class.

2

'We, the "People in Location"':
municipal ghetto & community action,
1907-1923

I am a German East Africa native in the employ of Paraskeva & Co. butcher. I reside and work at the Slaughter Poles. About 8 a.m. today Shilling and Joskie, Municipal Native Police came to my hut, they found a native Foromani with me in the hut. They arrested him, Joskie then asked me why Foromani was there. I told him he was previously employed there and that I intended seeing my master and having him taken on again. Joskie said I had no right to have [him] with me and that he would arrest me, he told me to hold up my hands for the handcuffs to be put on, I refused. Joskie then struck me a violent blow on the right ear with his fist. I fell down, some other natives who were with Joskie then held me down while Shilling struck me several times with a sjambok, the blood on my face was caused by the blow on the ear, the weals on my back were caused by the sjambok.

I did not refuse to go with the Police, but said I would go without being handcuffed, as I had done nothing.

(Statement by Tabora, 4 June 1910 (LG42/7, Sub-Insp., O.C., Town Det., B.S.A.P. to Town Clerk, 6 June 1910).

This chapter will investigate the development of the location system from 1907 to the early 1920s. The period was marked with events such as the re-opening of the location, the removal of 'free' African residents from the town, and the demolition of 'private locations' on the commonage; the establishment of a church reserve to the north of the location (1909); the employment of European full-time superintendent (1913), and the resultant abolition of the post of African headman. Another important event was the introduction of a monopoly on African beer, which provided the municipality with a vital means to finance its otherwise costly management of African affairs. The chapter will also explore the impact of these events and developments on the life of urban Africans, and the ways in which people reacted to them. Generally very unpopular with Africans, the 'locationisation' policies gave rise to a series of protest movements, including a storm of women's protest against the local authority's usurpation of the manufacturing and sale of African beer. Following such movements diachronically, one will notice a broad change, from a stay-away attitude at the beginning, to location-based mobilisation over living conditions in the post-World War I years. This may be viewed as pointing to the nascence of an African 'urban community' within the official ghetto.

As is plain from Tabora's bitter testimony cited above, Africans like his friend Foromani, who stayed outside the authorised areas at night, ran the risk of being harassed and arrested by the police. Foromani was convicted of trespassing and loitering under the vagrancy laws and sentenced to a £2 fine or 14 days hard labour.[1] He was just one of numerous Africans who were taken before the magistrate's court for relying on friends' hospitality in securing a sleeping place. One may wonder, then: if all the Africans who were not housed by their employers were obliged to reside in the public location, what kind of housing was provided there?

'It is the best compound that I have visited in the country.' This was the opinion of W. S. Taberer, the Chief Native Commissioner, after his inspection of the new location in 1908. According to him: 'The huts inside were kept scrupulously clean, and the surroundings left nothing to be desired. The rubbish deposits and latrines were kept in good order.'[2] Non-official visitors, too, expressed a favourable opinion. Among them was Henri Rolin, a Belgian academic who studied the 'law and administration of Rhodesia'. He wrote in the early 1910s: 'The location at Salisbury, which the writer visited, consists of rows of round huts made of corrugated iron within a large enclosure; there is an appearance of neatness and order.'[3]

One thing that impressed the European visitors must have been the spaciousness of the place. The location was erected on open terrain, surrounded by the veld rolling away to the horizon. Within the boundary was a collection of newly erected Kaytor huts, each built on a plot 50 by 50 feet, and standing in lines running east to west. The place had an impressive appearance of tidiness and regularity, as well as spaciousness. Moreover, the Kaytor huts represented an above-standard type of African housing in those days, for the 'native quarters' in the private industries invariably consisted of miserable shacks and the cheapest hovels.[4]

Yet this was a cursory impression, at best, and at worst a completely inaccurate one. In fact, the official estate was bitterly unpopular with the very people for whom it was built. Why? As we have seen, municipal involvement in African housing was the product of a demand for exclusion and control arising from the very structure of the settler town, and the scale of municipal housing was initially very limited in relation to the dominant servants' quarter/compound system. This gives us a clue to understanding the nature of the council's location policy.

Simply representing an exclusionist pressure, then, the policy was char-

Kaytor huts in the Old Bricks section, Harare township, 1958

Kaytor huts (Matank) were the first major form of municipal accommodation in the 'new location' established in 1907.

Source: National Archives of Zimbabwe, Harare, Photographic Collection.

acterised by utter disregard for the quality of tenants' lives. It was not at this stage that the problems of the 'indirect wage', and of the reproduction of African labour-power became an urban question. Acting as a landlord, rather than a social planner, the council was inclined to see the production of African housing in terms of revenue. This, together with the housing controls which enabled the council to charge a monopoly rent, led to a high rate of rent appropriation.[5] In 1907, rents in the new location were raised 100 per cent.[6] A man who occupied a hut with his family had to pay a monthly rent of 10s. at a time when few workers earned more than 15s. a month. Nor was this rental policy compatible with the standards of the real estate market: with the price of a Kaytor hut being £12, the annual return on the initial investment on building was as much as 50 per cent.[7] In any case, the apparently comparatively good quality of accommodation in the location had to be paid for by tenants themselves in higher rents.

Another major strand of the council's location policy was its preoccupation with control. The location was placed under police rule (the deployment of many policing staff to a very small location inevitably exerted an upward pressure on rents), and elaborate regulations were imposed. Tenants had to be regularly employed; that is to say, the African was given a 'privilege' to hire a hut from the council only in exchange for his service to the town economy. Visitors could not remain in the location for more than twelve hours. A relative or a friend who wished to stay with a tenant had to buy an official permit. Failure to keep one's hut clean constituted a crime. People could not leave the location after 9 p.m. The police and other managerial staff were empowered to enter any hut for inspection. Business activity of any kind was prohibited; and so forth.[8] The former policy of allowing tenants to erect their own huts was withdrawn.[9] People were now in the location purely on a monthly basis, so that the 'undesirables' were evicted quickly. Thus, in 1907, when the draft location regulations (framed in terms of the Native Urban Locations Ordinance) were sent to London for Imperial approval, officials of the Colonial Office commented on the regulations as being designed to 'make life on the location as burdensome as possible'.[10]

Understandably, people had an aversion to going to the location and resisted, if possible, being entrapped there. Already prior to 1907, when the council started to overhaul the method of location administration, most of the residents had deserted the location.[11] The new location, too, despite its seemingly improved appearance, was met with a unanimous stay-away attitude.

Resettling Africans & Popular Response

The new location, when started in October 1907, caused great anxiety for African urban dwellers. Shortly after its opening, a large number of Africans visited the location superintendent, asking for huts provided by the council, according to the superintendent, 'under the impression that they were to leave town. Then they found out that that was not the case [because the Ordinance (No. 4 of 1906) was not yet operative in Salisbury]. They stayed on in town'.[12] The result was that out of more than fifty housing units in the location only twelve huts were taken up.[13] A number of Africans renting rooms in town were evicted in the following months, but this hardly improved the position.

Yet with the approach of 1 May 1908 (the day when African 'free' residence became illegal), there was a rush of people seeking municipal accommodation. On 2 May the superintendent joyfully informed the town clerk that 'the whole of the huts at the location are now full, consequently until further accommodation is provided, it will be impossible to accommodate more natives there'.[14] But it soon turned out that people had come to the location only temporarily. By September 1908 ten huts found no tenants,[15] and this spurred the local authority to intensify its campaign against law-evaders. Blacklisted by authority were 'a number of post office boys and native women' on Dardagan's brickyard; 'several on Forbes' plot'; 'strange boys' sleeping with brickyard workers; six women 'in boys quarters at railway station'; '2 native women' at Ayrshire station; 'several natives' near Salisbury Street; 'some' behind Argus House and around Kennedy House.[16]

The problem of empty huts became more serious in 1909. In the winter of that year almost half of the huts in the location stood empty.[17] In their attempt to detect 'free' residents who should be forced into the location, the council and the police left no stone unturned: the places affected by official inspections included the servants' quarters on the Golf Club links, stores and yards in Manica Road and Second Street, a 'native eating house' near the railway station, dwellings at the top of Albion Street and on both sides of Pioneer Street, the railway compound, and brickyards.[18] In September 1909 the first exemplary punishment in terms of the Native Urban Locations Ordinance was inflicted on three drivers of Sena (Mozambican) origin, Douglas, Solomon and David, who shared a room in Pioneer Street.[19]

The Native Urban Locations Ordinance had an exemption clause. A former location resident, J. Fushtina, applied in 1908 for a special permit 'enabling his wife to live with him in town', with a letter of recommendation from his employer.[20] But far from obtaining it, Fushtina was warned by the council that he himself was 'liable to summary ejection by the police', for he was living neither on his employer's premises nor in the location. [21] With its own location underutilised, the council was all the more of the opinion that 'the exemptions granted be as few as possible', and that 'all native married women should reside in the Location'.[22] Indeed, by August 1909 the government had issued only nine permits for the whole of Salisbury − four to government employees, two to Sena traders operating outside the location, one to a David Moeketsi employed by the Anglo-African Trading Co., and two to wives and families.[23]

In mid-1909 there were, the police believed, 'few natives residing in Town except on premises where they are employed'.[24] Accordingly, the focus of evictions and removals to the location progressively shifted from inner to outer Salisbury. By the 1910s it was clearly fixed upon African settlements on various plots on the commonage.

Perhaps the largest of such locations was on the Wesleyan mission station near the cemetery. The station had been established in 1893, immediately to the south of the old municipal location. Together with the Epworth farm outside the town, it formed the first Wesleyan foothold for African evangelisation in the country. The place was inhabited by African Christians employed in town. In 1908, the station contained fifty-six huts and a chapel, with ninety adults and fifty or sixty children living there. It provided a day school in which a South African teacher taught fifty children.[25]

With the growing concern over African urban residence and the demolition of the old location in 1907, this 'independent' African community attracted official attention. In this case the Chief Native Commissioner took the initiative. In his letter to the council in October 1908 he made a virulent attack on the community: 'it is the filthiest hovel I have ever visited. It is in my mind a standing disgrace that such a location should be allowed to exist within the town area. . . . I am of the opinion that steps should be taken to place this location under the Towns Urban Locations Ordinance, 1906.'[26]

Alarmed by this challenge, the supervisor of the station, the Rev. John White, snapped back. 'We have held this ground for 15 years', he wrote to the town clerk:

During that time no serious complaint had been made of any nuisance by the Council. Indeed, the cleanliness of the place has been commented on by a member of your Council publicly. It is an open secret that the Council wish to take from us the right we have had, and I do not think that it would be difficult to get the Government to agree with you.[27]

In his view, 'the sanitary condition of the place is a question of administration. If it is declared unsatisfactory, and, after warning, no attempt made to remedy it, then drastic action would be excusable.'[28] He pointed out the people's aversion to living in the official location: 'it is not clear to me what practical benefit is going to accrue to anyone by the proposed step. For reasons they regard as sufficient, the natives will not live on the Town Location. Driven from our Reserve they will go to their homes or settle at some congenial place outside the Municipal area.'[29]

A negotiation followed, while the community remained. In mid-1909 the town clerk urged the police: 'you should at once proceed against any tenants there who are evading the law. The number of empty huts in our

Native Location has now reached 25, or half of the total number'.[30] But the police replied to this: 'as this location is outside the surveyed township, the Constabulary cannot take any action'. [31] So the Wesleyan location survived a little while longer. But in 1914, by which time the area had been developed as Bacon and Oil Factory sites, municipal pressure was again brought on the mission station. This time the Church gave in, and the people were resettled in the town location.[32]

Another important case of community removal took place on Blake's plot (also known as Esterman's plot), situated on the location road, halfway between the town and the location. On this freehold plot there were a laundry and an eating-house, as well as fourteen Kaytor huts which were let to African workers. Towards the end of 1912 this tenant community was declared illegal. Despite the landowner's claim to the right to make profits from his property, the police raided the plot on the night of 6 January 1913. They arrested all Africans living there who were not in Blake's employ. Some twenty Africans were prosecuted and ordered to reside in the municipal location.[33]

Affixing Churches to the Location

The first years of the century were the formative era of African churches in Salisbury. [34] The meetings and services of African Christians were initially held within town. The situation was soon frowned upon by the European community, which demanded removal of African congregations from the town centre.

The Anglican church was the first affected in this respect. They had had services and a night school 'in a wood-and-iron building near the old Cathedral' in Second Street since around 1899.[35] In 1905, when the expansion of the congregation necessitated an African church, the town council successfully located the new church, St. Michael's, outside the township, near Umtali Road.[36] But before long the choice of the site was regretted. After the opening of a new location, it became a policy to concentrate all the mission churches *within* the location. Confronted with the problem of empty huts, the council offered plots for missionary work in their efforts to make the location more attractive, and in 1908 the Salvation Army and the Presbyterians accepted the offer.[37]

The following year, however, the council rescinded the previous policy. They learned from the town clerk of Bulawayo, who had written:

Several of Native services are continued after 9 p.m. and as the necessary permission to be out late has been granted by employers to the boys concerned for the purpose of attending Churches – altho' [sic] may have no intention of doing so – we find it very difficult to control them. ... Our population at the

44

Location is about 700, and as on Sundays we get as many as 2,000 present, you can imagine the position is a thorny one and requires careful handling.[38]

Upon realising that the existence of ecclesiastical institutions would attract a 'crowd' and offer a pretext for strangers to be in the location, the council set aside in October 1909 a church reserve, situated *outside* but *adjoining* the location.[39] Some church leaders complained about this policy – because many Africans worked and slept within town – but the council overrode them. The Catholics were the first to come to the reserve.[40]

In the meantime, another reserve came into being. In early 1910 the Presbyterian Church (whose African members had been meeting in the criminal yard of the magistrate's court)[41] intended to build an African 'church and school' in Cameron Street in the Kopje area. The plan provoked a wave of protest from European neighbours. In a manner reminiscent of the citizen movement against the African tenants, Kopje residents sent petitions to the local authority, arguing that '[t]he noise and other inconveniences arising from the congregating of Natives will make the locality unsuitable for families to reside'.[42] The local authorities urged the Church to abandon its plans in the Kopje; as a compromise, another church reserve was demarcated, immediately south of the railway station, but not very far from the official location. A few years later this place became the site of the Presbyterian headquarters, under the care of the Dutch Reformed Church, for a huge contingent of Nyasalanders working and travelling in the colony.[43]

In this way, African religious services and schools disappeared from town. By 1910 the churches were all placed around the official location, except the Anglican St. Michael's, to the east of the town. As a result, churchgoers and school pupils were increasingly lured into the hitherto unpopular location area. Before long the location and its surroundings became a religious and educational centre for Salisbury Africans. The Catholic Church, for example, built a substantial brick church, St Peter's, there in 1910. A resident Jesuit Father was stationed there; he supervised a central day school at the location and number of 'kraal schools' outside Salisbury.[44]

By 1910 the various measures that we have seen – eviction, police raids, resettlement, and church removals – gradually yielded the desired effect on public housing. In that year empty dwellings in the location were slowly taken up,[45] and thereafter the location was usually fully occupied. The tenant community expanded rapidly. On the eve of World War I municipal housing comprised a total of 156 Kaytor huts, accommodating approximately 420 adults and 60 children.[46] It appeared that a certain number of town-based Africans were, at last, fixing their abode in the officially-designated area.

45

Canteen, Superintendent & Protest in Location, 1913-18

When the town council set out to consolidate location administration in the latter half of 1913, by setting up a beer hall and appointing a full-time European superintendent, the location once again witnessed an exodus of dissenting residents. Yet, on closer examination, the protest action in this period was not a mere repetition of the earlier, predominantly stay-away attitude. It increasingly assumed a new element of residence-based action, developing around issues of the state control of people's 'housing'.

Since beer controls prompted the most sustained popular struggle during and after the war, it seems worthwhile to review the history and nature of the beer question before 1913. To a great extent, the evolving patterns of beer controls in Salisbury resembled those of housing controls. In the 1890s beer restrictions were initiated, following the South African example, and they were redefined and institutionalised in accordance with needs of an emerging capitalist economy and society, first around 1900 and again after 1907.

As early as 1892 there was a talk among officials about how to regulate the making and drinking of traditional beer in the newly-established location, but the sanitary board's position at the time was that 'the evil had not become a noticeable one'.[47] This initial leniency faded, on paper at least, when the location regulations framed in 1895 banned the possession of beer in the location, and the restrictions were consolidated by Native Location Regulations (No. 181 of 1898) which enabled the 'inspector of locations' to check African access to alcohol.[48] Yet it was not until 1900 that 'township-wide' regulations were first effected in Salisbury. In that year the town council passed bye-laws prohibiting the beer trade (or the making and possession of beer in 'large quantities') within the Salisbury township.[49]

With the expansion of production and the growth of towns from around 1907 in the colony as a whole, new efforts began to link the labour 'problem' with the 'solution' of beer. In these years the mining industry tried to use the beer question as a means to secure an ample supply of African labour and to increase its efficiency. Thus, the mine owners' associations lobbied for a Kaffir Beer Ordinance which, on the one hand, 'would stop ill-gotten profits going to the kraals and would force the idle hundreds of the beer sellers to come out and work'[50] and, on the other, would confer the power to make and supply beer on employers and officials.[51]

A similar, though more diffuse, social process took place in towns, where official attention was riveted on African weekend beer parties, and the robust sub-culture these parties represented. In Salisbury such meetings were held in places like the location, the railway compound, brickyards, and market gardens, just outside the township, where the 1900 beer bye-laws

46

did not apply.[52] As a rule these gatherings involved drinking, singing, dancing, gossiping, and many other social activities, which attracted crowds of
leisure-hungry male workers, as well as prostitutes and beer traders, some
of whom were based in town and others who came in from local villages.[53]
The beer sold by traders fetched a high price, normally one shilling a mug,[54]
almost equivalent to a day's cash earning for the ordinary African worker.
To take the railway compound as an illustration, it was reported in 1910: 'a
good many of the natives employed in town are in the habit of frequenting
the Railway Reserve and ... they obtain Kaffir beer there which is brought
in to the Reserve by native women'.[55] One Saturday night that year the
place was the venue of a large function, attended by no less than 200 Africans, and pandemonium reigned to such an extent that 'the noise they were
making would be heard all over the town'.[56] All these aspects of the African workers' beer parties – unregulated alcohol consumption and leisure
activity, money-making outside wage employment, etc. – were viewed as
potential sources of trouble by the rulers of the emerging colonial town,
with their preoccupation with social order and work discipline.

The real drive for controlling a beer-related popular subculture began
around the end of 1909.[57] The very campaign against the 'free' African
settlements situated on the commonage was, in fact, compounded with vigilance against the 'free' beer parties which were also held there. The railway
compound was among the first subjected to such controls. In 1910 the railway management, at the instigation of the council and the constabulary,
allowed the police to pay periodical visits to the compound and forbade the
making or storing of beer on their premises.[58]

In the location, too, the weekend parties were under attack. In April
1910, in the course of a fresh effort to enforce beer regulations there, the
court found that the Native Urban Locations Ordinance (which repealed
the previous location regulations) had no provision to stop the sale of beer.[59]
This loophole led to a dramatic increase in the number of huts at which the
practice of making and selling beer was carried on, from three to 'no fewer
than 17'.[60] In August, however, the magistrate reconfirmed the illegality
of beer trade by convicting a number of residents in terms of the Sale of
Liquor to Natives and Indians Regulations (No. 240 of 1898).[61] More than
that, the council extended, two months later, the 1900 beer bye-laws to
the commonage,[62] thereby enabling the police 'to deal effectively with any
cases arising out of beer drinking on the Commonage, Railway Reserve, or
freehold plots within the boundaries of the Commonage'.[63]

Thus, in 1910 the sale of African beer was unequivocally defined as a
criminal offence in the whole of Salisbury. The hitherto highly visible link
between women traders and male workers/consumers, was driven under-
ground. The calabashes of beer brought into town for sale by village women
became a thing of the past. Workers' weekend parties were dispersed and
became less conspicuous. The drums containing large quantities of beer

were now 'usually concealed in the long grass or in pits'.[64] A need for quick brewing was felt so strongly that trade in 'a preparation of kaffir corn, crushed and cooked but not fermented' flourished.[65] Nonetheless, home brewing for personal consumption was not criminalised at this point – not least because it was widely believed that African beer was, after all, a time-honoured beverage and diet, and that consumption in reasonable quantities might have beneficial effects on the productivity of labour.

But even this legitimacy of private use was to evaporate, when news about the famed Durban system reached the BSA Company's territory. By 1909 the Durban municipality had created a system under which they set up a few centralised, municipally-controlled African beer halls, while imposing a total prohibition everywhere in and around the borough – the only exception being the municipal beer halls. Not only did the system yield, so it was claimed, a drastic decrease in the amount of African drunkenness, but it also proved financially profitable. In less than three years from its inception the Durban municipal beer fund showed accumulated profits of a staggering £22,000 – a remarkable achievement at a time when the problem of how to pay the cost of urban African administration racked official brains.[66]

These results quickly drew the attention of state functionaries throughout the subcontinent. In Southern Rhodesia the Native Affairs Committee of Enquiry of 1910-11 indeed recommended that an institution similar to the Durban system be established in Rhodesian towns,[67] and specific provisions were made in the Kaffir Beer Ordinance (No. 17 of 1911) to move in that direction. In 1913 both the Bulawayo and Salisbury municipalities launched beer canteens in their locations. The Salisbury canteen project was modest, and the council simply acted as a trader handling beer manufactured by South African Breweries.

Shortly before the opening of the canteen in September 1913, the manager of the Breweries boasted of the quality of their produce: 'All the boys in our employ regard it as superior to anything they can obtain in the locations, and the head boy of the Municipal Location states that it is the finest beer he has tasted.'[68] But what really happened was a boycott against this 'finest beer'. Most consumers stuck to their old drinking habits and patronised African beer sellers. 'During the first week in particular complaints were made', grumbled the town clerk, 'that the beer was sour, and some of the natives even said that it tended to make them sick. The sales ... are very trifling compared to what they should be'.[69] In reaction, the superintendent was given 'discretionary powers to take all legitimate steps to prohibit the unlawful brewing or possession of kaffir beer in the location'.[70] In mid-October the police repeatedly raided African homes in search of illicit beer, with the superintendent engaging an undercover agent 'to do nothing else but to go around and report where beer is being made' (see Figure 7).[71]

The crux of the matter was no longer the problems of 'Saturday and Sunday evenings', but the problems of home brewing and home consumption. After September 1913 the council was bent on curtailing home brewing as much as possible, not to mention stamping out beer traffickers, and this posture was underpinned by a material incentive. Challenging the activity previously considered legitimate or condoned, the council now invaded the private domains of consumption and home life. The new beer policy threatened the lifeline of the ordinary household in the location – like the one in which the husband consumed cheap home-made beer, while the wife gained a few shillings through backdoor sales in her efforts to supplement the husband's low wages[72] – and became a great catalyst in generating location-wide discontent.

African Headman vs European Superintendent

It was not only the beer question that gave rise to popular discontent at the time. In December 1913 the town council, obtaining a bonus from the canteen, employed an ex-B.S.A. Police officer, G. B. Reilly, as a full-time superintendent. Unlike his predecessors, Reilly was to supervise the location area alone.[73] In this way, the council intended to revamp the whole method of early location administration. To achieve a higher degree of control over the location community, they concentrated a great deal of power on the new superintendent.

In March 1914 the council interviewed the Chief Native Commissioner and obtained his accord on introducing new location regulations. These regulations included that 'every visitor to the Location must obtain a permit from the Superintendent', that 'the Superintendent should have power to arrest drunk and disorderly natives', and that 'it should be an offence to resist the Superintendent or the Headman in the execution of his duties'. In addition, the new regulations provided that 'brewing of Native Beer in the Location should be stopped'.[74] Meanwhile, the new superintendent was also made a special constable who could make arrests inside and outside the location.[75] Significantly, he took his residence in a cottage at the south end of the location, so rendering himself available for twenty-four-hour supervision.[76]

In short, direct rule by the European superintendent began. In February 1914 the Detective Department, in conjunction with Reilly, forayed into the location and rounded up those who possessed beer 'in large quantities', while the Native Commissioner came along to collect taxes; he arrested sixteen tax defaulters.[77] On top of this, the council tried to demolish the 'kitchens' put up by residents, which had so far been tolerated – because the Kaytor hut afforded no cooking space. These kitchens, made of scrap iron, were in practice used as extra rooms which served multiple purposes, from cooking and keeping firewood to accommodating people.[78] Insofar as they were 'immovable', the kitchens also provided a degree of security against eviction for the owners. Thus, the official plan to replace the existing kitchens by municipally provided, small, roofless kitchenettes invited strong indignation from residents.[79]

The tradition of transforming grievances into community action was not totally absent in the early days of the new location. By this time there had been some instances in which people united on the basis of the common status of tenant (as against a highly despotic landlord) and strove to defend or improve their immediate living conditions. In 1913 this development was significant enough for the Native Department to institute a 'safety valve', an officially recognised channel through which people's opinions could be heard. The Chief Native Commissioner wrote to the Administrator in September 1913: 'I have reason to believe natives residing in the location have in the past wished to lay certain grievances before the Town Council, but have been prevented from doing so by the Superintendent ... I would suggest that, with the concurrence with the Town Council, natives be informed that they may in such matters approach Mr. Carbutt, who will in turn lay the fact before the Council for final decision'.[80]

So it was that there developed collective efforts by residents to resist the municipal onslaught, beginning with the canteen. When the kitchen plan was announced, residents reacted: 'they consider that the [proposed] kitchen will be a hardship, instead of a benefit, and threaten they will leave the Location, if compelled to use them'.[81] The council stepped back on this matter, but people felt that they had had enough. At the end of February there was an exodus of protesting tenants. A few weeks later the location saw five empty huts, while 'no applications have been received for huts' and 'the Canteen takings are falling off considerably'.[82]

The local authorities were then shocked to learn that at the centre of unrest and opposition was no other than their own 'faithful servant', E. W. B. Makubalo, who had been the location headman for some time. In February 1914 Makubalo was reportedly 'inciting the people not to use the canteen'. 'On one occasion of late', the furious superintendent informed his superior, 'he has interfered with boys who were working for me because they gave me information about some beer in the location, and I am of the opinion that he is aiding and abetting the brewing of Kaffir beer in the location.'[83] In March, just before officials attempted to investigate and arrest him, Makubalo decamped.[84]

To understand why the head 'collaborator' in the location became a leader of popular opposition, it is important to remember that prior to 1914 the headman occupied the central position in day-to-day location administration. Legally, this was recognised by the Native Urban Locations Ordinance which required the approval of the High Commissioner for the appointment of a headman, as in the case of European officials involved in African administration. But perhaps the real reason for the importance of headmanship was simply the absence of a full-time European superintendent. Before December

1913 the superintendent's work was carried out by the town ranger, who also held the post of the compound manager, among others.[85] Hence, the task of everyday control in the location was assigned to the African headman and a few 'police boys', all residing at their place of work. Uneasily straddling the two worlds of the coloniser and the colonised, the headman was often overtaxed, and few remained in the post for more than a year.[86] But Makubalo was different. He was appointed as headman in 1911, and lived in the police quarters with his wife and four children.[87] In the course of time he exercised a considerable degree of authority, both legally and conventionally, over the location community. It was the headman to whom the night visitor had to report upon his or her arrival.[88] It was also the headman who was to explain new rules and regulations to the community. He supervised the manner in which residents made and consumed beer: 'it is customary [the town clerk wrote in 1911] for any tenant who wishes to make beer to notify the Headman, and the latter sees that the quantity made is not excessive'.[89] Makubalo took great pride in his workmanship,[90] an attitude which might be justified by the fact that during his tenure the location saw no empty huts. But the thrust of official policy from 1913 alienated this proud headman so thoroughly that he identified himself with his dissenting neighbours. A European newcomer abruptly usurped his position as 'induna' of the location and, moreover, introduced novel methods and procedures of community control, centred on the use of the police.

In April 1914 the town house received a protest letter signed by 'People in Location'. The writer was no doubt Makubalo himself.[91] In it the people bitterly complained about the reign of terror which had begun with the arrival of a new superintendent:

> We are trying to write this letter. Sir we have just got words to let you know that this new Superintendent of Native Location does not treat us well same as before. ... Some of us have been here nearly seven to eight years. But now they are leaving Location for the sake of this new master. They are leaving for farms to stay there. They are afraid of this new superintendent of Native Location. This master when ever he finds little bit of ndawa he goes very quick to the Police Station and tell them to have the boys run in. ... Plenty people have gone in the farms for the sake of him. Our women all have run away. Sir this month you will find that plenty boys have gone away from Location.[92]

The general tone of the letter hints that this protest action was underpinned by a sense of solidarity developed by the people who had shared a common living space in their daily lives. The dissenters were contemptuous of the heavy-handed ways with which the new superintendent handled community affairs, while extolling the past social order:

> The late John Smith and Mr. Winter [the former town ranger/superintendent] was

not doing like this, they been looking in Native Location very well. ... This new Superintendent does not understand to look after this place. ... We shall be very much pleased if you will kindly send Mr. Winter back in Native Location again.[93]

How did these residents view their ability to influence the council? The following passage gives us a clue:

Sir if you keep on this new master here you will see that in Native Location shall be no people. All have gone in the farms. If we see that Mr. Winter is coming again, plenty of us will go back again in Native Location. We got no more to complain. Only this. We are the people living in Native Location.[94]

Plainly, these residents tried, as they did over the kitchen issue, to use the threat of leaving the location as a means to negotiate with their 'landlord'.

In the event, the demands by Makubalo and others fell on deaf ears, but this agitation seems to have materially influenced the African attitude towards public housing during the World War years. As 'People in Location' warned, the number of unoccupied huts in the location rose from that time onwards. It reached 16 in March 1915, 25 in August, 29 in October, and finally 39 in November. The following year the situation remained unchanged.[95] That was not all. Beer sales began to shrink. Whereas in the municipal year of 1914/15 the town council managed to secure a net profit of £1,134, roughly equal to the rent revenue for that year, the same income dropped to £908 in 1915/16 and further to £533 in 1916/17, as shown in Figure 8.

The superintendent was on the horns of a dilemma. It was necessary to minimise private brewing in order to compel Africans to buy beer from the canteen. On the other hand, he was aware: 'if I am too strict with the natives, they will move out of the location, and so deprive the Council of revenue'.[96] If Africans were expected to patronise the location and the canteen at once, the screw had to be tightened from outside the location. So in early 1917 the police, in cooperation with the council, embarked upon a nocturnal house-to-house raid in search of trespassers.[97] The authorities also took a step to end private brewing completely. In March 1917 the administrator declared that the Salisbury urban area was a proscribed area in terms of the Kaffir Beer Ordinance, making the possession of home-brewed beer illegal. The proscribed area included a two-mile zone outside the town boundaries. [98] (To the dismay of officials, it failed to include the municipal location, since legally the location was not part of the Salisbury urban area, but a special area set aside by the administrator in terms of the Native Urban Locations Ordinance.) The fixing of the two-mile limit meant that official eyes were now fixed on African communities on suburban farms. This caused, in the opinion of a Native Department official, 'distinct hardships to natives residing within that area', who were 'now compelled to visit the Location if they want to drink'.[99]

An immediate outcome of these measures was an influx of people back into the location which was fully tenanted by April 1917 and thereafter entered a new phase of expansion.[100] However, the sales of the canteen continued to decline: in the municipal year of 1917/18 the canteen revenue plummeted to a mere £174, a critical level which forced the beer manufacturer to warn the council that the amount of trade did not 'make the continuance of the contract ...worth the while of the Brewery'.[101] Accordingly, at the end of the war the council hurriedly imposed a prohibition measure in the municipal location, except the canteen premises (in terms of the Native Urban Locations Ordinance).

The Location Community & Protest Against the Beer Monopoly & High Rents after 1918

At this juncture it may be useful to take a look at the nature of the location community around 1920. The residents may be divided into three categories in terms of the form of tenancy. First, there was a group of people who hired huts by themselves. They were often 'family people', with their children, more or less continuously living in the location.[102] Those who slept in employer-rented huts formed the second group. These people were typically 'bachelor' migrant labourers who would live with their workmates, often in overcrowded conditions. The third group comprised migrants who secured accommodation by organising a 'mess system' with their friends and compatriots. Some of them remained in town for prolonged periods, while others worked in town for limited periods or looked for jobs. One may add to this list yet another type, unregistered 'lodgers' of both sexes who would somehow make their way into the location.

In mid-1920 the location possessed a total of 247 huts, with a core population of about 760.[103] Of these, 45 huts were used as bunkhouses by private companies and the municipality, and five were occupied by the 'police and labourers'.[104] The remaining 197 huts were tenanted by African workers in their own names, around two-thirds of them housing the first group in our classification, i.e. 'family people', the rest accommodating the third group, the tenants sharing rent with others.[105]

The ethnic composition of the male inhabitants had a strong bias towards the groups whose rural homes were distant from Salisbury, and who offered longer periods of service in the labour market. 'One most notable feature with regard to the residents', the superintendent noticed in 1915, 'is that no local natives (Mashonas) reside in the location'.[106] In corroboration of this, an old Hararian, Antonio Chikereni, recently recalled: 'When I first came to the location [in 1919], only three Zezurus [Shonas of central Mashonaland] were living there. In those days my neighbours were Nyasas, Northern Rhodesians, and Portuguese Africans, and I myself as a son of a Portuguese

53

African who came from Kanyembe, though my birthplace is Sipolilo'.[107] Unlike the men, however, the female population had a strong local element. This hints at the frequency of unions between foreign workers and Shona women in those days.[108]

Women were allowed to live in the location only as wives to men who were in active employment. It was the official position to recognise a marriage only when it was registered with the government, but the majority of Africans did not pay heed to this, resulting in some leniency on the part of the officials. As a result, the location was a home for a large number of women with 'unregistered' marriages, many living with husbands for many years, whereas a few were the parties of unions of convenience, with a few 'prostitutes' cohabiting with men. Later, in 1936, the Native Commissioner, Salisbury, reported that out of the total of 800 women in the location, 650 lived with male partners. Of these, 150, or 23 per cent, had registered marriages. Of the 500 with unregistered marriages, he estimated, about 300 were 'regarded by natives as respectable women', while those frequently changing husbands were about 100 in number. He numbered the professional prostitutes as 50.[109]

It is a mistake, therefore, to suppose, as is often done, that '[b]efore the last war [of 1939-45] the African townships were occupied mainly by single tenants'.[110] In truth, the location had from its inception a marked concentration of 'long-service workers', 'town dwellers', 'married people', 'wives', 'runaway women', and other relatively proletarianised and/or urbanised elements.

In many ways, the location was a bleak place. The council's dual concern about regulation and revenue was present everywhere. The whole area was enclosed with a barbed-wire fence, with a few openings where the location police watched the comings and goings.[111] Inside there existed no amenities, no shops, no clinics, no churches, no schools – only the large municipal beer canteen. In 1920 a neighbourhood of 250 Kaytor huts, many of them now in a dilapidated condition, shared one borehole and three communal latrines, and there was not a single ablution facility for them (see Figure 10).[112]

Exactly like in the labour compound, the superintendent (nicknamed *katsekera* in chiNyanja, meaning 'one who locks out') and his police would start their daily routine with turning out residents to work. 'Scarcely a day passes', wrote the superintendent in 1921, 'without several natives being sent from the Location to their work who are simply malingering for the purpose of card-playing.'[113]

The desolate physical ambiance was further accentuated by the fragmentation and internal tensions of the community: ethnically heterogeneous, materially impoverished, and politically marginalised. In the post-war years the location was frequently the scene for 'faction fights' or group violence, in addition to a high incidence of drunkenness, gambling, brawls, bicycle thefts, burglary and arson.[114]

Superintendent D. McDougall and Salisbury location police, 1927

The European superintendent was nicknamed Katsekera, meaning the one who locks out.
'This name "Kasekela" was given to him [McDougall] by Africans. He had very clever and wise methods of settling African cases.
He used to settle them at once and did not like putting off till the next day' (Bantu Mirror, 2 Oct. 1943).

Source: Rhod. Her., 2 Dec. 1927.

Still, the location was not simply an instrument of control. As we will see in Chapter 5, African workers had been developing social institutions and associations at various places in industrial Salisbury. At the centre of this development were often 'old-timers' in town who had made the location their habitat. For this and other reasons, the location became the focus of African associational life, and the sorts of activities it represented – tea meetings, dances, football matches, beer drinking, religious gatherings, night schools, etc. And this transformed the official ghetto into a vital urban scene.

Bearing in mind these features of the location community, we now turn to popular mobilisation there. One factor that greatly influenced the post-war protest was the ravages of inflation occasioned by the war. In a matter of years, from 1914 to 1920, the prices of goods soared by 165 per cent, while the nominal wages for African workers rose only by 18 per cent.[115] That is to say, by 1920 the real African wages had dropped to less than half of their pre-war level. The overall impact might not have been so serious as far as rural migrants were concerned – partly because agricultural products fetched high prices in these years, and partly because while working in town they received rations and shelter from their employers; on the other hand, the African urbanites, fully enmeshed in the cash economy and perhaps less able to call on agrarian resources, were among the most vulnerable and bore the full brunt of the high prices.

The inflation dramatically sharpened the problems and social contradictions inherent in the colonial towns and industrial centres. In the production process it fixed African workers' attention on the problem of low wages, and this resulted in a great deal of African industrial action, including strikes, after 1918.[116] Simultaneously, the high prices and lower real wages posed an overwhelming threat, above all to the fragile family budgets of African residents, so highlighting various 'secondary forms of exploitation' in the consumption process.[117] With cash in short supply, men and women in the Salisbury location tightened the purse strings and turned to 'informal jobs'. But it was precisely at this moment that the local state tried to stop the consumption of low-cost home-made beer and to take over African beer trade. This made the location inhabitants quite sensitive and antagonistic to pressures stemming from state control of African housing. In defence of their interests, they came together and resisted as 'African tenants' herded together by the colonial state.

This point was clearly evident in a public meeting held on 2 January 1919. A few days earlier, at the end of 1918, new regulations had been promulgated prohibiting all kinds of private brewing in the location. [118] The meeting was held between location residents and officials, including the Superintendent of Natives and the town clerk. On that occasion the residents 'strongly objected' to the latest beer regulations. Contending that the people with families 'couldn't afford to buy beer' from the municipality, they asked for permission to brew a small quantity for their own consumption on Sundays, as they had been allowed to do in the past.[119]

The keynote of people's grievances characteristically concerned a crisis in domestic consumption. Since 'it was impossible to obtain sufficient dead wood on the commonage for their requirements', they asked: 'Could not wood be supplied' by the municipality? 'Some also wanted pieces of land given to them', which would help tide them over difficult times. In addition, the residents complained of high rents charged by the municipality, by appealing 'if the rent per hut could be reduced from 10/- to 5/-'.[120]

In a manner reminiscent of the events in early 1914, the officials were further told that '[i]n consequence of these new [beer] Regulations ... many natives would leave the Location, especially those with families'.[121] By this time, however, the action of deserting the location had ceased to be a major feature of the protest. Indeed, despite the above threat, and also the superintendent's fear of yet another exodus in 1920, no significant evacuation occurred.[122] Rather, after 1918 the tenants showed a marked tendency towards stabilisation and towards defining themselves as members of the location community.[123] As a conscious expression of this trend, the residents demanded in the meeting to enter the decision-making process in the location: they should be 'notified beforehand of any contemplated bye-laws affecting their welfare, to enable them to hold meetings and discuss such regulations, and submit to the Government their formal protest if they considered it necessary to do so, as they would have done in regard to Government Notice No. 487 [the latest beer regulations]'.[124]

So it was that the new beer regulations introduced at the end of 1918 appeared to cause a good deal of popular opposition. But in February 1919 the magistrate found these regulations, framed under the provisions of the Native Urban Locations Ordinance, *ultra vires*. As a result, 'residents ... gradually recommenced brewing small quantities of beer'.[125]

It was in the following year, 1920, then, that the authorities waded through the quagmire of beer laws. They passed the Kaffir Beer Amendment Ordinance (No. 21 of 1920), under which, in November, the administrator re-defined the proscribed area. [126] This covered the entire town of Salisbury, including the municipal location. The previous two-mile limit beyond the commonage boundaries was expanded to a five-mile limit in order to control more distant African settlements. The superintendent accordingly told the location residents that after 21 November the location must be completely 'dry', except the official canteen.[127]

On 27 November 1920 a woman named Ruisa, 'who had elected to test the validity of the new regulations was fined £2 for being in possession of 6 gallons of Kaffir Beer'.[128] Immediately a deputation was organised by the people in the location. On 29 November 'about 150 native women of all tribes', that is, practically all the female residents in the location, went to interview the Superintendent of Natives. The complaints and requests lodged by the deputation included that residents 'might be allowed to brew a small quantity of Kaffir beer'; that the monthly rent of 10s. should be reduced to the level of the Bulawayo location, i.e. 5s.; and that garden plots should be allocated to women.[129] With respect to two fundamental issues concerning beer and rent, nothing came out of this action. But the women won a concession in respect of land. By the end of 1920 the municipality allocated garden plots, in the south-eastern corner of the location, to 'married women and several women who lost their husbands during the Flu'.[130]

In the Christmas week some residents started making beer again.[131] The new year dawned with a decisive state offensive against the private brewers. Its destructive effect on the already poverty-stricken community was evident:

> There appears [observed the superintendent in June 1921] to be a reluctance to call in a doctor lately doubtless owing to the reduced circumstances occasioned by curtailing the brewing industry in some cases and I have arranged with the A.N.C. Salisbury to send any natives unable to afford a doctor to him that they may obtain a note of admission to Hospital.[132]

A new temper arose, and a search for new forms of activism began. On 10 January 1921, when five women and eleven men were taken before the magistrate for being in possession of beer, according to the press, 'Fully one hundred natives were congregated outside the Court'. The magistrate gave severe penalties to the prisoners. Two persons were fined £25 each, with the alternative of three months' imprisonment, and the fines imposed amounted to over £100 in total. 'The gang of natives outside took a keen interest in the proceedings, and when, by some unknown means, they heard the sentence almost as soon as it was delivered, there was much animated conversation and gesticulation. The hubbub became so great eventually' that the police were called in to disperse the crowd.[133]

The location inhabitants then adopted a measure to bypass the local channels and go directly to a higher power when, in May 1921, they sent a petition to the Legislative Council. The petition was addressed to none other than William M. Leggate, a spokesman for the settler farmers and a chief opponent of the municipal beer monopoly system in the legislature.[134] It was written by Enock Mankayi, a literate South African working in Salisbury, who had been elected to the executive committee of a Union Bantu Vigilance Association at its inaugural meeting in July that year.[135]

The petitioners, describing themselves as 'Natives living in the Location', asked for an amendment to the Kaffir Beer Ordinance and stated: 'If we may be refused we shall demand the government to abolish the Beer Hall as [it] is a money making place. ... Money is made not for our benefit. ... We ask the government to see how much money the Court made in fines for beer-making. ... We draw the notice of the government to the fact that Kaffir Beer to our mind is reckoned as food.' The underlying problem was again pinching poverty: 'We ask the Elected Members to consider our position in the Location regarding the Hut-fees which is ten shillings a month. We ask the Government to realise that we live by buying foodstuffs every day. We ask the Elected Members to see how we are affected by the high cost of living. We ask the Elected Members to ... make some places where we could be able to buy at lower prices.'[136]

Protest rumbled into the following year. In August 1922 some women in the location were in a restive mood, because the superintendent prohibited the women from entering the canteen after five o'clock. The next month they came out in a boycott of the canteen. 'For a time they managed to prevail upon the male customers to leave with them', causing a noticeable drop in the takings at the hall.[137]

By this time, however, the vigour of the post-war community action was undeniably on the wane, probably as inflation subsided after 1921. The beer protest, the linchpin of the popular mobilisation at the time, was entering a new phase. The municipality gradually succeeded in directing African beer drinkers to their canteen. Sales at the canteen showed an upward turn in 1919 and thereafter increased more or less steadily (Figure 8). Facing the high risk of competing with the town council, the African brewers, too, started adapting to a new reality. Especially in mid-1922 a large number of Africans turned to a safer brew, known as hop beer.[138] 'There is no law to stop the brewing of "Hop beer"', so commented the superintendent, 'since it is looked upon as a harmless household refreshment, but some of the old women have discovered that the addition of potato, water and sugar makes the brew much stronger'.[139] Within a few years hop beer became indispensable to African workers' recreational gatherings; as one complainant wrote in 1925: 'the disturbances nearly always occur late at night and mostly as the result of overindulgence in "Hop beer" which is brewed in large quantities throughout the location by the women'.[140]

Conclusion

By the end of the Charter Company's rule the maturing of the location system was apparent. African free dwellers had been expelled from the town centre; the tenant communities on the commonage had disappeared; African churches and schools had been shifted to the location area; the law unequivocally defined where the African workers were to sleep; the top-down machinery of control headed by a full-time European superintendent was built; and the beer monopoly system added a revenue-generating dimension to location administration. The location thereafter entered a new phase of expansion, with its total population rising to 1,738 in 1925 and then to 3,488 in 1930.[141] It was the symbolic expression of a non-integration attitude by the town's dominant groups, as well as the practical container for the 'spillover' from the private servants' quarters and compounds.

The growing state control of African housing, with an exclusionist emphasis, had far-reaching repercussions for Salisbury's history. One such was that it made the sphere of African living a site, potential or otherwise, of social conflict. To put it in the style of Castells,[142] it directly contributed to collectivising issues of living – securing a house, paying high rentals, making and consuming African beer, visiting friends and husbands, going out after 9 p.m., erecting a makeshift kitchen, collecting firewood, and engaging in market gardening – which would otherwise be private, individualised, and, in many instances, even innocent activities. The location policy concentrated a mass of Africans on one spot, under a single landlord, and in more or less the same living conditions. It therefore encouraged the location residents to think of themselves as members of one community, particularly when the oppressive edges of the system were felt. In this sense one can say that the development of the location system was inseparably linked to a story of African social movements seeking a living space in city.

It has often been pointed out that the pre-World War II Salisbury was a politically quiet town, compared with its sister town in the south-west, Bulawayo. Such might be case – since the local Shona communities rarely aired their grievances in the urban context – but this should not lead us to assume that there was little popular mobilisation in early Salisbury. The foregoing pages have clearly shown that a lot of urban protest took place over restrictive housing policies. The movements were initially character-ised, as the 1914 letter of the 'People in Location' indicates, by attempts to avoid using the location, a tendency to live on suburban farms, and the threat of vacating the location. Consequently, the location repeatedly saw vacant huts – a striking situation, since the African housing question in later periods was almost always synonymous with a housing shortage. However, with the advancement of the municipalisation of African housing, including beer controls, and of the relocation of people, the position changed. After around 1920, discontent was seldom expressed in the form of moving out of the location, which was usually fully occupied. The popular mobilisation was now more location-based, and more concerned with issues directly rel-evant to location life, including, as the case of the public meeting of January 1919 demonstrated, requests to the authorities for participation in deci-sion-making process about the welfare of residents. The change seems to underline the coming into being of an African urban community with some internal coherence within the location. This is remarkable, in view of the fact that the men and women in question had diverse linguistic-cultural backgrounds, most being new arrivals from the countryside, and having only recently taken up residence in the location (see Figure 9).

Notes

1   D/4/7/13, case 604 of 1910. Trespassing was the most common African crime in early Salisbury. In 1911 out of the total of 1,756 Africans taken before the Salisbury magistrate 343, or 20 per cent, were charged with trespassing (under the provisions of the Natives Pass Ordinance (No. 10 of 1902) as amended), and the corresponding figures for 1924 rose to 1,186, or 30 per cent, out of 3,987: D/4/7/13-14; J/5/1/3.

2   LG/42/6, W.S. Taberer, C.N.C., to Secr., Adm.'s Dep., 21 Oct. 1908.

3   H. Rolin, *Rolin's Rhodesia*, trans. D. Kirkwood (Bulawayo, 1978), 145.

4   Phimister writes (I. Phimister, 'African labour conditions and health in the Southern Rhodesian mining industry, 1898-1953', in Phimister and van Onselen, *Studies in the History of African Mine Labour*, 106): 'they (Kaytor huts) cost £11 each, a price which the mining industry generally considered 'prohibitive', and even the rich Globe and Phoenix built only sixty. After the reconstruction period, Kaytor Huts were somewhat more widely used'. Later on, the position was quite different, as Saidi writes (W. Saidi, *The Old Bricks Lives* (Gweru, 1988), 29): 'Not many were excited about living in these tanks [the Kaytor huts in the Harare township in the 1950s] which were occupied mostly by migrant workers from Portuguese East Africa and Nyasaland. Moreover, they were generally so overcrowded that their occupants were the first to succumb to any widespread disease in the township.'

5   Thus the Chairman of the Native Affairs Commission of 1930 had to warn the Premier in 1931: 'We regard it as of the utmost importance that it should be made impossible in the future for Native finance to merge into and become indistinguishable from municipal finance. We foresee a serious source of inter-racial antagonism if the position is not safeguarded once and for all': S482/789/39, H.M.G. Jackson to Minister of Native Affairs, 14 Jan. 1931.

6   The council originally planned for a more drastic rent hike, which met opposition from the High Commissioner: LG/47/16, Town Clerk to Chief Secr., Adm., 28 Nov. 1907.

7   S86, Native Affairs Commission (Salisbury Municipal Location) 1930, Report.

8   At the beginning more than half of the expenditure for the location was accounted for by 'salaries' and 'labour': Revenue and Expenditure Account, in *Mayor's Minutes*, 1909-10.

9   At the beginning of the century, however, this practice was being replaced by the policy of erecting municipal buildings: LG/52/20, T. L. Knapman to Town Clerk, 10 June 1903.

10 Public Record Office, London, C.O. 417/438, minute of Grindle on Selborne to Elgin, 25 Nov. 1907, quoted in J. M. Mackenzie, 'African labour in the Chartered Company period', *Rhod. Hist.*, I (1970), 49.

11 See the section, Town Location in the Years of Urban Growth, in Chapter 1.

12 LG/52/6/1, J. Smith, Location Supt., to Town Clerk, 21 Nov. 1907.

13 *Ibid.*

14 LG/47/16, Town Clerk to Chief Insp., S. R. Constabulary, 2 May 1908.

15 LG/52/6/1, Memo. by Supt., 7 Sept. 1908.

16 LG/47/17, Town Clerk to V. Dardagan, 23 Sept. 1908; *Ibid.* Town Clerk to S.R. Constabulary, 6 Oct. 1908.

17 Ranger's report, in *Mayor's Minutes*, 1908-9.

18 LG/47/17, Town Clerk to Secr., Gold Club, 20 Apr. 1909; *Ibid.*, Town Clerk to Chief Insp., S.R. Constabulary, 23 Nov. 1909; LG/47/18, Town Clerk to Chief Insp., S.R. Constabulary, 14 Jan. 1910; *Ibid.* Town Clerk to General Manager, B. & M. Railways, 18 Feb. 1910; LG/52/6/1, J. Smith to Town Clerk, 2 Mar. 1910.

19 *Rhodesia Herald*, 16 Sept. 1909; D/4/7/12, cases 944, 945, 946 of 1909.

20 LG/47/17, Town Clerk to C.N.C., 10 Sept. 1908.

21 *Ibid.*

22 LG/93/9, Council Minute, 8 Sept. 1909; LG/52/6/1, Town Clerk to C.N.C., 14 Sept. 1908.

23 LG/42/6, Magistrate to Town Clerk, 31 Aug. 1909; *Rhodesia Herald*, 10 Sept. 1909.

24 LG/38, Delahay to Sub-Insp., S.R. Constabulary, 14 July 1909.

25 LG/52/6/1, J. Smith to Town Clerk, 19 Nov. 1908; LG/38, Rev. John White to Town Clerk, 23 Nov. 1908. For an account of the Wesleyan work in the Salisbury area, see R. Peaden, 'The contribution of the Epworth Mission settlement to African Development', in T. O. Ranger and J. Weller (eds), *Themes in the Christian History of Central Africa* (Berkeley, 1975), 135-51.
26 LG/42/6, W.S. Taberer, C.N.C., to Secr., Adm., 21 Oct. 1908.
27 LG/38, Rev. J. White to Town Clerk, 17 Nov. 1908.
28 *Ibid.* Rev. J. White to Town Clerk, 23 Nov. 1908.
29 *Ibid.*
30 LG/47/17, Town Clerk to Chief Insp., S.R. Constabulary, 11 Aug. 1908.
31 LG/38, Sub-Insp., S.R. Constabulary, to Town Clerk, 17 Aug. 1908.
32 LG/47/22, Town Clerk to Supt., Wesleyan Mission, 14 May 1914; LG/47/24, Town Clerk to A. Walton, 27 May, 8 June 1915: LG/47/25, Town Clerk to A. Walton, 24 June 1915; LG/38, A. Walton to Town Clerk, 3, 14 June 1915; Jesuit Archives, Harare, Box 132/1, 'Johanny: Burbridge's estimate of the parish statistics', 14 Aug. 1929.
33 This paragraph is based on LG/47/20, Town Clerk to O.C., B.S.A. Police, 25 Jan. 1912; *Ibid.*, Town Clerk to Honey, Blanckenberg, & Ross, 29 Feb. 1912; LG/42/9, H. C. Maline to O. C. "E" Troop, 5 Feb. 1912; LG/38, Roberts, Letts & Gill to Town Clerk, 14 Jab. 1913; D/9/7/15, case 28 of 1913.
34 An analysis of the 1911 census data shows that almost twenty-eight per cent of the Africans in Salisbury claimed to be Christian, whereas it was estimated in the same census that only one-sixteenth of the adult Africans in the colony were receiving 'a certain amount of religious training' at mission churches. C/5/2/12-16; S.R., *Report of the Director of Census ... 1911*, 17.
35 Hist. Mss Collect., MISC/MU 1, Samuel Muhlanga. History File.
36 *Rhodesia Herald*, 24 Aug., 28 Sept. 1905, 18 Sept. 1906.
37 LG/38, C. Clark to Town Clerk, 9 June 1908; LG/47/16, Town Clerk to Salvation Army, 25 June 1908; LG/38, S. Dornan to Civil Comm., 13 Aug. LG/47/17, Town Clerk to S. Dornan, 27 Aug. 1908, 12 Jan. 1909.
38 LG/38, Town Clerk, Bulawayo, to Town Clerk, Salisbury, 3 Sept. 1909.
39 LG/93/10, Council Minute, 22 Sept. 1909.
40 LG/47/17, Town Clerk to Rev. Gartlan, 23 Sept. 1908.
41 LG/38, Rev. H. W. Cochran to Town Clerk, 10 July 1906.
42 *Ibid.* Petition to Mayor and Councillors, 15 Jan. 1910.
43 See LG/38, Rev. Adshade to Town Clerk, 18 Oct. 1910; H.M. L. du Toit, 'The Church of Central Africa-Presbyterian', in P.S. King (comp.), *Missions in Southern Rhodesia* (n.p., [1959]), 70. The DRC mission was transferred to the location area in 1935: LG/93/34, Commonage and Gardens Comm. Minute, 8 Oct. 1935.
44 Jesuit Archives, Harare, Box 41/5, 'Notes on the Zambesi Mission, 1924'; A. J. Dachs and W. F. Rea, *The Catholic Church and Zimbabwe* (Gwelo, 1979), 92-3.
45 LG/93/10, Council Minute, 12 Jan. 1910; LG/52/6/1. J. Smith to Town Clerk, 13 Oct. 1910.
46 Ranger's report, *Mayor's Minutes*, 1912-13; LG/52/6/1, G. Reilly to Town Clerk, 3 Mar. 1914.
47 *Mash. Her. Zamb. Times*, 5 Mar. 1892.
48 A/2/4/1, Milton, Actg. Admin. to High Comm., 27 May 1898; Ranger's report, in *Mayor's Minutes*, 1898-9.
49 Gov. Notice No. 54 of 1900.
50 *Rhodesia Herald*, 2 Nov. 1910.
51 *Rhodesia Herald*, 15, 22, 25 Nov. 1907, 20 May, 17 Nov. 1908, 25 Feb. 1909; *Debates*, I, 21 May 1909, 47. For a detailed discussion on the subject, see van Onselen, *Chibaro*, 166-72.
52 But a measure of control was imposed in the location under the provisions of the Native Location Regulations (No. 181 of 1898). For beer parties held on the commonage, see among others LG/47/7, Town Clerk to C.N.C., 11 Jan. 1910; LG/52/6/1, Location Supt. to Town Clerk, 11 Nov. 1909, 4 Apr. 1910; *Rhodesia Herald*, 15 Feb. 1901, 12 Mar. 1902, 16 Sept. 1909, 8 Aug. 1910.
53 For beer sellers coming from outside the town, see *Rhodesia Herald*, 30 Nov. 1894, 27 Oct. 1909, 26 Sept. 1911; LG/52/6/1, 11 Nov. 1909. On the production of beer by village women

in this period Elizabeth Schmidt writes: 'it was evident to many households that female beer brewing ... was a more profitable use of female labour time than their involvement in field work' (idem, 'Women, Agriculture, and Social Change in Southern Rhodesia, 1898-1934, with Special Reference to the Goromonzi District', Univ. of Zimbabwe, Hist. Dep., Seminar Paper, 1986, 5).

[54] Rhodesia Herald, 13 Apr., 9 Aug., 23 Dec. 1910, 31 Jan. 1911.

[55] LG/38, Town Clerk to General Manager, B. & M. Railways, 15 Feb. 1910.

[56] Rhodesia Herald, 30 Mar. 1910.

[57] LG/93/10, Council Minute, 27 Oct. 1909; Ibid. Commonage and Markets Comm. Minute, 21 Jan. 1910; LG/52/6/1, J. Smith to Town Clerk, 11 Nov. 1909, 4 Apr. 1910.

[58] LG/47/18, Town Clerk to General Manager, B. & M. Railways, 15 Feb., 24 Mar. 1910; LG/38, Town Clerk to District Engineer, B. & M. Railways, 29 Sept. 1910; Rhodesia Herald, 30 Mar., 29 Apr., 243 Dec. 1910.

[59] Rhodesia Herald, 13 Apr. 1910.

[60] Ibid. 9 Aug. 1910.

[61] Ibid. 18 Aug. 1910.

[62] Gov. Notice No. 280 of 1910.

[63] LG/47/18, Town Clerk to O.C. B.S.A.P., 28 Oct. 1910.

[64] LG/52/6/1, H.S. Winter to Town Clerk, 17 May 1915. See also Rhodesia Herald, 31 Jan. 1911.

[65] Ranger's report, in Mayor's Minutes, 1910-11.

[66] J.M. Orpen, Natives, Drink, Labour (East London, 1913), 65. For more recent studies on the Durban system, see M. W. Swanson, '"Durban system": Roots of urban apartheid in colonial Natal', African Studies, XXXV (1976), 159-76; P. la Hausse, 'The Struggle for the City: Alcohol, the Ematsheni and Popular Culture in Durban, 1902-1936' (Univ. of the Witwatersrand, History Workshop Paper, 1984).

[67] S.R., Report of the Native Affairs Committee ... 1910-11, 12.

[68] LG/38, Manager, S. A. Breweries, to Town Clerk, 27 Aug. 1913.

[69] Ibid. Town Clerk to Manager, S. A. Breweries, 9 Oct. 1913.

[70] Ibid. Town Clerk to Manager, S. A. Breweries, 9 Oct. 1913. Steps were also taken against illicit brewing at brickyards, the Hatfield estate and other places outside the location: LG/47/21, Town Clerk to E. E. Oudaille, 24 Oct. 1913; Ibid., Town Clerk to District Supt., Town Police, 24 Oct. 1913.

[71] LG/52/6/1, H.S. Winter to Town Clerk, 13 Oct. 1913.

[72] Thus the superintendent stated in early 1914: 'I find most of the residents brew their own beer, but not in sufficient quantities to enable me to prosecute' (LG/52/6.1, G. B. Reilly to Town Clerk, 19 Mar. 1914).

[73] LG/93/11, Commonage and Markets Comm. Minute, 7 Nov. 1913; LG/38, Reilly to Council, 21 Nov. 1913; Ibid. Town Clerk to Reilly, 1 Dec. 1913.

[74] LG/38, Memo. by H. L. Lezard, 13 Mar. 1914. See also LG/47/22, Town Clerk to Honey and Blanckenberg, 1 May 1914.

[75] LG/47/22, Town Clerk to G. B. Reilly, 12 Mar. 1914.

[76] Mayor's Minutes, 1913-14, 4. This was one of the recommendations made by the Native Affairs Committee of 1910-11, in Report of the Native Affairs Committee ... 1910-11, 11.

[77] LG/52/6/1, Reilly to Town Clerk, 3 Mar. 1914.

[78] Ibid. Reilly to Town Clerk, 19 mar. 1914.

[79] Ibid.

[80] N/3/20/2, C.N.C. to Secr., Dep. of Adm., 25 Sept. 1913.

[81] LG/52/6/1, Reilly to Town Clerk, 20 Feb. 1914.

[82] Ibid. Reilly to Town Clerk, 19 Mar. 1914.

[83] Ibid. 3 Mar. 1914.

[84] Ibid. 1 Apr. 1914; 1914; NSA/2/9/1, Asst. District Supt., B.S.A.P., to Supt. of Natives, Salisbury, 6 Apr. 1914.

[85] The town ranger would inspect the location only a few times a week. See Ranger's weekly reports, in LG/52/20; Mordecai's statement, in case 1032 of 1908, D/3/21. After the appointment of a full-time superintendent and Makubalo's incident the headman system was stripped of all its original contents and ceased to exist in 1923, when the town council

decided to dispense with it (LG/76/2, Commonage and Gardens Comm. Verbatim report, 6 June 1923).

[86] One headman complained to the council, writing: 'I think that this job is very dangerous and perilous to me' (LG/38, John A, Chirwa to Master, 7 Feb. 1910).

[87] LG/47/19, Town Clerk to E.W.B. Makubalo, 26 Jan. 1911; LG/52/6/1, Winter to Town Clerk, 7 Aug., 22 Nov. 1912.

[88] J. Smith's statement, in D/3/5/21, case 1032 of 1908; LG/47/20, Location Supt. to O.C. B.S.A.P., 20 June 1912.

[89] LG/47/19, Town Clerk to Secr., Umtali Sanitary Board, 1 Aug. 1911.

[90] Makubalo claimed that he had been a headman 'carrying all the responsibility on my shoulders' (LG/38, Makubalo to Town Clerk, 14 Feb. 1914).

[91] Both the handwriting and the content of the letter suggest this. Cf. LG/38, People in Location to Town Clerk, 3 Apr. 1914, and *Ibid*. Makubalo to Town Clerk, 14 Feb. 1914.

[92] LG/38, People in Location to Town Clerk, 3 Apr. 1914.

[93] *Ibid*.

[94] *Ibid*.

[95] LG/52/6/1, Supt.'s reports, 31 Mar., 31 Aug., 1 Nov., 1 Dec. 1915, and 3 Feb., 1 Mar. 1916.

[96] LG/52/6/1, Reilly to Town Clerk, 13 May 1915.

[97] *Rhodesia Herald*, 23, 25 Nov. 1916; LG/47/26, town Clerk to Comm., B.S.A.P., 24 Nov. 1916; *Mayor's Minutes*, 1916-17, 6.

[98] Gov. Notice No. 113 of 1917. See correspondence in LG/52/12, A/3/21/34.

[99] NSA/2/7/1, W.S. Taberer to C.N.C., 17 Apr. 1917.

[100] According to the location superintendent's report (*Mayor's Minutes*, 1916-17): 'The increased demand for accommodation was caused by the Municipality regulations relating to natives living in town and on the commonage being more strictly enforced, and by the introduction of regulations prohibiting the brewing and possession of kaffir beer.'

[101] LG/93/16, Commonage Comm. Minute, 31 May 1918.

[102] By 'family people' I mean not only 'properly married' couples, but also those in temporary unions. The management did not allow, in principle at least, the presence of single women in the location, as the superintendent reported in 1920: 'young native women occasionally arrive from kraals and with the assistance of the C.I.D. are at once sent home' (LG/52/6/2, Location Supt., to Town Clerk, 7 June 1920). Thus 'independent' women often entered unions, temporary or not, with male tenants, thereby remaining in the location.

[103] LG/52/6/2, Location Supt., to Town Clerk, 30 June 1920.

[104] *Ibid*. 31 Aug. 1920.

[105] It was reported in *Rhodesia Herald*, 28 June 1920: 'There are at present 135 natives living in this location with their wives and children.'

[106] Location Supt.'s Report, in *Mayor's Minutes*, 1914-15.

[107] My interview with Antonio Z. Chirekeni (b. 1910), Highfield, Harare, 21 Apr. 1985.

[108] In 1921, 524 African females lived in Salisbury, of which 320, or 61 per cent, were of Southern Rhodesia origin, whereas their male counterparts accounted for 40 per cent of the total male population (Figure 11). In 1930 out of the total of 679 women living in the location 426, or 63 per cent, came from within the colony, whilst the total male population there was 2,352, out of which 1,024 or 44 per cent were Southern Rhodesian Africans (Figure 12).

[109] S1542/S12, N.C., Salisbury, to C.N.C., 9 Sept. 1936.

[110] G.C. Passmore, *Local Government Legislation in Southern Rhodesia* (Salisbury, 1966), 19.

[111] The fence was erected in 1912, the western gate being the main entrance: LG/52/6/1, J. Smith to Town Clerk, 14 Nov. 1911; Ranger's Report, in *Mayor's Minutes*, 1911-12. In 1924 the northern gate was closed permanently. Commenting on the residents' protest against this action, the Assistant Native Commissioner, Salisbury, stated: 'if proper control of the Location is to be expected, one entrance, and one only, should be allowed' (S138/41, Asst. N.C., Salisbury, to Supt. of Natives, Salisbury, 13 Mar. 1924).

[112] LG/52/6/2, H. E. Hicks, M. O. H., to Town Clerk, 20 June 1920.

[113] Location Supt.'s Report, in *Mayor's Minutes*, 1920-1.

[114] For 'faction fights' see LG/52/6/2, Location Supt. to Town Clerk, 30 Jan., 31 Oct., 31 Dec. 1920; LG/52/6/4, Location Supt. to Town Clerk, 30 May, 30 June, 31 July 1922; *Rhodesia Herald*, 22 Jan. 1920, 25 July 1922. Criminal statistics for the location can be found in Location Supt.'s Reports, in *Mayor's Minutes*, 1917-18 to 1920-1.

[115] N/3/33/2, Report and attached schedules, 22 Nov. 1920.

[116] See Chapter 4.

[117] Note that in these years a number of protests occurred against the stores which charged 'extortionate' prices for goods: van Onselen, *Chibaro*, 222-3. In 1914 the Salisbury location residents complained 'about the high prices charged by the store keepers for foodstuffs', see LG/52/6/1, Location Supt. to Town Clerk, 14 Sept. 1914.

[118] Gov. Notice No. 487 of 1918.

[119] N/3/20/2, W. S. Taberer, Supt. of Natives, Salisbury, to C.N.C., 3 Jan. 1919.

[120] *Ibid.*

[121] *Ibid.*

[122] LG/52/6/2, Location Supt. to Town Clerk, 30 June 1920.

[123] One of the reasons for this stabilisation was no doubt a growing shortage of housing in the location in the 1920s, which became so serious that in 1923 even a practice of paying premiums for obtaining accommodation was alleged: LG/52/23, Town Engineer to Actg. Town Clerk, 14 June 1923.

[124] N/3/20/2, W.S. Taberer, Supt. of Natives, Salisbury, to C.N.C., 3 Jan. 1919.

[125] LG/52/12, Location Supt. to Town Clerk, 28 Feb. 1919.

[126] Gov. Notice no. 582 of 1920.

[127] LG/52/6/2, Location Supt. to Town Clerk, 30 Nov. 1920.

[128] *Ibid.*, D/4/7/27, case 3016 of 1920.

[129] LG/42/14/14, Taylor, C.N.C., to Town Clerk, 1 Dec. 1920.

[130] LG/52/6/2, Location Supt. to Town Clerk, 30 Nov. 1920.

[131] *Ibid.*, 31 Dec. 1920.

[132] LG/52/6/3, Location Supt. to Town Clerk, 30 June 1921.

[133] *Rhodesia Herald*, 11 Jan. 1921; D/4/7/28, cases 80-95 of 1921.

[134] His. Mss Collect., LE/3/1/2, E. Mankayi to W. M. Leggate, 16 May 1921. Note that there was considerable opposition to the municipal monopoly system among non-urban employers and landed interests, as well as missionaries and temperance promoters. In 1923, for example, a motion was proposed in the legislature to stop the extension of the system to Gatooma, which was narrowly defeated by 10 votes to 8 (*Rhodesia Herald*, 2 July 1923).

[135] *Rhodesia Herald*, 25 July 1921.

[136] His. Mss Collect., LE/3/1/2, Mankayi to Leggate, 16 May 1921.

[137] LG/52/6/4, Location Supt. to Town Clerk, 30 Sept. 1922. It was in line with this tradition of protest that the women successfully staged a two-day boycott against the beer hall in the late 1920s, which forced the superintendent to repeal his previous order not to brew hop beer: S85, Native Affairs Comm. of 1930, Evidence by Rusiti and Munyoma, and by J. Moeketsi.

[138] Location Supt.'s Report, in *Mayor's Minutes*, 1921-2; LG/52/6/4, Location Supt. to Town Clerk, 31 Aug., 30 Sept. 1922.

[139] City of Harare, Town Clerk's Dep. Files, 28/10/6R, 1/9/, J. 1, D. McDougall to Town Clerk, 3 Feb. 1925.

[140] *Ibid.*

[141] Location Supt.'s Reports, in *Mayor's Minutes*, 1924-5, 1929-30.

[142] Cf. Castells's polemic observation for the tenant unions in the Parisian Grands Ensembles (Castells, *The City and the Grassroots*, 94): 'Since the relative homogeneity of living conditions made it easier for residents to realise the commonality of the urban problems from which they were suffering, the socialisation of housing led to the socialisation of protest, overcoming the individual relationship between landlord and tenant. It is in this sense that we can think of the formation of a new type of movement: a collective consumption-oriented trade unionism that paralleled at the residence place what capitalist concentration of production and management has triggered in the form of labour unions at the work place.'

3

Straddling town & countryside:
the rise of black suburbia

Prior to the end of World War I people frequently adopted a stay-away attitude towards public housing, leaving many huts in the location unoccupied. The alternative residences they often chose were legally known as private locations, which were situated on European farms just beyond the municipal boundary.[1] By 1918 considerable numbers of African men and women had packed up and left the town. On suburban farms, Africans obtained plots from landowners under rent-paying agreements. They put up huts, lived with their families, cultivated land, raised cattle, and brewed African beer (although the latter not on the mission farms). They created autonomous hamlets, and commuted from there to the town. By the early 1920s there arose a chain of African settlements in outer Salisbury, with a distinct mode of life and culture. With the implementation of the Land Apportionment policy, such settlements became less prominent after 1930; yet they lasted in some form up until the mid-twentieth century.

This chapter will address the beginning and growth of this black suburbia in early Salisbury. It will discuss the localities, magnitude and nature of the African suburban settlements, as well as government's reactions and countermeasures, as in the establishment of the No. 2 Location for married Africans in 1922. Reference will be also made to the life histories of a few individuals who were actually part of this suburban life. We will find that the outer town was both a focus of African material accumulation through dual participation into wage labour and peasant agriculture, and a cradle of African modern politics in Mashonaland, promoted by a small group of mission-educated men – suburbanites who were employed at better-paid positions in and around Salisbury.

The Development of African Suburban Settlements

The development of African suburban settlements in Salisbury got under way in the first decade of the twentieth century. It accelerated during World War I and probably reached its peak around the early 1920s. In 1915 the town ranger took the trouble to investigate such settlements. He found that there were 21 huts or rooms on G. Haupt's farm (Greendale), 39 on A.V. Williams's farm (Lorelei, around the present Msasa), 77 on M.T.C. farm (south of Hillside), and 51 on Hatfield Estate.[2] The list was far from exhaustive. Additionally, we know from other sources, such as private location agreement records, that Epworth mission farm (also known as Chiremba's Kraal) was inhabited by 50 Africans employed in town in 1920; Brown's farm (Arlington Estate, situated around the present Harare International Airport) by 69 tenants, nearly all employed in town, in 1918; Waterfall Induna by 14 families or 70 people in 1925; St Mary's farm, Hunyani, by a dozen workers in 1925; and Ventersburg farm (south of Mabvuku) by at least 10 tenants in 1917. Evidence also shows, though later, in 1929, that Donnybrook farm (Mabvuku) had 14 tenants.[3]

Tantalisingly patchy and incomplete as these data are, they do at least serve to reveal the magnitude of the issue. It may be said that the total number of huts, or formal tenants, or families, was around a little over 350 at any one time in the decade between 1915 and 1925. Assuming that one can get an idea of the population size by multiplying this by five, the aggregate population in private locations may be estimated at 1,750 or more. Given that the 1921 population census gave the number of African women in Salisbury as only less than 500,[4] it seems certain that a very significant proportion – possibly more than half of the African 'townspeople' – lived outside the town.[5]

One important factor which gave impetus to the growth of African suburbs was the policy of racial exclusion operating in the settler town. A clear correlation existed between the town council's housing restrictions and people's exodus from town. In the first years of the century, African 'independent' dwellers tended to move into the inner town. This trend was reversed when the imposition of a strict location system from 1907 caused an overall outwards migration. This was first observed by the town ranger in his annual report for 1908-09: 'many of the natives who used to rent huts in the location are now to be found on Avondale or on farms adjoining the Commonage'.[6] The second phase of exodus took place in the wake of the introduction of a beer canteen and an aggressive location policy in 1913-14. Attributing the problem of empty huts directly to the beer controls, the location superintendent complained in 1915: 'The location ... contains not more than a fraction of the people for whom it was intended, owing to the number of private locations situated immediately outside the common-age boundaries, which have grown considerably of late.' (See Figure 13.) The superintendent wondered 'if a law could be introduced prohibiting the squatting of natives within a certain radius of the town'.[7]

Resistance to urban control, however, was only one factor contributing to a widespread and continuous exodus. Another important factor was a conflict between the logic of the urban system and that of agrarian capital over suburban settlements. The early years of the century, especially after 1907, witnessed the first systematic efforts by the colonisers to tap the country's land resources. This development caused the removals of numbers of Africans into Reserves, but it also gave rise to numerous instances of African 'squatting' on what had forcibly become European land. With land generally underutilised, and labour scarce, agrarian capital often desired that African communities remained on, or came onto, its land in the capacity of either labour-suppliers, rent-payers, or sharecroppers.[8] In the Salisbury area farmers and landowners were willing to have Africans employed in town as 'rent squatters' on their estates. This happened, ironically, at the very moment when white Salisbury was out to shift urban Africans into the municipal location.

The urban authorities' onslaught on what they saw as the uncontrolled African suburban communities was thus neutralised by the exigencies of rentier landlordism. A high court judge commented on this in 1925: 'if you want to expel a native, the right to do so would have to come from the owner of the land, and if he refused you would be in an impasse. Apparently some of these owners must be drawing very considerable revenues from these private locations near to the towns'.[9] Certainly, it was primarily the question of revenues that patterned the landlord/tenant relations on the private farms. The landlord gave little thought to the daily activities of his tenants, provided that rents and fees were regularly paid, and that his possessions, such as trees and wild animals, were protected.

Moreover, the notion of 'social control' held by agrarian capital was not identical to that of the urban authorities. A farm-owner's letter that appeared in a local newspaper in 1915 illustrates this point. Angrily responding to the council's criticism that M.T.C. farm was a sanctuary for illicit beer drinking, the 'owner' of the farm, I. Gallagher, expressed his own opinion on the beer question:

> Mr. Evans ... is certainly guilty of misrepresentation in saying that there are droves of boys coming here to drink. It is all a yarn ... Most of the boys here are my work boys. There are 35 licensed boys. Mostly boys employed in public offices. It is convenient to their work, and they were well treated by me. ... The law gives the kaffirs certain privileges, one of which is that they can brew kaffir beer for their own use. Quite right; the boys work much better when they get a small quantity of kaffir beer.[10]

The position was further complicated by an administrative problem. The locality was too rural to come under the control of the urban authorities. Yet it was too urban to be supervised by the Native Commissioner's office: 'They are supposed to be under the Native Commissioner of the district', stated a former Native Department official in 1925, 'but you will find that the Native Commissioner goes out to these places very seldom indeed, and therefore not much control is exercised. ... I think that periodical visits should be made, and the headman of the location should be responsible to the Native Commissioner as well as the owner of the farm.'[11]

It is now apparent that the private locations on peri-urban farms afforded more freedom to urban Africans. There, they did not have to constantly contend with the onerous rules and regulations of the town location. Suburban settlements were self-organised and autonomous communities, often with headmen and sometimes with governing institutions.[12] People would set up and join these communities by using a network of friends, compatriots, and co-workers. Consequently, the tenant village on Haupt's farm, popularly known as Agrippa, was largely a Manyika community; that on Waterfall Induna comprised non-indigenous people; the members of the Zinyengere village on Epworth farm were Nyasalanders; M.T.C. farm, Ventersburg farm, and some other farms were almost the preserve of government employees.[13]

There were further attractions to farm life. There was, for instance, better security of tenure on farms, so that the suburban homestead frequently became a 'permanent home', especially for foreign workers, who had no rural home in the colony. Free from the noise, coarseness and squalor endemic in the poverty-stricken, predominantly male society in town, the suburbs offered a serene, pastoral environment, one which perhaps was more congenial to family life. For Christians, some settlements were conveniently located for attending the churches and schools provided at the mission farms, like the Wesleyan Epworth, the Catholic Chishawasha, and the Anglican St. Mary's, Hunyani. One may add to such a list Waterfall Induna owned by a Zulu, Frank Sixubu, who sponsored in the 1920s an industrial school run by a Zulu Anglican teacher, Abraham Twala.

People went to suburbs for economic reasons as well. They could live on farms relatively cheaply. The mission farms charged only nominal rents, in order to encourage Africans to move in (and presumably, thus be more likely to convert to Christianity). At Epworth mission in 1915 the rent was 5s. per annum and, if the tenant was a cattle-owner, a dipping fee of 2s. for each beast.[14] The private farms demanded much higher rents, ranging from around £3 per year (or 5s. per month), as at Haupt's, Williams's, and M.T.C. farms; Arlington estate charged £1 per year.[15] This meant that the running of private locations was an extremely lucrative business for the landowners: in 1906, for example, a farm of about 1,000 acres near Salisbury changed hands for £165,[16] so that a score of tenants would pay the price of the farm in the matter of a few years. Some officials even feared that such a high level of rent appropriation might embitter race relations.[17] Even so, it paled before the level of rental charge at the Salisbury municipal location, where a monthly rent for a hut was 10s., more than double the standard rates on farms.

Furthermore, farms granted the option of renting a plot for agricultural purposes – whereas the municipality made it a policy not to lease commonage gardens and plots to the Africans.[18] Suburban dwellers, often the womenfolk, indeed hired plots and engaged in market gardening, while also raising cattle, thus enhancing their family incomes. Of the importance of this agricultural potential for the livelihood of low-income people, John Moeketsi, a Sotho worker of the Anglo-African Trading Co., stated in 1925: the Ventersburg tenants 'say that they want to do some cultivating', because 'the wages of the husband would not be able to support them in the [municipal] location'.[19]

For all these advantages, suburban life did have some disadvantages. The most serious one was perhaps that it was inevitable that a worker would have to travel a long distance to and from work in town, every day or every weekend. Under certain circumstances, as in the case of defaulting rent payment, tenants were evicted by their landlords, while on the mission farms, church regulations, like the prohibition of brewing beer, were enforced.[20] On balance, however, it is clear that Salisbury possessed a highly rugged social terrain, whose periphery provided, in general, a less repressive and more congenial residential space for Africans than the European-dominated centre.

Two Zones of African Suburbia

By 1920 Salisbury's African suburbs comprised two identifiable zones, representing different modes of life and culture. One was an area adjacent to the town boundary where there was a relatively high concentration of individuals and households that actively participated in beer trade, prostitution, and other forms of business which met migrant workers' leisure-time needs. The other zone was further afield, about eight miles or more from the town. It was largely inhabited by 'family people', comprising long-service workers, perhaps mission-educated, with above-standard wages, their wives, who were often involved in market gardening, and their children.

The 'inner zone' flourished as the local authority succeeded in enforcing tougher beer and housing controls in town. Soon after the opening of an official beer hall in 1913, together with the enforcement of stricter regulations on the private making and consuming of beer, the traditional beer nexus between brewers and consumers, women and workers shifted from the town to suburban areas, such as Hatfield estate, M.T.C. farm, and Haupt's farm.[21] In reaction, the authorities passed, as we saw in the previous chapter, a series of beer regulations, extending prohibition in 1917 to two miles, and three years later to five miles, from the commonage fence. In the 1920s the 'island of freedom' had receded to Williams's farm, even further away from the town.

To understand what was going on on Williams's farm, it may be useful to look at the life history of Mary Nyrenda, a key figure in the 'affairs' of the farm. Mary, a Sotho woman, was the leader of a syndicate of African *femmes libres*, or 'prostitutes', in Mashonaland. Earlier, she had lived in the town location with her husband, Robert, who was employed in town, and her niece, or daughter, Annie. The police informed the location superintendent about her in October 1920:

> This woman, Mary Nyrenda, has lived with various Europeans since her residence in this Territory. ... She used to travel round the mines with other native females for the purpose of prostitution. During recent years she has made Salisbury her headquarters, but has also travelled round various mines in Mashonaland. She was recently convicted with the case of Rex vs. Wennburg, who was charged and convicted with supplying liquor to natives; she was found drinking in this man's room with her daughter Annie and another woman Maria Jenkins. ... As you are aware, it is a daily occurrence for this woman, together with her daughter and others, to be seen outside the Native Canteen at your Location waiting on natives to stand them drinks, and to solicit, though not in such a manner as to arouse suspicion or render them liable to prosecution. This woman was acquitted on the recent charge against her of 'keeping a brothel'.[22]

Perhaps, the officials regarded Mary as masterminding the growing women's beer protest after 1919.[23] At the time of the enforcement of total prohibition towards the end of 1920, the superintendent ousted the Nyrendas from the location on the grounds that 'they are responsible for the barter of native women and set an example to other natives who would otherwise fear to indulge in this traffic'.[24] This led to the residence of Mary, Robert and Annie on Williams's farm.[25] Before long these people and their neighbours turned the farm into the 'most notorious' place in the Salisbury area. Little cultivation took place here, with residents ingeniously turning to a trade of hosting weekend beer parties and other 'recreational' activities for Salisbury workers. 'The amount of crime on that farm', an official deplored in 1925, 'is enormous, and even then we do not get to know half of what is going on'.[26]

In the latter half of the 1920s, Williams's farm was regularly raided by the Salisbury police, whose mobility was now greatly improved by the use of motor vehicles. These actions effectively suppressed the 'vices' of Williams's farm, forcing the 'shebeen queens' and the like, including the Nyrendas, to leave the place.

If the stereotype of the inner zone was roistering and criminality, that of the outer zone, such as Epworth, Ventersburg, Donnybrook and St. Mary's, was sobriety and respectability. In the latter zone, the urban merged with the rural, in that farms there would come to contain not only villages of 'family people' whose breadwinner worked in town, but also villages of local Shona peasants. Agriculture, especially for the town's markets, was a prominent activity in the both types of villages; so it was perhaps more than a matter of coincidence that the outer zone developed in the well-watered valleys of the Mukuvisi, the Ruwa, and the Hunyani (the Manyame) – an area relatively densely populated in the precolonial era.[27]

A pertinent question now arises as to how Shona rural history intruded upon the landscape of African suburbia. As is well known, the African communities in the Salisbury district, close to the citadel of colonialism, experienced the impact of colonial rule in a most devastating and traumatic way – via labour recruitment, taxes, rinderpest, the wars of conquest, the loss of ancestral land, the dispersion of peoples, and so forth. Yet, those communities displayed a remarkable degree of resilience, sticking to their 'own ways'. To meet the ever-growing cash needs, they sold agricultural products, rather than labour, to the colonial economy.[28]

The influence of the money economy was felt quickly: 'Very few Mashonas whose kraals are within a day's walk of Salisbury [a newspaper reported in January 1893] care to trade for salt or limbo [cloth]. They prefer money, and have doubtless learnt to come in and do their own shopping.'[29] When faced with the crises of the late 1890s, including the defeat of the 1896-97 uprisings, the local Shona stepped up farming activities for both subsistence and marketing purposes. As the Native Commissioner of the Salisbury District reported:

> The crops reaped in 1900 were unusually heavy, the natives being able to sell large quantities of grain. ... I understand the cultivation of grain has greatly increased in this district. It is quite the usual thing for a native to have three gardens. The first he will tell you is for his year's food, the second to make beer of, the third for trade.[30]

As the frontier town of Salisbury evolved into a modern urban centre, the economic interactions between Salisbury and its African hinterland were intensified. The business in African produce, albeit dominated by European traders, was brisk enough to stimulate a few Africans, like a Seke-based farmer, Muzeya Chanakira, to become traders before World War I.[31] Some of the goods were directly brought into the town for sale by African peasants themselves, as a labour-hungry European farmer near Salisbury complained in 1902:

> ... it is common knowledge that the amount of labour [the local Africans] will volunteer for will be infinitesimal, and this will grow less and less as long as they are allowed to come into town and hawk fowls, eggs, pumpkins, grain, etc., without having to pay any sort of license to the Government. They pass my place in hundreds, carrying mostly about five fowls each, and return to their respective

kraals with from 12s. to 15s. Should their hut-tax be due, or they require a few shillings, all they have to do is to take a journey to Salisbury, and in one day they have all they want.[32]

This evolution of a pre-colonial society into a modern peasant society was also evident in patterns of settlement. 'In order to become and remain a successful peasant', as Ranger has noted in the Makoni context, 'it was necessary first and foremost to have access to markets.'[33] Some households and communities in the recently demarcated Chinamora and Seke Reserves indeed showed a tendency to cluster at the points near the market, i.e. the town and main roads.[34] While some Africans were resettled into Reserves, others remained, or even came to settle, in the 'European land' near Salisbury.[35] They became peasant 'squatters', setting up their own villages, in some instances side by side with the villages of urban workers.

The case in point was the farm of St. Mary's, Hunyani, owned by the Church of England after 1903. Two social processes combined to give rise to the tenant community there. On the one hand, there was a migratory movement of Seke peasants towards the southern bank of the Hunyani. As a result, the Anglican farm, situated precisely in that locality, received an influx of Seke people that apparently reached a peak around 1911.[36] On the other hand, Africans employed in Salisbury sought to build homes on the farm. Their initial entry was rather slow because the place was so remote, 14 miles away from the town, but by the 1920s the farm had become a popular residential area. 'We constantly have', stated an Anglican bishop in 1925, 'applications from people in town to allow them to go out there and live.'[37]

There were five villages at St. Mary's in 1925. One of them was reserved for the people who were working in town, the rest being for local Africans. In total, 50 men, 50 women, and 75 children lived on the farm. All the inhabitants took up serious agricultural production for markets.[38]

Some of the St. Mary's inhabitants were doing well in riding the waves of social change set in motion by the advent of colonialism. Surely this was the case with a Noah, a Christian Shona of local origin. From 1914 to 1916 he was employed at the Anglican Cathedral in town, thereafter going back to his rural home in the Seke Reserve. In 1923 his connections with the church helped him obtain a better-paid job as a messenger at the Department of Agriculture. In the meantime, Noah married and had three children. He built a home on St. Mary's farm, from where he travelled daily to Salisbury. He had a garden plot on the farm, for which he paid an annual rent of 5s., and where his wife grew mealies, rapoko, monkey nuts, and beans. All this was still only part of his livelihood: he was also trying to establish himself as an entrepreneurial farmer in Seke, probably by channeling his urban incomes into agriculture. He was among the first Africans to introduce ox-plough cultivation in Seke, where his land and cattle were under the care of his brother.[39] To Noah, 'squatting' outside the town apparently meant many things: the ability to remain in continuous wage employment and to have a regular cash income from it; to lead a family life near his place of work (and to live away from the repressive environment of the town location); to utilise family labour for market gardening; and to build up a wealthier peasant household in his natal community.

The Establishment of No. 2 Location:
Myth & Reality of the 'Native Garden Village'

If the European citizens zealously defended urban turf against an equal African presence, and the colonial economy steadily revolved around the migrant labour system, this should not make us insensitive to the fact that there was also a movement, or a tendency, among colonists in favour of creating a class of African wage-earners resident within urban areas. Thus, the Salisbury municipality built, in 1922, the so-called 'No. 2 location for married Africans'. Promoters of such a policy advocated building African suburbs, or 'garden villages', where long-service workers could settle with their families in more or less pastoral conditions. The imagery of these settlements bore remarkable resemblance to the existing African suburbs, but their major practical function was to stop these very things. This section will study the official ideology and practice in respect to the African suburbs, with particular reference to the history of the No. 2 location in Salisbury.

Two circumstances, among others, combined to give rise to early advocacy for married housing. First, for all its advantages and opportunities, the migrant labour system, as it developed in the early years of colonialism, was not totally trouble-free for European employers. It posed them such headaches as the unreliability of short-service labour, the unavailability of female labour for domestic employment, the moral chaos of a sexually unbalanced community, and the rapid accumulation of lumpen proletarian, rather than proletarian, elements in towns. To the extent that such problems were real, attention would turn to the merits of a stable labour service, a stable family life, and a stable urban community.

This kind of logic can be clearly seen in the deliberations of the Native Affairs Committee of 1910-11, one of the first official organs which publicly advocated the provision of married housing.[40] The committee bemoaned conditions in urban areas:

> There is, however, very little semblance of home life in any location, and we think this accounts for a good deal of the disorder and immorality which is reported to be prevalent in them. Forms of recreation are few, other than gambling and drinking. This naturally attracts indifferent characters, and those natives who are law-abiding and quiet have to suffer.[41]

It was felt that these vices, associated with migrant labour, could best be counterbalanced by the virtues of family and community, associated with stabilised labour. So the committee stressed the need of 'the better class of native' being given 'an opportunity of improving his surroundings' and suggested that special housing be provided for a minority of regularly employed and better-paid Africans. Since women were at the centre of family and community, it was further recommended that 'garden plots be granted, at a reasonable rent, to the occupants of the location. This would give the wives of men who are away at work all day some legitimate means of occupying their spare time, instead of spending it in a less wholesome manner.'[42]

Yet another circumstance leading to the case for married housing concerned the existence of the 'independent' African suburban settlements. Relatively free from official controls, those settlements would be categorically frowned upon or stigmatised by colonists. The same committee of inquiry of 1910-11, for instance, noted that 'In the vicinity of many towns' there were 'private plots where natives of doubtful character congregate[d]', and suggested that 'squatting on plots in the vicinity of towns should be absolutely prohibited'.[43]

The idea of creating an official suburb was first advanced in the context of the Bulawayo region. Emerging at the heart of the precolonial Ndebele state, and rapidly developing into the largest industrial centre in the Rhodesias, colonial Bulawayo had been plagued by a serious 'squatter problem' since the turn of the century – as former subjects of the Ndebele nation came to congregate on peri-urban farms like Hyde Park, Tshabalala, and Rangemore,[44] apart from the municipal location, with young male residents even becoming permanent wage labourers. After 1914 the central government tried to organise a 'Native suburb' as a counter-measure to this situation, but the proposal was soon stymied by white public opposition.[45] A similar process, though on a smaller scale, developed in the colony's capital town, where the municipality, counselled by the government, undertook the married housing scheme. Here the idea was translated into reality in 1922.

The issue had first been raised by the Southern Rhodesian Missionary Conference in June 1920. The Conference, which met in Salisbury that month, criticised squalid conditions both in the Salisbury and Bulawayo locations and, as at the previous conference of 1915, called for making special provision for the housing of married Africans.[46] The criticism, when reported in the press, so upset the council that Mayor George Elcombe refused to receive a missionary deputation on the subject.[47] Nevertheless, following this event the possibility of providing married housing began to slip onto the municipal agenda.[48] At the time, it will be remembered, urban Africans were living through tough times, caused by wartime inflation, stagnant wages, the Spanish influenza epidemic, and the municipal monopoly of African beer. Discontent was simmering in the location. The situation sufficiently alarmed the town council for it to take an unlikely interest in the subtler aspects of what may be termed social control. A sign of change in this direction was apparent in December 1920, when the council, in reaction to earlier African women's complaints over the total prohibition of African beer and other issues, offered garden plots to women living in the location.[49]

However, it was an eviction case cropping up the following year that prompted the officials to draw up a married housing project. At the beginning of 1921 the people living in the private location of the Arlington estate were given notice to leave. 'About 200 males', with an unknown number of women and children, were affected. The majority of them were married and 'permanently employed' in offices and stores in town. The community appealed to the Native Department for assistance in finding an alternative place to live. Like many other African suburbanites, they were 'adverse to settling in the Municipal Location' and wanted 'land some distance from Salisbury which will enable them to return home in the evening, and where the women will have scope for occupation in their gardens'.[50]

In response, Native Department officials realised that this could be a model case of replacing a free African neighbourhood with an official settlement. The Chief Native Commissioner and other top officials of the Department met town councillors to review the matter, and the municipality agreed to set up a model 'native village'. H. S. Keigwin, a key figure in formulating and implementing the new Native Development policy which aimed at harnessing the dynamics of African social change,[51] unofficially offered his service in building this village.[52]

It immediately transpired, however, that the parties involved held quite different views on the proposed village. The Africans concerned wanted a replica of their old community, thus preferring a new home on the edge of the town. The local authority regarded this as a beer-brewers' conspiracy to evade control. They intended to place the settlement as close as possible to the existing location, because they did not wish, in their words, 'to forego the necessary control which would have to be exercised in maintaining the discipline in this settlement'.[53]

Government officials, for their part, envisaged the settlement in terms of their own Native Development policy. An important ideological thread of the policy was an asymmetric way of evaluating town and countryside, in which countryside was seen as representing positive values, such as family, community, peace, and order, as against the supposed growing evils of urbanism and 'detribalisation'.[54] In this paradigm, reminiscent of the urban/rural contrast elsewhere in the world,[55] the urban African worker ought to be a half-ruralist, and the settlement to be a 'garden village' with a degree of horticulture. This description should perhaps make us to wonder if this was not simply a copy of the existing 'respectable' African suburbia. The Native Department held a middle-of-road position as to the locality of the proposed settlement, suggesting that the settlement should be detached 'a mile or two away from the present location'. The department warned the municipality that the Arlington estate tenants would not move into the new settlement if it were to be located so near the town, as proposed by the town council.[56]

The town council's view prevailed in the end, however. In May 1922 a No. 2 location, or a married location, was opened immediately to the south of the main location, across Ardbennie Road (Figure 2). It came under the supervision of the existing location administration. The new location began with a dozen one-roomed pisé huts with kitchens and yards, to which a number of more permanent buildings, two-roomed brick cottages with kitchens and yards, were added shortly afterward. A tract of land near the location was earmarked for gardening. A monthly rent of 15s. was charged for a brick cottage, which may be considered quite reasonable, given that the monthly rent of a single room unit in the main location was 10s., and the cost of building a cottage £130. Only 'properly' married Africans were allowed to rent the new accommodation. Most of the first occupiers were church people, some self-employed, 'who roam[ed] around mending beds, boots, etc.'[57]

The area quickly became a stylish elite neighbourhood. The residents were so home-conscious that every cottage, it was reported in 1924, 'gave the appearance of a smart cosy home with front and back vegetable garden and fowl run and water supply'.[58] The place made sharp contrast with the main location, a poorer neighbourhood where single male migrants, married people, and widows and other 'marginals' lived. In his novel, *The Old Bricks*, William Saidi wrote of how ordinary residents looked at the new location later on: 'Most occupants nursed the ambition of one glorious day fleeing the overcrowded squalor of the Old Bricks for the comparative luxury of ... New Location, where people lived in genuine married houses.'[59] The new location both brought about and highlighted social differentiation within the African urban community (Figure 14). It arguably seems to have functioned as ballast for a poor, amorphous, and potentially conflict-ridden urban society.

The new location was widely publicised as the first garden village in Southern Rhodesia,[60] but its accomplishments fell far short of what its elegant appellation would imply. In fact only a variation of the standard urban location, the place hopelessly lacked the symbols of pastoral life. For example, the agricultural plots intended for the use of women, one of the key components of the village concept, were hardly utilised by residents, owing to constant pilfering by poor neighbours.[61] Not surprisingly, the new location failed to attract residents of the Arlington estate. 'It is a well known fact', reported the location superintendent in 1922, 'that many of the married natives for whom a pressing need for providing accommodation apart from the old Location occurred have gone to live at Williams Farm where they augment their incomes in the old fashioned way.'[62]

Nor were the accomplishments of the No. 2 location impressive at the quantitative level. As time went on, the municipal interests in married hous-

Cottages at the married location, 1927

'The married quarters were in themselves a revelation.
Constructed solidly of brick and iron, they contain living-room, bed-room
and kitchen. Most of the stoeps were flower-bordered, while the ubiquitous petrol
can was to be seen hanging from many of the roofs and containing flourishing
flowers. ... there is a plot of ground behind each house, which the occupiers use
for growing their own vegetables, and the provision of poultry runs.'

Source: Rhodesia Herald, 2 December 1927

ing dwindled, not least because married housing yielded little revenue, and could even be a financial burden.[63] By 1930 the brick cottages in the new location numbered 71, and the figure remained the same in 1939.[64] The main location, on the other hand, expanded by leaps and bounds. The council built the last batch of Kaytor huts in 1921 and then switched to the erection of brick blocks of four rooms (later to be known as Old Bricks). The total number of brick rooms rose from a humble figure of 64 in 1924 to 680 in 1930 and to the peak of 1,712 by 1939.[65] It is clear that the municipal building policy prior to World War II was almost exclusively oriented towards single-room housing units, with the No. 2 location remaining a tiny showpiece.

As the case of the No. 2 location shows, the idea of a garden village, or married housing, was highly controversial among the Europeans, especially when it came to its practicality. In fact, even the central government, apparently the chief advocate of such an idea, had various opinions about it. The government pursuit of the matter thus unfolded only in a prosaic manner. The Land Apportionment Act of 1930 did have provisions for establishing Native Village Settlements near towns, as well as prohibiting rent tenancy in the European area (other than in the Bulawayo area which had its own regulations), but these provisions were not enforced for some time. After 1935 the government started to construct two village settlements, one for Bulawayo and one for Salisbury, which became respectively the Luveve Village Settlement (opened in 1936), and the Highfield Village Settlement (opened in 1937).[66] These projects, essentially a rehearsal for future action, were so small in scale that they hardly had an impact on African residential patterns. A noteworthy ramification, however, was that the central government's experiment of building cottages at the minimum cost at Luveve and Highfield was emulated by the Salisbury municipality in the early forties, when the latter constructed the so-called Jo'burg Lines at the south-eastern corner of the main location.

The slow increase in the provision of married housing, by both municipal and central government, meant the slow decline of the 'independent' African suburbs. In the early 1930s the administration made a policy to discourage 'the establishment of any new Private Locations within 20 miles of the larger towns',[67] but the existing private locations tended to be tolerated. It was estimated that in 1938 the total number of urban Africans living outside Salisbury was 2,100 – 450 heads of family and 1,650 dependents.[68]

The whole situation changed after World War II. At the end of the war the authorities took decisive steps to introduce the 'White City' principle to Salisbury. Within a short space of time, less a decade after 1947, the Harare location or township expanded enormously; 'home life' was brought in by the construction of new houses in a section known as 'National'; all the Africans accommodated or trading in the city (except domestic workers and the like) were removed; and the outlying African suburbs were demolished.

The brick block of four rooms, Salisbury township, 1948

'*The brick buildings, each providing four single-room housing units, represented the main type of the location's housing from the mid-1920s to the 1950s. The verandahs and kitchenettes were often used as extra rooms. One can still see some of these buildings in New Lines, Mbare.*'

Source: African Weekly, 29 December 1948

The project of married housing no longer denoted primarily a palliative to the evils of the migrant labour system. It was now directly linked and dynamically tuned to exigencies of the mid-century colonial/capitalist system – the need for both stable labour by the colonial economy, especially by its secondary industry, and administrative measures to cope with pressures of African urbanisation, and a demand for territorial segregation by various sections of European society. It is revealing to note that the nomenclature of married housing itself underwent a change over these years – from 'garden village' (or 'village settlement') to 'township': from something connoting ruralism and farming to the one predicating urbanism and wage labour.

Case Studies: Black Suburbia as a Focus of Accumulation & Modern Politics

This section is devoted to recording the life histories of a few individuals who left an indelible mark on the history of the African Salisbury, and who spent much of their lifetimes in its peri-urban zone. This approach inevitably makes our narrative somewhat anecdotal. All the same, by looking into the particular experiences of 'historical actors' we wish to further concretise and deepen our understanding of the meanings and significance of Salisbury's periphery.

Two themes, among others, will be highlighted. First, we will illustrate and emphasise that the urban periphery was a geographical focus of African accumulation and peasantisation through *dual participation* in wage employment and agricultural production. Closely related to this is the second theme – that the peri-urban zone of Salisbury was a cradle of modern African politics. Although my material pertains to the Rhodesia Native Association (RNA), which is the earliest political association formed by educated youths in Mashonaland, this is not a study of African politics as such. Rather, I supply only so much of the data on RNA leadership as I consider relevant for an understanding of the position of the emerging 'elite' within the social and spatial structure of Salisbury's African community.

Elizabeth Musodzi & Others: Chizhanje & Ventersburg Farm

Few women who lived in early Salisbury were more celebrated than Elizabeth Maria Musodzi Ayema. The recreation hall of the Harare African township is named after her. From around 1910 'Mai Musodzi', with her husband, Frank Ayema, and children, lived in a place known as Chizhanje (in the vicinity of the present Mabvuku, on, or next to, Ventersburg farm). By the late 1930s they left the place and became 'genuine' residents in the

81

municipal location, although the Ayemas had rented a cottage in the No. 2 location since the mid-1920s.[69] Musodzi exemplified the 'respectable' African woman, her position in the moral spectrum being directly opposite to women like Mary Nyrenda. Prior to her death in 1952, she was the representative of the women's community of the location, sitting on the committee of the African Welfare Society, as well as on the (first and unofficial) Harare Native Advisory Board for many years. She was also the founder and chairwoman of the Harare African Women's Club (established in 1938), perhaps the first women's voluntary, 'non-ecclesiastical' association in the country. Mostly by way of the women's club, she was involved in the first-aid classes of the Red Cross society, the sewing and kitting classes, and many other community activities. Musodzi played an important role in improving the welfare of African women and reforming African home life in the Harare township.

Her children were also a large part of community life in Harare. The eldest, Lucy Chabuka (1909-1956), took over Musodzi's position as the leader of women's movements after 1952. One of her sons, Moses Ayema (1916-1984), a teacher and a journalist with the African Newspapers, was a founder member of the African National Congress and first chairman of its Harare branch. Another son, Francis Joseph Ayema (1919-1963), was a builder who was as active in public affairs as his brother Moses; a member of the Reformed Industrial and Commercial Workers' Union (Reformed ICU), Joseph often served on the Harare Native Advisory Board.

Musodzi's paternal family belonged to Chief Hwata's people. In 1890, when Fort Salisbury was built by the 'pioneers', she was a small child living in a village in the Mazoe Valley. In 1896-97 the Hwata, along with other indigenous polities, took up arms to resist European encroachment. They were badly beaten, and Musodzi's parents were killed. The surviving children, three in all, found themselves among the war refugees and orphans who came under the care of the Catholic Mission at Chishawasha, about 15 miles east of Salisbury. Musodzi attended the Convent of the Sacred Heart at Chishawasha. Around 1908 she married a Lozi policeman, Frank Joseph Ayema, who was also Catholic.

Musodzi became a key member of the female section of the early Catholic congregation around Salisbury. Coming to live at Chizhanje, she distinguished herself as an industrious, successful agriculturalist. In 1925 a Jesuit Father extolled Musodzi by depicting her as a torchbearer of Christian virtues in the darkness of paganism and superstition:

> She started a plot by paying £3 a year, at the other side of the Cleveland Dam, five miles from town. It is very rich soil there. The people who are out there are beer brewers, but this woman has come under some Christian influence, and some four years ago she produced one bag of mealies. The following year she produced ten bags, and last year she produced five bags mealies, five bags monkey nuts, five bags of rice, 50 pumpkins, and 35 bags of rapoko. This year she is on a fair

Elizabeth Musodzi and the Red Cross Society, Harare township, 1948

Left to right: Elizabeth Razika (Chihota),
Lucy Chabuka (Musodzi's daughter), Elizabeth Musodzi.

'Lady Kennedy, the President of the Red Cross in Rhodesia,
presents a Red Cross badge to Mrs Franks [Musodzi],
Commandant of the African Detachment, Salisbury Location.'

Source: African Weekly, 18 Feb. 1948.

way to supplying the oil factory with monkey nuts as she was much taken up with some Spanish Bunch, three acres of which she has under cultivation. At any rate it is expected that she will have a splendid crop. There is another tenant near by, who has been much struck with her methods of agriculture and industry, and who has emulated her example and produced 15 bags of mealies. All the others put her success down to magic, and ask her to supply them with seed which they assume must have been doctored with "muti" to have produced such good results. Others say that she is a witch.[70]

Musodzi would employ three workers in her agricultural venture,[71] and all this suggests that her contribution to the material welfare of the Ayema family was substantial.

Women's undertaking of market gardening, a common feature of the African suburbia, was not alien to the precolonial African tradition, in which day-to-day agriculture had been done by women, but the past seems to have been modified to serve the present in this case: Musodzi's extraordinary involvement in public affairs, which were supposed to be primarily men's business, was apparently predicated on her ability to earn substantial incomes on her own.

One of Musodzi's neighbours on Ventersburg farm was John Mfokazana. The Mfokazana family provided another case of women's gardening and 'dual participation'. Mfokazana was a mission-educated Ndebele, working for the Stationery Department from the very early days up to his retirement after World War II. Mai Mfokazana, assisted by her children and two hired Africans, laboured on an agricultural plot of 20 acres: in the words of her husband, 'Some we eat ourselves and some of the produce I sell'.[72]

Bammi Mukandawiri & Epworth Farm: The Origins of the RNA

The Wesleyan Epworth farm, located to the south-east of Salisbury, had been occupied by a large number of Africans since the early days of colonial settlement. It was a popular residential area for African Christians working in town, partly because of its proximity to Salisbury. Like St. Mary's, Hunyani, the farm possessed two types of settlements, indigenous and foreign, that is, a settlement of Chiremba's people, who had been in that locality since the precolonial days, and one of foreign workers employed in town, who in many instances had spouses hailing from local villages. This made the mission farm a great crossroads of different cultures and ways of life – town and country, the alien and the autochthonous, and Christianity (Methodism) and tradition.

Japhet Y. 'Bammi' Mukandawiri, popularly known as Bammi (possibly meaning headman or leader), was a long-time resident on Epworth. He was born at Nkata Bay on the Lake Nyasa and educated at the Kongwe Mission.

At the turn of the century a young Bammi joined one of the earliest Tonga labour migrant groups coming into Southern Rhodesia. But, unlike many of his colleagues, he did not return home. He stayed, worked and lived in Salisbury, associating himself with the Wesleyans. He married a Wesleyan woman of local origin and built home on Epworth around 1914. Shortly after World War I Bammi was elevated to 'boss boy' at the Farmers' Co-op., remaining in that post until his retirement in 1948. A cheerful, sociable person, always cracking jokes, he was a very popular figure in Salisbury.[73]

Bammi's daughter, Kate Chitumba, born at Epworth in 1918, recalls the livelihood of her family at Epworth: 'I think he [Bammi] was earning very little money because he had a big family and it [his natal community] is very far from Zimbabwe'.[74] To supplement the father's incomes the mother and daughters tilled the land:

> They growed [*sic*] beans, peas, maize, and tomatoes to sell in town. We took care of our gardens ourselves. We use[d] to go to town twice a week. Tuesday and Friday. To go and sell the vegetables and buy food too. We use[d] to carry our vegetables on the bicycles. Other families who had no bicycles had to carry them on their heads in baskets. The money earned from selling was used to buy food and clothes, e.g. meat, sugar, bread, flour, etc. Many people walked from Epworth to town daily.[75]

With such 'dual participation', the Mukandawiris lived a peaceful, stable, and relatively affluent life. The eldest daughter, Kate, was sent to a boarding school at Waddilove. Shortly after World War II, she joined the teaching staff of Chitsere School, the first government primary school in the Harare township.

By 1948 Bammi was able to save enough money to buy a farm at a purchase area in the Mt. Darwin district, where he eventually retired, spending the rest of his life as a small farmer.

At Epworth Bammi was a leader of the tenant community and would busy himself, as a catechist, with chasing people to attend church and school on Sundays. Chairman of the Nyasaland, Northern Rhodesia Association, he was visited for advice and assistance by those migrants coming from his home country. He worked for the welfare of Salisbury's Africans in many ways, for example by sitting on a committee of the Salisbury Native Welfare Society in the late thirties and the forties. He was also a founding and long-time member of the Rhodesia Native Association, the first African 'modernist' political organisation in Mashonaland.

The life history of Bammi Mukandawiri, when combined with those of Elizabeth Musodzi Ayema, John Mfokazana, and also Noah, present a fairly solid picture of the type of people who settled in suburban areas, as well as the way they organised their lives there. Such people were often better-paid, long-service African workers – government employees, 'boss boys', and the like – who lived with their wives and children. By locating themselves at the

Bammi Mukandawiri and the Salisbury Native Welfare Society

Committee members of the Salisbury Native Welfare Society, 1939
Left to right – sitting : Bammi Mukandawiri,
the Rev'd Darikwa, W. J. T. Ollyn (Sports Organizer)
Left to right – standing : Joseph Mandabve, H. C. Finkle (Secretary),
Timothy Kanyowa, Thomas Sambo

Source: Bantu Mirror, 12 Aug. 1939

urban periphery, they sought to 'straddle' wage labour and peasant agriculture in order to expand their incomes. This livelihood pattern makes a striking contrast to that of both the majority of Salisbury's Africans, who struggled to meet cash needs by physically 'circulating' between town and country, and the denizens of the inner town, whose survival rested almost exclusively on meagre urban incomes.

Some suburban dwellers in Salisbury indeed arose as dynamic accumulators of wealth by the early 1920s. Most revealing in this regard was the fact that they were themselves employers of African labour: 'The wage-earners in town [a missionary observed in 1925] hire a boy [or 'boys'] to plough for them. Quite a number of boys are hired in that way.'[76] In the most advanced stage of this social evolution were often local Shonas, since they were more advantageously positioned in terms of access to land, marriage, networks of people, and other 'resources'. This was pointed out by Job Ngangelize, a Xhosa settler employed in Salisbury, when he gave evidence before the Land Commission of 1925: 'Some of the local natives are very wealthy, especially some of the natives who are working here, and if they saw some natives buying land, they would certainly follow their example'.[77]

The economic ascendancy of a group of educated, entrepreneurial worker-peasants in the Salisbury area had important implications for African intellectual and political history. It would place such people at the forefront of a social change taking place throughout the colony in those years; African Christians, hitherto a cultural minority in the African society, were becoming a self-assertive, influential social force. This change of tide is well-recorded in the case of Chishawasha. At one level, resentment towards colonial rule never disappeared there: 'Even now after so many years', a Chishawasha missionary deplored in 1925, 'most of the older Natives make little difference between the Missionaries and the rest of the White population: they are, to the Natives, all at once in taking the best of their lands and making the Blacks the servants of the Whites'.[78] On the other hand, as Vambe and others noted, growing numbers of people, especially youths, had started to look at their own future in terms of the new social order imposed on them, realising the values of education and training provided by the church.[79] This climate led some of the early Christian converts, especially those who had managed to build wealthier homesteads, to view themselves as qualified leaders in uplifting and modernising African life.

It was such people, in the words of the press in 1923, 'habitually employed in town [Salisbury]' who launched the Rhodesia Native Association in 1919.[80] A novelty of the RNA's message lay in its promotion of supra-tribal, territorial unity among the Africans. Its constitution stated that it aimed 'to exhort, guide, lead the natives as to ways of pure, upward, peaceful, and good and right living in their homes', and 'to secure mutual understanding and unity of action among the various tribes in Southern Rhodesia.' The RNA wanted to play the role of a political intermediary between the colonial authorities and the Africans, by assisting 'the Government in every possible way, especially in keeping it informed of Native Public Opinion', and by helping 'the natives in directly representing them to the Government in all matters affecting native life and welfare in towns and elsewhere'. Much of the wording of the constitution was almost identical to that of the Nyasaland Native Association movement[81] (which had been started in 1912 by the Christians educated at the Livingstone Mission and was spreading southwards after World War I). This congruence, coupled with the fact that the RNA's first president, Eli P. Nare, was a Sotho teacher of the Presbyterian Church, working among Salisbury's Nyasaland migrants, and the first general secretary was Bammi Mukandawiri, an educated Nyasaland Tonga, strongly suggests that the RNA was born as a southern version of the Native Association movement in the north.

The local support for the RNA came mainly from Epworth residents employed in town.[82] They included Bothwell Zata, an interpreter of the Native Department, and Amos Zhakata, an evangelist who later became a Jeanes Teacher, as well Bammi Mukandawiri.[83] It may be noted parenthetically that it was also Epworth (Chiremba section) members of the RNA, including Aaron Jacha and Rev. Matthew Rusike, who, together with activists in Bulawayo and other places, founded the Southern Rhodesia Bantu Congress in 1936.[84]

Abraham Chirimuuta & Seke Reserve: The Development of the RNA

The intimate nexus of the RNA, Christianity, and entrepreneurial worker-peasants – and therefore the suburban origins of African modern politics – may be further illustrated by looking at the biography of Abraham Zindoga Chirimuuta. The RNA's history was very much associated with this person in the memories of the people in later periods.[85]

According to his eldest son, Ben Chirimuuta, Abraham Chrimuuta (who died in 1975) was born at Uzumba, Mrewa around 1895. A severe famine attacked Uzumba sometime before World War I, pressing him to look for wage employment. He went to Salisbury and became a 'garden boy' there. Keen on learning, he joined the local Wesleyan community and attended a night school at the mission station near the town, where he laboured his way as far as Standard VI. These Methodist connections led him to associate with the RNA from its earliest days. Chirimuuta combined his struggle for literacy with a struggle for skills, and entered apprenticeship to learn the tailoring trade at a garment factory, where he eventually became a 'boss boy'.

As was often the case with people of a similar socio-economic profile, Chirimuuta came to live in the urban periphery. He married a Wesleyan woman of Seke and established his homestead at Kudyarawanza in Seke in the early 1920s.[86] We find here yet another case of 'dual participation'. While living in the Reserve, Chirimuuta worked as a head tailor on Edinburgh farm near his home. At the same time, he increasingly established himself as an enterprising peasant, engaging in market gardening with the assistance of family labour and a few employed hands. A proud owner of a plough and oxen and a Scotch cart, he was by 1930 a main promoter of the Seke Native Farmers' Association, one of the progressive farmers' associations which sprang up throughout Mashonaland at the time.[87]

Chirimuuta became increasingly prominent in politics, as well. By the end of the 1920s he was a familiar figure in public meetings and events in Seke and the Salisbury district, representing the educated section of the African community. He voiced grievances and requests before the colonial government on behalf of the old traditional leaders. In 1928, when the RNA held its second conference, he was elected president, so becoming the first Shona president of the RNA.[88] His presidency continued until 1952, when he was replaced by Isaac Samuriwo.[89] In the late fifties, when the storm of African nationalism gripped the whole country, old Chirimuuta was still part of African politics as organising secretary. In February 1959, when the colonial government declared the state of emergency, he was arrested and spent some time in a detention camp.

As the 1920s progressed, the RNA's constituency expanded from Salisbury out to the Shona provincial areas. Everywhere the leaders of the RNA were men like Chirimuuta, though agrarian issues in these places assumed a more important position than in the Salisbury area. The first secretaries of the Fort Victoria and Umtali branches of the RNA, John Hungwe and Valentine Saungweme, were both proverbial entrepreneurial farmers with Christian education in their respective areas: Hungwe was one of a few Africans in the Fort Victoria district who could purchase a farm in the supposedly European area and Saungweme was a leading market gardener in Zimunya Reserve near Umtali town. Like their Salisbury counterpart, the RNA's provincial branches focused their efforts on thrusting a modernist force into the power structure dominated by the Native Commissioner and the chief.

Conclusion

In the first two decades of the twentieth century African 'townspeople' increasingly resided on the fringes of Salisbury. By locating themselves beyond the borders of the town, they freed themselves from noxious regulations and sordid conditions in the European town, retained a degree of autonomy in their lives, had access to land at a lower cost, and enhanced their earning capacity through the sale of beer or agricultural produce. In the 1920s the suburban dwellers in the outer zone constituted perhaps the majority of such people. This zone (stretching, in a semi-circular way, from Seke, St Mary's, Waterfall Induna, and Epworth to Chizhanje, Ventersburg, Chishawasha, and Domboshawa/Chinamora) was particularly dotted by villages of educated Africans. They would participate simultaneously in wage employment in town and peasant agriculture in the country. The serene landscape of such villages concealed the unfolding of a dynamic social history. They were becoming a focal point of the social, economic advancement of Christian worker-peasants, and, therefore, of African modern politics, as represented by the Rhodesia Native Association.

The African suburbs continued to exist, though they were increasingly regulated by the government after 1930, up until mid-century. The other side of the coin was that it was not until the latter date that the private locations on farms near Salisbury were categorically prohibited under the provisions of the Land Apportionment Act. The early official projects of married housing, such as No. 2 location (1922), and the Highfield village settlement (1937), were little more than showpieces, or experiments, although a lot of publicity was given to them as being 'garden villages'.

The growth of the suburbs entailed the dispersion, rather than the concentration, of African residence. Quite apart from the army of rural migrants billeted by European employers at servants' quarters and compounds in town, the African urban dwellers were residentially segmented into two groups: the one living in the municipal location, and the other on the farms, mission stations, etc. outside the town. In the course of time each of these African wards developed their own neighbourhood institutions, representing different values and different life modes.

In his study of the 'African Voice' Ranger states that 'Organisations like the Rhodesian Bantu Voters' Association or the Rhodesian Native Association ... seldom spoke for the interests of urban workers as such', and that 'the associations were much more concerned with things like dipping fees, de-stocking, and land shortage than they were with urban wage rates or the conditions of work for unskilled labour in the towns'.[90] But at the same time he makes a point which does not fit snugly into the above observation:

> In these towns [Bulawayo and Salisbury] the urban members of the associations lived in municipal locations along with thousands of African workers, drawn both from Southern Rhodesia and from far outside its borders. ... The urban members of the associations shared with these workers common grievances about living conditions even if not about working conditions.[91]

This last point is not supported by the evidence reviewed here, at least not for Salisbury, where members of the RNA, or educated Africans in general, stayed away from the inner town.

The values and behaviour of the RNA members were, then, more coherent than Ranger suggests. Despite their strong connections with wage labour and urban life, the RNA's Christian members, in common with many other Africans, were all against being reduced to landless, culturally uprooted urban proletarians. By situating themselves in African suburbia, they were able to pursue, often successfully, the life strategy of becoming members of a wealthier, modern peasantry. The RNA was, in short, an *urban* organisation, with a *rural*, or *anti-urban* orientation. It thus remained aloof from issues and problems directly emanating from the colonial urban/capitalist system. It was instead much concerned with such issues as those of keeping a moral integrity of Africans against what were supposed to be the bad effects of city life, and establishing a modernist influence in African areas. By the post-World War II years, when the Native (or African) Association regained its vigor, it had thus transmuted into an organisation almost exclusively of Reserve leaders in Mashonaland.

This point brings us to a salient feature of African social movements and politics in early Salisbury: the urban grassroots movements, like location/township movements and trade unionism, tended to evolve 'spontaneously', or in separation from the 'purely' political aims of educated men. The case in point was the long history of uneasy, entangled relationships between the Industrial and Commercial Workers' Union (ICU) and the RNA/Congress: in 1929, when the ICU made its appearance in Salisbury to campaign against low wages and bad working conditions, RNA men were far from sympathetic. This rivalry was to be repeated in the postwar years, when the Reformed ICU and the RNA/Congress vied with each other for leadership in the Harare township.

Behind this phenomenon lay, it may be argued, great 'sociological' dissimilarities between the location residents (or those living in the inner town) and the suburban dwellers. In a schematic way, the location residents, for instance, were highly 'cosmopolitan' in composition, as they were frequently 'foreigners' coming from various parts of southern and central Africa (though their wives were typically of local origin). They had only weak, if any, connections with the Shona countryside, as against the strong rural connections of the suburbanites. In addition, many of the location residents depended heavily on wages and other urban incomes for survival; some of them could even best be described as proletarians and the urban poor. The suburban life, on the other hand, was marked by 'dual participation', a peasant life mode, and at least the possibility of upward social mobility. The spatial separation in residence was just part of, or perhaps yet another catalyst for, this 'class' differentiation. The following resolution of the RNA's 1929 conference gives us an idea of how far the inner and outer Salisbury had become differentiated:

> We all know and admit sometimes that the Location was built for workers, people who are in employment, who need a place of rest with or without their families. If one takes this question today, the Location is no longer a place for

Public meeting of the Reformed ICU
Source: By courtesy of Solomon Davis-Maviyane, Sunningdale, Harare.

workers, but a cesspool of drunkenness and immorality, a place and a home to house wanderers. In many cases a good number of decent Natives have refrained from hiring any huts in the Location ... although they are employed in the Towns yet they have chosen the outside places in order to keep their families away. ... The Location have deprived of parents their children, husbands their wives, and children their mothers. Unless the Government can take steps to have this matter investigated or appoint a commission, we do not know what will happen to our next generation.[92]

Notes

[1] Throughout this chapter the term farm is used in a very broad sense, denoting even the land owned for speculative purposes, and also land held by ecclesiastical bodies.

[2] LG/52/6/1, Winter to Town Clerk, 17 May 1915.

[3] LG/52/6/1, Ranger to Town Clerk, 17 May 1915; N/5/1/4, N/5/1/12-16, S235/447-449, Private location agreements; *Rhodesia Herald*, 28 June 1920; S96, Memo. by W.G. Webster, Evidence by F. Sixubu.

[4] C/6/4/5, 1921 census, table re. Africans in Salisbury. According to this, the total number of African females in Salisbury in 1921 was 524, which included children.

[5] It may be useful to note that in 1920 the municipal location housed 135 African men living with wives and children: *Rhodesia Herald*, 28 June 1920.

[6] Ranger's Report, in *Mayor's Minutes*, 1908-9.

[7] Location Supt.'s report, in *Mayor's Minutes*, 1914-15; LG/52/6/1/, Reilly to Town Clerk, 13 May 1915.

[8] For a general discussion on the subject, see J. K. Rennie, 'White farmers, Black tenants and landlord legislation: Southern Rhodesia 1890-1930', *Journal of Southern African Studies*, V (1978-9), 86-98.

[9] ZAH/1/1/1, Evidence by C. H. Tredgold.

[10] *Rhodesia Herald*, 20 Apr. 1915.

[11] ZAH/1/1/, Evidence by W.S. Taberer.

[12] The suburban settlement usually had its own headman system which regulated disputes, etc. within the community: *Ibid.* my interview with Kate Chitumba (b. Epworth 1918), Mbare, Harare, 16 Oct. 1987. Even at Epworth, controlled by the mission authorities, the community had a considerable influence on daily affairs, as Peaden wrote: 'Permission to reside had also to be obtained from the mission authorities, but the evidence suggests that it was equally, if not more, important [for a foreigner] to have made an alliance with the community itself' (Peaden, 'the Epworth Mission settlement', 141).

[13] N/5/1/12, 15, Private Location agreements, Greendale, 1918, 1915; ZAH/1/1/1, Evidence by F. Sixubu; *Ibid.* Evidence by J. Nfokazana, S. Matiza, et al.; Peaden, 'the Epworth Mission settlement', 141 and 150.

[14] N/5/1/15, private location agreement, Epworth, 1915. However, the rent was raised to £1 per year in 1929, with the exception of those residents who entered the 1915 agreement: S235/447, Private location agreements, Epworth,1936.

[15] For Haupt's farm, Williams's farm, and Arlington estate see respective private location agreements in N/5/1/12, 15. For M.T.C. farm see D/3/5/39, case 1582, 1915.

[16] *Rhodesia Herald*, 17 Jan. 1906.

[17] See correspondence in A/3/21/53.

[18] But they leased, as an exception, plots near the town location to a few Sotho workers, like Eli. P. Nare and J. Moeketsi: LG/52/6/4, Mason to Town Clerk, 15 May 1922; ZAH/1/1/1, Evidence by Moeketsi.

[19] ZAH/1/1/1, Evidence by Moeketsi.

[20] On the other hand, the mission farms tried to attract Africans by providing schools

and other services. For the church regulations of Epworth and St. Mary's, Hunyani, see S235/447, private location agreement, Epworth, 1936; S96, Memo. on St Mary's mission by W.G. Webster, 7 Mar. 1925.

21 LG/47/21, Town Clerk to District Supt., Town Police, 24 Oct. 1913; A/3/21/34, Staff Officer, B.S.A. Police, to Secr., Dep. of Adm., 8 May 1918.

22 LG/52/6/2, Asst. Supt., C.I.D., to Location Supt., 11 Oct. 1920. For Mary, Robert, and Annie before 1920, see also D/3/5/49, case 1893, 1919.

23 See Chapter 2.

24 LG/52/6/2, Mason to Town Clerk, 1 Dec. 1920. See Also LG/47/33, Town Clerk to Location Supt., 29 Oct. 1920.

25 D/3/5/62, case 68, 1924; *Rhodesia Herald*, 12 Jan. 1924. According to Stanley Chidyamatamba (my interview, Highfield, Harare, 13 Feb. 1989), in the 1930s Mary Nyrenda was back in the municipal location, where she was active as the 'queen' of the Manyika Burial Society and still dominating the so-called underworld.

26 ZAH/1/1/1, Evidence by Tredgold. For additional information about the same farm, see *Ibid*. Evidence by J. R. Rowland and A.C.I. Burbridge. It will be seen that the focal point of beer controls progressively shifted to the outer area over the years. The position in 1927 was summarised by the police as follows: 'A certain amount of brewing takes places at Private Locations within the prohibited area but this is decreasing yearly and [because] the brewers are leaving to reside outside the prohibited area, the latter should be extended another five miles; this would make it almost impossible for natives in the Salisbury Labour Area to obtain Kaffir Beer other than at the Location Canteen. With the use of motor transport the Law could be better enforced ... Motor transport has been used of late with good results' (S138/53, Comm., B.S.A. Police, to Attorney General, 29 Apr. 1927).

27 C.N.C. Chuma, 'The Impact and Effect of Land Alienation in the Greater Harare Region, 1890-c.1920' (Univ. of Zimbabwe, Hist. Dept., B.A. Honours Paper, 1983), 6.

28 See among others N/9/1/6, Report by N.C., Salisbury, for 1906.

29 *Rhodesia Herald*, 21 Jan. 1893.

30 N/9/1/4, Report by N.C., Salisbury, for 1901, quoted in Chuma, 'Land Alienation', 18. For an analysis and account of African social change in the early Salisbury district as regards to women, see Elizabeth Schmidt, 'Women, Agriculture, and Social Change in Southern Rhodesia, 1898-1934, With Special Reference to the Goromonzi District' (Univ. of Zimbabwe, Hist. Dep., Seminar Paper, 1986).

31 My interview with Kupara Chanakira, Highfield, Harare, 13 July 1987. The report by the Native Commissioner, Salisbury, for 1911 (in N/9/1/14) read: 'One native in the Seke Reserve has purchased a light wagon, and is doing well in riding transport for traders and others. Another has taken out a Hawker's Licence, and is also doing well'.

32 *Rhodesia Herald*, 2 Jan. 1902.

33 Ranger, *Peasant Consciousness*, 31-2.

34 For example, the southernmost part of Chinamora and the northernmost part of Seke.

35 It was estimated that in 1911 the total number of such people in the Salisbury district was 2,353, as against 14,666 Africans living in the Reserves: N/9/1/14, Report by N.C., Salisbury, for 1911.

36 *Ibid*.

37 ZAH/1/1/1, Evidence by W. G. Webster.

38 S96, Memo. by Webster, 7 Mar. 1925; My interview with Patrick Pazarangu (b. 1915, d. 1989, brought up at St Mary's), Mbare, Harare, 29 Mar. 1983.

39 ZAH/1/1/1, Evidence by J. Mwela, Noah, et al.

40 Some mine owners held such a view earlier at the beginning of the century: van Onselen, *Chibaro*, 76-8. The Conference of Superintendents of Natives held in 1909 also stressed the necessity of married housing: Report by Conference of Superintendents of Natives, in S.R., *Report of the Native Affairs Committee of Enquiry 1910-11*.

41 *Ibid*. 11.

42 *Ibid*. 12.

43 *Ibid*. 11, 12.

44 By the mid-1920s the efflux of people from the town took place on such a scale that 'The

Roman Catholic Mission people removed their Church [from the town] because their adherents had moved away': ZAH/1/1/2, Evidence by T. E. Vawdrey.

[45] The Southern Rhodesia Missionary Conference, *Proceedings of the Southern Rhodesia Missionary Conference ... 1920* (n.p., the Conference, n.d.), 4.

[46] *Ibid.*

[47] *Rhodesia Herald*, 28 June 1920.

[48] LG/52/6/2, Mason to Town Clerk, 31 Aug. 1920.

[49] LG/52/6/2, Location Supt. to Town Clerk, 30 Nov. 1920.

[50] All the quotations in this paragraph, from LG/42/15, H. J. Taylor, C.N.C., to Town Clerk, 18 Mar. 1921.

[51] For a useful discussion of this change, see M. C. Steele, 'The Foundations of a "Native" Policy: Southern Rhodesia, 1923-1933' (Simon Fraser Univ., Ph. D. thesis, 1972); Phimister, *An Economic and Social History of Zimbabwe*, 139-45.

[52] *Rhodesia Herald*, 2 May 1921.

[53] *Ibid.* 28 May 1921. See also LG/42/15, Mason to Town Clerk, 5 Apr. 1921.

[54] See for example H.S. Keigwin's speech at the 1920 missionary conference, which was reported as follows: 'The native lived in his own native country, in the reserve, and that surely was the place where they should get at him. The Cape Colony Native Land Committee had made a great point of that, that the native should be kept as far as possible in contact with the land, and that thus only could he and his family live and maintain themselves under healthy conditions. ... It was astonishing when one got outside how enviously people spoke about the system of native reserves in Rhodesia.' Appendix II, in the Southern Rhodesia Missionary Conference, *Missionary Conference ... 1920*.

[55] A classic work on the urban/rural contrast is R. Williams, *The Country and the City* (London, 1973).

[56] *Rhodesia Herald*, 28 May 1921.

[57] LG/52/6/4, Mason to Town Clerk, 30 Sept. 1922.

[58] *Rhodesia Herald*, 31 May 1924.

[59] W. Saidi, *The Old Bricks Lives* (Gweru, 1988), 29.

[60] See for example *Rhodesia Herald*, 31 May 1924.

[61] S86, Native Affairs Comm. of 1930, 43. However, women's gardening itself continued to flourish at various places along the Mukubusi.

[62] LG/52/6/4, Mason to Town Clerk, 30 May 1922.

[63] ZAH/1/1/1, Evidence by T. R. Rowland.

[64] S86, 4; Report by M.O.H., in *Mayor's Minutes*, 1938-9.

[65] Location Supt.'s Report, in *Mayor's Minutes*, 1923-4: S86, 4; Report by M.O.H., in *Mayor's Minutes*, 1938-9. Saidi's assertion that it was in 1938 that the Old Bricks was first instituted is not correct (Saidi, *The Old Bricks Lives*, 73).

[66] Of the nature of the Highfield project, A. C. Jenning wrote to the Town Clerk of Salisbury in 1934: '... the Natives who would primarily have to be accommodated in the proposed [Highfield] Native Village Settlement are those, who being definitely employed within the Municipality, are living outside the Municipal area as tenants under Private Location Agreements on privately owned lands other than Mission farms': S1542/V4, Jennings to Town Clerk, 11 Dec. 1934.

[67] S235/448-9, Actg C.N.C. to N.C., Salisbury, 21 Jan. 1933.

[68] City of Harare, Town Clerk's Dep. Files, 41-20-6R, 15/54, J. 2, Secr. of Native Affairs to Town Clerk, 27 July 1938.

[69] The account of Musodzi's life history here is based on my interview with L. Chabuka (a grandson of Musodzi), Pioneer St., Harare, 10 Nov. 1988; my interview with E. Chihota, Workington, Harare, 22 Nov. 1988; *African Weekly*, 26 June 1944, 28 July 1948, 23 July 1952, 6 Aug. 1952, 27 Aug. 1952, 22 Dec. 1954, 25 Apr. 1956.

[70] ZAH/1/1/1, Evidence by Burbridge.

[71] *Ibid.*

[72] *Ibid.* Evidence by Mfokazana. See also ZBJ/1/1/2, The Native Production and Trade Commission, 1944, Evidence by Mfokozana.

[73] The account of Mukandawiri's life is based on my interview with Kate Chitumba, Mbare,

Harare, 16 Oct. 1987; Letter from K. Chitumba to this writer, 6 Nov. 1987; *Bantu Mirror*, 11 Apr. 1936, 28 Jan. 1939, 6 Mar. 1943, 29 Jan. 1944; *African Weekly*, 5 July 1944, 6 Sept. 1944, 7 May 1952.

74 Letter from K. Chitumba to this writer, 6 Nov. 1987.

75 *Ibid.*

76 ZAH/1/1/1, Evidence by Burbridge.

77 *Ibid.* Evidence by Ngangelizwe.

78 Jesuit Archives, Harare, Box 41/5, Notes on the Zambesi Mission, Chishawasha, [1925].

79 Vambe writes of this change following the death of Chief Mashonganyika in the mid-1920s (L. Vambe, *From Rhodesia to Zimbabwe*, 5-6): 'The majority now leaned towards the European way of life, thought and social behaviour. It was as if the death of the Chief had freed them from their tribal vows. There were no more rain-making or spirit dances, nor any of the rousing drum-beating song assemblies that often made tribal life so distinctive. ... Suddenly they seemed to be rejecting *ChiSwina* (Shona) culture wherever it was in conflict with their new beliefs. With the death of the Chief, they seemed to seize the chance to escape from their old existence and were trying to make a giant leap into this new dynamic system brought by the Europeans.'

80 *Rhodesia Herald*, 11 Sept. 1923. Historians have given various dates for the inception of the RNA: See for example J. R. Hooker, 'Welfare associations and other instruments of accommodation in the Rhodesias between the World Wars', *Comparative Studies in Society and History*, IX (1966-7), 59; Peaden, 'the Epworth Mission settlement', 147; Ranger, *Peasant Consciousness*, xi; Phimister, *An Economic and Social History of Zimbabwe*, 151. Yet documentary evidence clearly shows that the RNA was founded in 1919: S2584/73, S. D. Sandes, Detective, B.S.A.P., to Supt., C.I.D. 4 Mar. 1927; S482/114/8/48, The Comm. of Enquiry into Native Disturbances, 1948, Evidence by Baminingo; *African Weekly*, 22 July 1953, 9 Nov. 1955, 28 Aug. 1957.

81 The rules and regulations of the RNA, in S2584/73, J. S. Mokwile to C.N.C., 27 Nov. 1924. For their Nyasaland counterparts see J. van Velsen, 'Some early pressure groups in Malawi', in E. Stokes and R. Brown (eds), *The Zambesian Past* (Manchester, 1966), 376-412.

82 Peaden, 'The Epworth Mission settlement', 147-8. Epworth was to produce a series of leaders of the Native Association and the African (Bantu) Congress. Apart from those just mentioned, they included Rev. M. J. Rusike, Rev. J. Chiota, Aaron Jacha, Patrick Rubatika, and Josiah Chinamano.

83 *Bantu Mirror*, 25 June 1938; *African Weekly*, 23 May 1945; S85, The Native Affairs Comm. of 1930, Evidence by Zata et al.

84 The Bantu Congress was inaugurated in November 1936, not in 1934, as has been often accounted: S2584/73, Minutes of the All Bantu Conference ... on the 11th November 1936, in Memorandum of Meeting held in the Chief Native Commissioner's Office ... February 27th 1947..

85 Much of the account of Chirimuuta's life is based on my interview with his eldest son, Ben Chirimuuta, Kambuzuma, Harare, 17 Oct. 1987.

86 According to Peaden, Chirimuuta once lived at Chinamano of Epworth (Peaden, 'the Epworth Mission settlement', 148), but Ben Chirimuuta says that his father never lived at Epworth (my interview with Ben Chirimuuta, 17 Oct. 1987).

87 See for example S138/72, E.D. Alvord to Dir. of Native Development, 21 Aug. 1930.

88 *Rhodesia Herald*, 2 July 1928.

89 *African Weekly*, 23 Apr., 30 Apr., 7 May 1952.

90 T.O. Ranger, *The African Voice in Southern Rhodesia* (Evanston, 1970), 138, 140.

91 *Ibid.* 139.

92 Hist. Mss Collect., MA/15/1/1, N. H. D. Spicer, Private Secr. to Premier, to Mayor, Salisbury, 15 July 1929.

Part Two

The Emergence of Migrant Workers as a 'Class'

4

Migrants & labour protest:
a strike movement after World War I

Though Salisbury possesses no voluntary or any other band, street music is being well provided for by the parties of Mashona labourers on the public works. The voices are equal to any number of drums and fifes. The massive refrain of their chant, englished, is generally
> "we are hungry and tired,
> we will work for the white men no longer".
> *Rhodesia Herald*, 12 April 1895.

In sub-Saharan Africa the period immediately following World War I was punctuated by stirrings of industrial discontent among African workers. In settler-dominated southern Africa, there was also a spate of strikes by European workers. The places affected ranged from Freetown to Cape Town, from Lagos to Lourenco Marques, from Nairobi to Johannesburg and many other employment centres. Southern Rhodesia was no exception. In the period from 1918 to 1921 African workers mounted strikes and work stoppages in towns, railways, mines, and other places throughout the colony. None of these disputes was more than a 'skirmish', involving limited numbers of workers, and lasting a short while, but together they constituted a strike movement or movements. The first part of this chapter is an attempt to describe this upsurge of labour protest. The strike wave was perhaps the earliest of its kind in the colony's history and much of it has so far remained in obscurity; it deserves to be recounted in detail.[1]

Such an account, with its exclusive focus on protest, and protest in the workplace, may lead us to a conclusion that these strikes marked an early emergence of 'worker consciousness', as well as a rapid proletarianisation of peasantries – perhaps much earlier and more rapid than has usually been thought. Yet we ought to be wary of this kind of view. At that particular juncture of history, it must be emphasised, the migrant labour system was still developing, and most of the African labourers were, in truth, rural cultivators who entered towns as part-time wage earners. The African reality thus embraced tremendously diverse sociological terrains. To understand any particular episode of worker protest, then, one has to place it within the wider economic, social and cultural world of the migrants; to see industrial action as part of a more general strategy; to realise the inter-connections between work experience and location or compound life, and between urban and rural life; to envisage workers as also past and future peasants, as kinsmen, as members of various communities. The second half of the chapter tries to answer some of these questions. It thereby aims to clarify the particular 'logic' of the migrant's industrial protest and to explore the significance of such protest in the context of the country's social history.

Background

Two changes, among the many and complex socio-economic developments that converged around the time of World War I, are particularly important when looking at the rise in industrial protests at that time. As already discussed in Chapter 2, one change was a sharp increase in prices following the outbreak of the war, which coincided with stagnant wages during the same period. The result was perhaps the most drastic drop in real wages in the history of the country.[2] The consequential impoverishment of African workers was so glaring that it prompted Native Department officials to comment: 'Natives can no longer afford to buy blankets and clothing as they used to, and are resorting to the wearing of skins and other primitive garments' and 'the majority of boys working on mines and farms are clad in sacks'.[3]

With this drop in real wages there arose new circumstances favourable to industrial action: a scarcity of both European and African labour. The bargaining power of the European workers was considerably strengthened as white Rhodesia was heavily mobilised for the war, with the industries feeling a keen shortage of skilled manpower. Thus, during and after the war almost all categories of white labour, including railway and mine employees, artisans, shop assistants, civil servants and even the police, attempted to cope with biting inflation by organising strikes and deputations as well as forming trade unions and a Labour party.[4]

African labour, too, became very scarce. The high wartime prices for peasant produce, the decline of real wages, and the demand by the military for African manpower, all militated against an ample supply of African labour to industries. Still more importantly, the country's industrial centres were devastated by the influenza epidemic in October and November of 1918, which severely disrupted the established patterns of African labour supply. As it was reported:

Apart from the temporary and local results of the epidemic such as the pell-mell flight from many labour centres and the natural reluctance to return to what were regarded as centres of infection, many natives coming to the Territory in search of work were induced by fear to turn back to their homes before they even crossed the border; this influence affected not only the stream of independent labourers, but also those proceeding under the aegis of the Rhodesian Native Labour Bureau.[5]

In understanding the implications of labour shortage the African workers were hardly slower than their European counterparts. 'Since the recent influenza epidemic', wrote the *Rhodesia Herald* in December 1918, 'many natives have got the idea into their heads that there is a scarcity of natives and are consequently demanding higher wages'.[6]

An African Strike Wave after 1918

The initial stirrings of discontent remained isolated, as in two mine workers' strikes: one in which the miners employed at the Globe & Phoenix mine demanded increased wages in November 1918, and the other involving the sanitary workers at the Wankie colliery who opposed the introduction of a new work procedure in March 1919.[7]

But powerful undercurrents for change began to surface by mid-1919. On 14 July 1919 the African railway employees in Bulawayo went out on strike. The cessation of work involved 570 workers – practically all the Africans employed at Bulawayo station and railway workshops – and continued for three days. It occurred in the wake of a European dispute, only a day after the end of a two-day nation-wide strike by the European railway employees which won them higher war bonuses. On the first day of the African strike the workers refused negotiation of any kind, only sending a deputation to demand a wage increase. The following day the Native Department intervened and held an 'indaba' with the strikers. But the workers' attitude remained uncompromising. They demanded a wage of 5s. a day. 'The reason that 5/- a day or £7 10s. a month, had been fixed upon was because it was "what the white men got"'. The management answered this hard stance with the summary discharge of all the strikers.[8]

Meanwhile, perishable goods were rapidly accumulating at the station, although the coaling of locomotives and other necessary work was kept going by European workers. On the third day the authorities made a concession and managed to bring the workers to the negotiating table. The outcome was that 'the natives receive the same daily or monthly wage as at present, but that at each month end each man who has been employed for a year or more will receive an additional amount, which will vary according to the number of years he has served on the railway'.[9]

At a glance it may appear that these concessions were not particularly impressive; but, in view of the colony's labour record in which African industrial action had previously been subjected to criminal sanction or to extrajudicial punishment, they were quite remarkable. The news of the Bulawayo 'success story' spread quickly. The first to follow the example were the 'loco. boys' at the Que Que railway station, who walked out about two weeks later. Now that both state and management were determined to nip the apparent strike fever in the bud, thirteen workers were promptly arrested for 'refusing to obey the employer's lawful commands' under the masters and servants laws. 'The sight of seven or eight policemen parading the loco. boys to the Court House', it was reported, 'had the desired effect of bringing the remainder of the boys employed in the other departments to their bearings.'[10]

The quick reaction of the authorities notwithstanding, after the railway disputes came a series of similar actions in other industries. The most notable were the work stoppages staged by municipal employees in major urban centres during the latter half of 1919. On 6 August, eight days after the incident at Que Que, the Salisbury municipal workers struck, causing 'something of a sensation ... in Municipal circles'. That morning a crowd of between 300 and 400 marched to the Town House to intimate that work would not recommence unless a higher rate of pay was granted. The town engineer-cum-compound manager met the strikers, and the police were called in, resulting in thirteen arrests. The rest were eventually persuaded to work in the afternoon, when the Town Clerk promised an investigation into their grievances. The apparent 'ringleaders' were dismissed, and those arrested were convicted at the court for 'refusing to obey', each with the sentence of a fine of £2 or a month's imprisonment with hard labour.[11]

The Bulawayo railway strike also had repercussions within the town itself. It was followed, according to the Native Commissioner, Bulawayo, 'by a similar movement among the natives employed by the Municipal Council'.[12] Little is known about this dispute. However, when a few more municipal strikes and disputes simultaneously occurred in provincial towns in early December, it was quite evident that these events were only part of an African strike wave, which was set in motion, at least in the opinion of the press, by 'the example of the Salisbury municipal native employees, or some other form of unrest'.[13]

On 1 December the local authorities of Umtali and Gatooma were surprised to find their African employees refusing to work. In Umtali the workers demanded wage increases, while in Gatooma dissatisfaction centred on the adoption of a thirty-day ticket system in place of the practice of paying wages by the calendar month. Meetings with management or a Native Department official were held, where investigation into the matter was promised; and when some participants began to waver, the leaders or those still defiant were rounded up by the police. In Umtali thirty-four workers, and in Gatooma eleven, were prosecuted.[14] Concurrently with these disputes, further unrest was found among the Gwelo municipal workers over low wages and the adoption of the ticket system. In this case the existing wage scales seem to have been reconsidered, with the result that a possible work stoppage was averted.[15] In these months there were also parallel developments in various other places. Difficult as it is to find evidence about domestic workers, their discontent, in Bulawayo at least, came to be more frequently evinced shortly after the July railway strikes. As a local newspaper reported in September: 'Numerous cases of troublesome and obstreperous servants have recently occupied the attention of the Magistrates'.[16] Moreover, in January 1920, closely following upon the municipal strikes and unrest, as well as a number of European mine employees' walkouts, two mines are known to have witnessed incidents of collective action. 'At the Bushtick gold mine ... the workers voiced their need for higher wages'.[17] At the Shamva mine the workers successfully boycotted the mine stores which allegedly charged extortionate prices for goods. The Chief Native Commissioner attributed the success to the 'thoroughness of organisation' and a high degree of sophistication in the workers' tactics. 'The leaders influence and control the rest', he commented, 'by means of harangues and debates, and by the circularising them with notices, pamphlets and other propagandist literature.'[18]

As in the African labour movements after World War II, the epicentre of protest was Bulawayo, then the largest industrial centre in the colony. In May 1920 a newspaper remarked upon a new development: 'A movement among local native employes [*sic*] to secure increased wages in view of the high cost of living has been brought to [the] notice of the municipal authorities.' 'The originators of the movement are boys employed in the mechanical trade', residing at the town location. These workers, being employed at scattered places in relatively small numbers, organised themselves into a residence-based community through which they endeavoured to redress injustices at workplaces – an interesting fusion of issues of work and living. They held several meetings at the location and sent a petition to the superintendent. The town council then 'brought it to the notice of the public bodies, and large employers of native labour of the town'.[19]

This chain of events in Bulawayo was crowned several months later with yet another walkout by municipal workers, which ended in probably the largest single prosecution of workers, no less than 103, in the period under review. On 24 January 1921 labourers employed at the Road Department of the Bulawayo Town Council stopped working at mid-day in protest against heavier workloads imposed by Europeans overseers. Consequently, twenty-one workers were arrested for 'leaving work' under the masters and servants laws. The following morning their co-workers 'of many Tribes', living in a compound, went on strike. According to the court hearing held later, the workers' complaints were that 'whilst working they were not given enough time for rest'; that 'they had too much work to do'; that 'they

103

objected [to] being hit about and sworn at'; and also that 'they were not very much satisfied with the wages they were getting'. The arrest of eighty-two Africans on the charge of 'refusing to obey' resulted, and all of them, together with those in custody from the previous day, were imprisoned with hard labour.[20]

The task of this section, cataloguing the cases of industrial action, would be incomplete without making reference to two further strikes that occurred in 1921. One erupted at the Wankie mine in September 1921, of which C. van Onselen wrote: 'The miners' right to sell beer was threatened in this case through the actions of a compound 'policeman'; so they came out on a two-day strike which ended only when the police had been called in and marched them back to the pithead.'[21]

The last case was unusual. It involved the ricksha pullers working in Salisbury. On 3 February 1921, after having marched to the Town House in protest against police harassment, they stopped hauling rickshas throughout that morning. Tension between the ricksha workers and the police had a long history, since those who demanded strict work discipline were not the private employers but the municipality and the police. The ricksha puller normally hired a vehicle for 3s. a day from a European proprietor and operated as an independent, self-employed worker although his pass was still signed by the proprietor and his accommodation was provided by the same.[22] However, the local authority strictly regulated the behaviour of the pullers in the street. In January 1921 one worker, in his dash for a customer, mistakenly bumped into a European woman. An accident such as this in settler-dominated society was a real scandal, and the police thereafter became so zealous in enforcing the ricksha bye-laws that within the space of one week they had made a score of arrests. It was this police high-handedness that elicited the workers' mass reaction, which shows that strike action was not just the preserve of those relatively well-placed for combined action, like the municipal labourers or those employed at the railways and mines.[23]

This listing of African industrial protest in 1918-21 is probably far from exhaustive. An examination of prosecutions for 'refusing to obey' in criminal registers, as shown in Figure 15, strongly hints that there were many more protests than have so far been listed. The Salisbury magistrate's court, for instance, heard in October 1919 two cases of 'refusing to obey', involving fourteen workers of the Labour Bureau's Letombo Camp. The Gatooma court from August to December 1919 dealt with at least three cases of the same nature, resulting in the conviction of a score of wood-cutters.[24] But it is hoped that I have managed to etch the main outlines of the postwar African industrial action. It is plain that African industrial protest swelled in the wake of World War I. It appears that the peak of the wave was a period from July 1919 to January 1920, especially its last two months. Thereafter the course of events becomes somewhat hazy, but one can certainly say that the period of 1920-21 was marked by a relatively high incidence of worker protests.

As 1922 progressed, however, strike action was less frequent, and the labour movement was at low ebb in subsequent years. This trajectory of development may be attributed, in part, to the fact that from 1921, runaway inflation noticeably subsided, while African real wages were very slightly upwardly readjusted. Yet the most important reason for the downturn of labour movement activity was no doubt an increase in the labour supply from around 1920, following the end of improved conditions which had briefly prevailed after the influenza epidemic. Thus, 'market forces' decisively swung against African labour, especially after the collapse of the prices of livestock and grain in early 1921 and the ravaging drought of 1922, both driving many indigenous peasants into wage employment.

Similarly, from the latter half of 1925, when African labour once again was in short supply (primarily due to the competition for labour with the Northern Rhodesian mines and the rapid expansion of settler agriculture in the colony), according to the Chief Native Commissioner, 'Native labourers have become unsettled, and prosecutions have increased under the masters and servants' enactments',[25] and 'between December 1925 and October 1928', Phimister has noted, 'five strikes and four work stoppages took place on various mines scattered throughout the country'.[26]

Aspects of Ruling-Class Reaction

One of the characteristic attitudes taken by officials towards African labour militancy in 1918-21 was to pretend, consciously or subconsciously, not to be impressed: in the official mind, this kind of thing could not and should not have been happening in a young colony like Southern Rhodesia. The Native Commissioner, Bulawayo, for example, made only a passing remark on the Bulawayo strikes in his annual report for 1919 and quibbled: 'In each instance the strike, if strike it may be called, was short lived and of no immediate importance'.[27]

Behind such assumed indifference, however, there existed considerable alarm and exasperation among members of the ruling class. And how could it be otherwise, when the African labour protest was viewed as a component of the contemporary rash of industrial disputes, both white and black, throughout the subcontinent? What was most worrying was the possibility of European labour actions stimulating the radicalisation of African workers, a development which had recently been taking place on the Witwatersrand to the south.[28] An editorial in the *Bulawayo Chronicle* expressed such anxiety in response to the African railway strike of July 1919:

Here we have a repetition of the recent experiences on the Rand, except that

105

there is no sign of the movement extending. The natives have more than imitated the European workers in that they have asked for the increase of their pay by 100 per cent. . . . we may now mention that there were said to have been some irresponsible attempts while the European strike was on to get the natives out [on strike] also. We cannot believe that any responsible organiser of white labour would have advocated such a step.[29]

Both the state and capital instinctively thought that labour disturbances might pose a serious challenge to the future of the colony – which, they believed, was poised for a great postwar development. This was made explicit by an industrialist, when he stated in 1919: 'Rhodesia will be quite out of competition for capital and settlers once economy in the cost of production and *freedom from Labour turmoil* cease to offer compensations for the relatively low-grade of our great ore bodies' (Italics mine).[30] The issue was so serious that the administration deliberately delayed the repeal of wartime Martial Law as late as 1920.[31] They did so ostensibly on the grounds of the imminence of further European labour unrest, but much of their concern, one may suspect, rather lay with the prospect of militancy spilling over into the African labouring masses.

Native Department officials, for their part, were forcibly reminded by the African strikes of how much African societies had changed since the establishment of colonial rule. They saw the strikes as an early sign of African urbanisation – a notion which tallied with the administration's new Native Development Policy. One such official, the Native Commissioner, Lomagundi, wrote in his report for 1919: 'though undoubtedly some of the younger generations are acquiring ideas on the question of employers and employment which were unknown until recently, this is only natural with the examples before them and can be expected to increase as time goes on'.[32]

With this realisation of the inevitability of African social change came a re-examination of the prevailing master and servant relations. After 1919, for example, Native Department officials repeatedly warned the employers that the African wage rates had dropped 'to a degree which is becoming unsafe'.[33] Men like the Native Commissioner, Umtali, went as far as to argue for state intervention in labour relations. The same Commissioner found some of the labour-coercive arrangements unsatisfactory:

Portents have not been lacking that the demands for increased wages on the part of Europeans culminating in success where strikes are resorted to, are not without their influence and reaction upon the native labourers. The latter ... are conversant with the white man's methods of combating the increased cost of comodities [sic], yet when he attempts to imitate them he finds he is liable to be dealt with criminally. Moreover the Native is often thrown out of work when his European overseer strikes and so suffers loss of wages while the European gains.

He is left without means of effectually representing his claims and abstract justice is simply conveniently denied him. These unhappy conditions must inevitably result in fostering general and dangerous discontent. That is a consummation we must be prepared to guard against.

He advocated creating something like a Native Labour Board as a safety valve:

> As the natives are not permitted to resort to agitation to gain what they consider to be their rights in this respect, a medium for the fair and effective representation of their claims with power to remedy their just grievances when ascertained, should be provided as an act of grace.

> I have already submitted a report embodying a representation that certain provisions of the Native Labour Regulations Ordinance of 1911 designed to secure the welfare of the natives attested thereunder should be made applicable to all native employees, whether recruited thereunder or not.[34]

But this was a voice in the wilderness: the idea of the establishment of a Native Labour Board remained a heresy until after World War II. Nor did the suggestion of a measure of comprehensive state intervention material-ise. The last point was not totally unsupported, however: it in fact partly reflected the very thinking of the BSA Company administration. In October 1919, shortly after the railway strikes of that year, the medical director wrote to the administrator:

> I would add that there is a good deal of sickness always occurring amongst both European and Native employees on the Beira and Mashonaland Railways, and I am constantly receiving complaints of the accommodation provided for the staff, especially natives, even at such places as Bulawayo and Salisbury, and I am frequently asked why the Government insists on certain regulations being applied to mines whilst the railways are allowed to house and feed their native employees as they like. The conditions of the housing of natives on the railways certainly to my mind require some investigation.[35]

In response, the government imposed in 1920 certain standards concerning rations, housing, sanitation, etc. on the railway compounds in terms of the Native Labour Regulations Ordinance (No. 16 of 1911).[36]

The reactions described above should serve as indices of the ruling class assessment of the potential of the African labour protests for social change. It is plain that the impact of the protest was substantial – certainly more so than one might be led to believe by its subsequent obscurity. Our evidence thus renders support to van Onselen and Phimister's well-known thesis, that the conventional notion that the African rural migrant went astray when immersed in unfamiliar industrial conditions overlooks or underes-timates the ability of African workers to adapt to new realities, and 'there was a well developed worker consciousness [among African workers] from the very earliest days'.[37]

However, we must also immediately agree with Sharon Stichter's caveat that 'this worker consciousness was specifically a "migrant" one'.[38] It is grossly inadequate, indeed, to look at the subject exclusively in the light of the capital/wage labour nexus, since capitalist domination over the rest of society remained rather superficial, with indigenous agriculturalists being only partially incorporated into the wage-labour economy. Such a 'dualistic' reality inevitably had an important bearing upon the organisation of the work process, and on the consciousness and behaviour of the worker, as a number of scholars have recently argued.[39] To demonstrate how far this notion is useful for the study of African urban/labour history is the burden of the following pages. We first turn to a more rigorous examination of one particular migrant group.

Migrants' Life Strategies: Tonga Municipal Workers in Salisbury

The Salisbury municipal strike in August 1919 involved virtually all Africans employed by the town council, but the leading group was the Tonga, or Zambesi, sanitary workers.[40] Most of them came from Monze and other places on the Tonga plateau, north of the present Kariba Dam.[41]

The Tonga plateau formally came under the rule of the BSA Company in 1899. By 1904 the Company started to collect a tax in the area with a view to pushing Tonga men into wage employment in Southern Rhodesia as well as to financing the cost of local administration. The cash needs of Tonga families increased at the turn of the century, but how could they be met? Northern Rhodesia was then such a backwater colony that it created virtually no market for the sale of their agricultural produce. In 1906 the railway from Southern Rhodesia was driven through the heart of the plateau to link up with the Congo, which led to the alienation of a tract of plateau land along the railway. This area, connected to the mines and towns south of the Zambezi, had been subjected to the operation of labour recruiting agencies since as early as the 1890s. These circumstances, together with the fact that the late nineteenth century had been an era of tribulation for many Tonga communities (because of exactions by the Lozi and the Ndebele, as well as poor rains, locust attacks, and other natural disasters), combined to set in motion a large-scale Tonga labour migration to the south from the very early years of colonial rule.[42]

The majority went to seek work in Bulawayo and Matabeleland, while a few trekked to Salisbury and Mashonaland. By 1900 Tongas were turning up in the employ of the Salisbury municipality. Their average length of service at the beginning of the century was twelve to eighteen months.[43] Their relative rural insecurity, combined with the unpopularity of the municipal works, made the Tonga almost exclusive suppliers of labour to the town council, they thus occupying one of the lowest positions in the job hierarchy.

As municipal workers, the tasks they performed involved manual work in a revolting odour and dust, and physically exacting labour under the tropical sun. Yet the wages and rations they received were notoriously meagre: the cost of municipal labour per head was almost equivalent to, or sometimes even lower than, that of convict labour hired out by the government.[44] Also the employer's expenditure on housing was kept at an irreducible level: the workers were crammed into shacks at the compounds where they slept on old packing cases and iron bunks.[45] Of the conditions there the sanitary inspector wrote in 1915:

> Taken generally, the Compound is, in my opinion, very far from being in a sanitary condition ...
>
> Native Quarters. They are of wood and iron, two continuous rows of square rooms varying in size from 10' square to 20'x10', of an average height of 8'-6". They are badly lighted and ventilated, smoke begrimed, dirty, and so crowded as to make proper cleaning almost impossible. Twelve rooms accommodate 114 natives. ... All these quarters, except two rooms, have only earth floors, thereby completing the difficulty of effectual cleansing. As many as 15 natives are occupying one room 20'x10' ...
>
> Bathing and washing. No bathing or washing facilities are provided, whereby natives could be encouraged to wash themselves and their clothing, thereby improving the health conditions of the Compound.[46]

Along with these low wages and grossly inadequate housing, there existed a wide range of institutions, both private and public, to ensure work discipline and maximum labour efficiency. The compound system was just one example. The workers were discouraged from living elsewhere. They were expected to sleep in the compounds, where the managerial philosophy characteristically centred around discipline and punishment. In the compound manager's own words in 1903: 'Treatment: A firm hand. Always keep your word. Punish well when required. Do nothing by halves . ... A child with a man's vice'.[47]

Up to this point the position of Salisbury's Tonga municipal workers is remarkably similar to that of Stephen Thornton's Tongas employed by the Bulawayo municipality.[48] Like their Bulawayo counterparts, Salisbury's Tonga workers apparently personified arrested proletarianisation *par excellence*. They were most severely pinched between rural poverty and harsh urban conditions, consequently migrating back and forth between town and country to keep themselves afloat. It is primarily on this basis that Thornton presents a model of the militant Tonga worker. Such a construct contains elements of truth, surely, but I would argue that the construct must not be carried too far. The urban African strike record is far richer than Thornton apparently believes.[49] The criminal registers indeed reveal

Zambesi workers at cleansing station, sanitary farm, Salisbury, c. 1912

'We use a large enclosed van [drawn by oxen or donkeys] in the rear of which is
built a tank of wood... The fore part of van carries about 250 clean buckets nested
in each other. Contents of buckets are emptied into tank and dirty buckets nested
in van in lieu of the clean ones... At the Cleansing Station all buckets pass through
three tanks being scrubbed in the first two and dipped in liquid disinfectant in the
third. ... Seven natives are employed to each van handling 500 buckets per night.'
(LG/38, Memo. [by Town Clerk, Salisbury, 1912])

Source: D/3/5/30, case 1392, 1912.

extremely complex patterns of inter-ethnic worker involvement: the Que Que railway strikers convicted in July 1919 comprised eight Atonga, four Sena and one indigenous African; the Salisbury municipal strikers who met the same fate the following month were three Shona and ten aliens; their Umtali counterparts in December 1919 were eighteen Shona and fifteen aliens; the Bulawayo municipal strikers who went to gaol in January 1921 were forty indigenous and sixty-two alien Africans, besides one unidentified person; and so forth.[50] The evidence available hardly allows us to say with any certainty that the Tonga sanitary workers were more prone to act militantly than other migrant groups.

Nor were the Tonga workers in Salisbury permanently ensconced in a state of labour migrancy. The Tonga migrants, or any of the other groups for that matter, in fact possessed their own life strategies (or 'resources'), in terms of which they interpreted, interacted with, and changed their societal conditions – a theme about which Thornton had little to say, despite the fact that people's history proper starts from this point.[51]

Labour migration was closely tied to the strategies of African rural households to obtain cash incomes. At the beginning of the century Tonga agriculturalists were heavily dependent on wage employment for survival. 'It was not unusual in Plateau Tonga communities', Vickery writes, 'for thirty to 50 percent of the eligible males to be away in the South at a given time in the years 1904 to 1915, especially early in the period'.[52] (It may be of interest to note that the comparable figure for Southern Rhodesia as a whole was roughly between 10 and 20 percent.[53]) However, an interesting feature of early Tonga life was that people innovatively used savings from wage labour (and the incomes from the sale of agricultural produce) for strengthening the economic basis of their households. As the twentieth century advanced many Tongas increased cattle holdings, introduced ox-plough cultivation and exported agricultural products. This process of becoming peasants was pronounced especially from the late 1910s onwards, when the Katanga and then the Northern Rhodesian mines created a sizable market for African rural produce. Accordingly, the Tonga plateau ceased to function as a major reservoir of cheap labour for southern industries and became known for its sale of agricultural products to northern industries.[54]

This social alchemy emphasises that our protagonists were something more than the passive victims of the forces of proletarianisation. They had clearly-defined goals of their own when entering wage employment. As John Hambote, a Tonga peasant, has recently recalled: 'In those days a man would save money more when working, just waiting to take it back home with him. When he decided to go home he would buy a few clothes, then bring the rest back to buy cattle. People didn't go there to "eat bread" but to come back and be rich.'[55]

In this light, the archetypal Zambesi worker was a man of frugality, carefully sparing every penny which he earned from work. (Otherwise, it would have been impossible for him to save up to, say, £4 – the average sum the Bureau workers brought home with them – out of his 'starving' wage.[56]) Thus he was, as it is not difficult to imagine, very much attuned to changes in the working conditions and prepared to resist any tendencies to undermine his little economies and the integrity of his goal.

The Zambesi workers' first major protest occurred in the 'boom' years of 1908-11. In this period the mining industry began to demand a large share of the colony's African labour supply, and the industry's working conditions were somewhat improved, owing in part to the imposition of the minimum standards on rations, housing, etc. by the government (which considered its action necessary for the long-term development of the mining industry). Meanwhile, the colony's capital town expanded rapidly. The municipal works lagged behind this urban growth, and the burden of catching up tended to be placed upon the shoulders of the municipal employees.

In May 1909 workers refused to receive their Sunday allowance of meat 'on account of it not being sufficient', and a strike resulted. In a manner reminiscent of the 1919 strike, they tried to proceed 'to the Town House to discuss their grievances', marching 'in a body armed with sticks and axes'. Dete, Mangwali, and ten other Zambesi workers ended up behind bars on the charge of 'refusing to obey'.[57]

Thereafter, employment by the municipality became unpopular with the Zambesi workers, who instead increasingly looked to employment on mines. In a situation where 'No natives from Southern Rhodesia will undertake the work',[58] their attitude was serious enough to force the employer to review terms of employment. As the compound manager complained in October 1910: 'I beg to suggest that the Municipal Compound labourers should have their meat rations increased by half. Labour is getting scarce lately. And the Mining Compounds are trying to get the Zambeza [sic] Natives ... [by] giving higher wages, better food. All the Council Native Labour has been Zambeza natives ... and it's only Zambeza natives that care to do the work. So it would disorganise the Compound to lose hold of those now, and something must be done'.[59]

Another wave of discontent came in 1919-20, when the 'moral economy' of the migrant labour system once again collapsed. The dramatic wartime inflation seriously ate into the already meagre wages of workers, who responded by practising every possible retrenchment: blankets and clothing were less often bought, while humbler clothes like sackcloth were more commonly worn. Indignation among workers must have been widespread. Worse still, the end of the war opened opportunities for the expansion and streamlining of industrial activities. The municipal services, which had previously been curtailed to the minimum due to wartime needs, suddenly grew. This often resulted in intensified work pressures on each worker. In Salisbury the compound was incapable of accommodating an expanding labour force, and so some municipal workers were forced to sleep in the open: also the town council introduced a new system of rationing to economise on food bills.[60] In August 1919, shortly after the railway disputes, the municipal workers attempted a surprise walkout. Discontent rumbled into the following year, when the Town Engineer's Department was troubled by the workers' slow-down in protest against the supply of the poor quality of meat.[61]

Migrants' Labour Action: The Bulawayo Railway Strike

Industrial relations which developed under the system of labour migration in the early colonial era defy easy analysis. The system provided a number of advantages for employers. Migrants were low-skilled labourers with high rates of turnover, so that workers could be easily discharged, or taken on, in accordance with the needs of capital. They were not particularly amenable to a permanent labour organization – another plus from the employers' perspective. Since migrants usually left their families in rural areas, employers did not have to bear the full cost of the 'reproduction of labour-power'. Despite all this, however, one cannot say that capital's hegemony over African labour was particularly strong. With one leg in the rural economy, workers retained, potentially or in fact, a considerable degree of independence from the demands of capital, so that they could relatively easily withdraw their labour from the market. As a result, the migrants' protest behaviour tended to assume its own characteristics as compared to that of lifetime wage workers.

This last point may be illustrated by looking into the example of the Bulawayo railway strikers in June 1919. One thing which characterised this strike from beginning to end was the workers' efforts to overcome the disadvantages of 'replaceable' unskilled labour. These workers set the timing of action exactly at the moment when their position vis-a-vis the employer became strong. The strike occurred not only at the time of labour shortage, but also immediately after the European employees' strike, when the management were most keen to avoid further trouble and maintain an industrial truce. (In general, the wavelike character of the African protests and their simultaneous occurrence with the European disputes seem to indicate that African workers tried to take advantage of the situation created by the preceding disputes, whether European or African.)

Given the labour-coercive apparatus, it is quite natural that an overriding concern of the strikers was how to avoid victimisation, especially police intervention. This was evident in the fact that on the second day of the Bulawayo railway strike, the workers went to the police station, not to the management, first thing in the morning. They explained the legitimacy of their downing tools to the police authorities: 'Very shortly after 8 o'clock in the morning a body of about a hundred put in an appearance at the Police Station and stated their grievances, or rather announced that as the white men had obtained an advance they also wanted extra pay. ... They forthwith set out, in some sort of military order, for the railway station where they, for the most part, squatted down near the general offices'.[62] The workers' action was as highly organised as if they were demonstrating that the asset of migrants lay in the power of numbers, rather than the strength of skills and continuity: 'From the south end of the platform a view could be obtained of the native huts on the town side of the line and here it was evident that the main body of the dissenting ones were assembled, for hundreds of natives could be seen congregated in small and large groups, each of which appeared to have its speaker or speakers who could be seen gesticulating and haranguing their listeners'.[63]

Later on the same day a meeting was held between Native Department officials and a crowd of well over 500 workers. In that meeting officials made various suggestions to appease the strikers, but 'the boys had one reply, that they wanted a wage of 5/- a day and that unless their demands were conceded they would at once leave for their "kyas" [i.e. their rural homes]'. In reply, the Native Commissioner declared that 'all natives employed on monthly contracts would be signed off, but would receive no wages for this month, while daily paid labourers would be paid off tomorrow and all were to leave the railway's property forthwith'. The workers were now set to lose both jobs and shelter, but 'the announcement was received by the boys with loud cheers'.[64] Obviously, the participants in this dispute were rural migrants who were less vulnerable to the threat of being thrown into the street than stabilised workers.

The threat used by the railway workers was a typical labour action in the early days, i.e. desertion. They deliberately presented what was really meant as a strike (a temporary withdrawal of labour in order to improve work conditions) as a desertion (a permanent withdrawal of labour). The state also issued the threat which may be considered a typical employer reaction in those days, i.e. summary discharge. It did so to bring the strikers to 'their cooler senses'. [65] It was only after this ritual exchange of threats that negotiation really started.

The following day railway management proposed that the strikers select nine delegates for negotiation – an extraordinary turn of events, for even in the 1945 railway strike which erupted in Northern and Southern Rhodesia 'African workers never met management officials at the bargaining table ... Government and corporation officials refused to recognise African workers as negotiating partners'.[66] To the proposal the workers replied that they 'were afraid that if a deputation were appointed it would be clapped in gaol, or otherwise summarily dealt with'.[67] It was only after the management had repeatedly promised that there would be no victimisation that the workers accepted the proposal. Furthermore, not being so naïve as to believe in the managerial promise, the workers unilaterally changed the subsequent meeting into a two-hour mass bargaining session, when 'the deputation appointed by the strikers, which instead of nine comprised 50 boys representing all departments concerned met the Acting General Manager'.[69] Thus John Iliffe's observation for Tanganyika that early African strikes and stoppages were frequently 'of the anonymous, ostensibly leaderless type designed to prevent victimisation' seems to be applicable to our case.[6]

Going to Gaol Together:
Municipal Strikes in Bulawayo, Gatooma & Umtali

In some ways the Bulawayo case cannot be considered as representative. Workers elsewhere were usually unable to make use of the power of numbers. For them the results of industrial protest were in all probability either instant discharges, and/or exemplary arrests of some, and the return of the rest to their jobs. Despite, or perhaps because of, this prospect dissenting migrant workers invented a remarkably militant strategy – going to gaol together.

Since certain industries like settler agriculture were very vulnerable to a sudden withdrawal of labour, workers not infrequently opted for being sent to gaol as a method to win concessions or embarrass their employers. This tradition seems to date back to the very early days of colonial rule: a European farmer in Mashonaland bitterly complained at a farmers meeting in 1901 that 'in every seed-sowing and harvest season his whole native labour had been taken away, the boys having been hauled up before the magistrate'. According to him:

> No master could avail himself of the [masters and servants] law's benefits during seed time or harvest, because of the loss he would incur personally. He had either to pay his boy's fine [to get him back immediately] or lose his servants during these two most important periods of the year. . . . That acted as a direct encouragement to the native, who very quickly saw that he could annoy and disobey his master with impunity in this way. . . . If he were fined or imprisoned he would go home and boast of it. He was looked upon as a sort of hero if he had done time in the Salisbury gaol.

The farmer went on to say that the employer 'had consequently felt himself compelled to take the punishment of his boys into his own hands'. But a private punishment did not always achieve the desired effect, 'because native telegraphy [*sic*] was so highly developed that if you ill-treated a boy, before sunset tomorrow it was known 50 miles away', with no labour forthcoming thereafter.[70] Hence the state stepped in as an impersonal agent of discipline. In order to deter such action and other forms of labour 'misconduct', the Masters and Servants Ordinance (No. 5 of 1901) provided for harsh forms of penal sanction. First of all, since it was believed the Africans did not fear gaol, and also because employers often wished to get the 'disobedient' workers back as soon as possible, the main emphasis of the punishment under the Ordinance was not on long periods of imprisonment but on penalties to make gaol life most painful – hard labour, spare diet, and solitary confinement – apart from rather heavy fines. Furthermore, the law provided that the servant imprisoned must return to the same master to finish his contract, plus the period he was in prison. And if the convicted servant was employed on public works, he might be sent back as a prisoner to do the same work as he had performed before. Notwithstanding these stringent penalties, however, some strikers, notably municipal workers, resorted to the act of 'going to gaol' in the years after World War I.

The municipal strike in Bulawayo in 1921 was consistently filled with intrepid behaviour of this sort. On 25 January of that year, when a second group refused to work, they were 'marched down to the police station, where they were given the choice of being arrested, or going on with their jobs'. And '73 boys preferred to be arrested'. At the magistrate's court all the workers involved in the dispute were sentenced to a fine or imprisonment with hard labour, but 'the fines were not paid, the natives saying they would go to jail'.[71]

The same attitude was apparent in the strike by the Gatooma municipal workers, when, on 2 December 1919, all those convicted (except one) opted for one-month hard labour.[72] On the previous day their Umtali counterparts adopted the same line. A fine of 10s. or seven days hard labour imposed by the magistrate 'was treated as a joke' by the prisoners. The town clerk, much annoyed with the prospect of labour trouble after this, 'promised to go into the matter of wages' and even made an offer 'to advance their fine if they went back to work'. Nonetheless, the workers in the dock remained in a defiant mood and 'they all selected to go to prison'.[73] Their uncompromising attitude invited a flippant comment from a European reporter: 'Luckily, however, their punishment will be made to suit the crime and poetic justice meeted [sic] out as they are now employed, in convict garb, and under unusual discipline, in doing the same work as they were doing before. The Government, however, gets the money for their work and the municipality saves the food bill.'[74]

In such ways, then, these workers turned the 'court of justice' into a 'counter-theatre' where they tested and celebrated their own values of justice and solidarity. By opting for imprisonment together, they eliminated the danger of strike-breaking within their own ranks. One can only hypothesise a high level of industrial morale behind such concerted action. It is difficult to assess the effectiveness of this kind of action as a method of pursuing immediate material advances, but the tone of the above-cited farmer's complaint and the Umtali town clerk's eventual conciliatory attitude clearly suggest that the act of 'going to gaol' was not totally ineffectual, although it demanded considerable sacrifice on the part of labour.[75] This 'embodied' method of collective bargaining, too, seems to have something to do with the fact that the workers in question were essentially 'industrial guerrillas', only partially incorporated into the wage labour economy of the towns.

Conclusion

One implication which emerges from recent studies of agricultural and peasant history is that the evolution of the migrant labour system (and of the articulation of the capitalist and indigenous economies, which underpinned the system) was far from a simple, linear process.[76] The patterns in which African agriculturalists entered the labour market varied widely from one region to another. Vickery neatly summarises such differentials: 'South of the Zambezi, the rate of labour migration increased steadily, in some cases after an initial low period due to produce sales. In the North, migration rates became high immediately after taxation and rose even higher thereafter.' Yet still a few others areas, like the Tonga plateau, 'had a high rate to begin with, but the rate gradually fell, as participation in the produce markets increased'.[77] The meanings of wage labour (or peasant production) also varied considerably between individuals, homesteads, and villages within the same region. So, we ought to conceive of the migrant system as something like a patchwork of diverse and conflicting elements, developing as individuals occupied various positions in the peasant/proletarian continuum. To discuss such a subject in aggregate terms brings the risk of oversimplification.

Yet all the same, generalisation is necessary and useful. Arrighi was one of the first to outline the evolving patterns of the migrant system in the colony. Originally, out-migration from rural communities was a novel phenomenon, as it often took place only under the pressures of compulsion and persuasion. But in the course of time, wage employment increasingly became an important means of subsistence for a great many Africans. This transformation came to surface particularly around the early 1920s, Arrighi argued. Earlier, the rate of participation in the labour market by indigenous Africans remained relatively low, being between 10 and 15 per cent during the first years of the century, and about 20 per cent after the early 1910s, but it showed a marked increase in the early 1920s, reaching close to 40 per cent in the middle of that decade. He also noticed a new trend in out-migration: 'while before 1922 African participation in the labour market did increase in periods of falling real wages, after that year it always increased irrespective of whether real wages were falling, rising, or remaining constant'.[78] In short, labour migration assumed a 'necessary', rather than 'discretionary' character by the early 1920s.

This 'greater responsiveness to wage employment opportunities', however, should not be equated with the universal end of peasant prosperity, leading to permanent migration to towns. It was not at this stage that a crisis in peasant agriculture and permanent urbanisation became conspicuous themes in the country's social life. Rather in the context of the period under review 'greater responsiveness' to wage labour primarily meant the expansion and institutionalisation of labour migration. That is to say, the practice of rural households sending out their male members to the labour market became a common and regular one. Vambe vividly illustrates this change in a Shona village at Chishawasha near Salisbury:

> ... things soon returned to their daily rhythm after the deaths of Chief Mashonganyika and Mizha [in the mid-1920s]; in fact our existence became increasingly active. Most of the men had jobs in Salisbury, developed a sense of ambition and worked hard to add to their material possessions ... Disregarding the Missions sermons, which reviled material wealth as a barrier to the Kingdom of God, these people were spurred on to furious endeavor, as if they thought that they were being left behind by their neighbours in the race for earthly affluence and prestige. . . . It hardly seems possible that the tribe had once absolutely refused to work for money and had had to be coerced by white people with the sjambok. . . . At least the majority of them accepted the idea of employment, together with its unrelenting disciplinary code which demanded regular hours, obedience and responsibility to those who hired them in return for wages.[79]

At this point, Stichter's formulation concerning African migrant labour becomes particularly interesting. She argues that migrants can be defined as a social class:

> Migrant labour is a distinct form of labour use congruent with labour-intensive, low-wage, low-skill production. The individual migrant is partly involved in two different modes of production. It follows that migrants are in a particular class position, different from that of fully proletarianised workers. Migrants are a class, in the minimal sense of occupying a definable place in the structure of production.[80]

Without going into the lengthy discourse on what constitutes a class in colonial African history, I simply wish to state that Stichter's way of defining the 'structure of production' and an economic class is unique yet reasonable. It seems to me that the notion of migrants as a class is serviceable, especially in that it immediately brings us to the question of whether or not we can observe class-related behaviour and consciousness peculiar to migrant workers. Stichter's answer to the last question is affirmative:

> They [migrants] have also at times acted as a class in the larger sense – that of engaging in individual and collective actions aimed at furthering their class interests. Their strategies of class action are particular to their migrant situation, and tend to be distinct from those of more fully proletarianised workers.[81]

With little modification, many of our findings and assumptions in this chapter seem to fit snugly into Stichter's paradigm. Given a wave of workplace protests staged by migrant workers on the one hand, and the development of widespread, institutionalised labour migration on the other, it seems plausible to speak of the emergence of migrant workers as a social class. But before drawing a firm conclusion, let us recall our original perspective. We questioned the validity of the position, often held by historians of African labour, that assumes the primary influence of the production process on workers' thoughts and actions. Instead we suggested that attention should be paid to 'the wider economic, social and cultural world of the migrants', embracing not only work but also life; not only town but also country. Thus an important question which logically arises is how migrants behaved outside their places of employment. Could we find 'class-related' actions in this sphere, too?[82] It is to this question that we now turn.

Notes

[1] A few scholars, however, have noticed signs of the radicalisation of African workers after 1918. See for example E. Lee, 'The trade union movement in Rhodesia, 1910-1924', *Rhodesian Journal of Economics*, VIII (1974), 224-5; C. van Onselen, *Chibaro*, 221-4.

[2] See correspondence in N/3/33/2.

[3] S.R., *Report of C.N.C. for the Year 1919* (Sess. Paps, A2, 1920), 2; N/3/33/2, N.C., Goromonzi, to Supt. of Natives, Salisbury, 2 Nov. 1920.

[4] See Murray, *The Governmental System*, chapter 7; Lee, 'The trade union movement', 215-37; I. Phimister, 'White miners in historical perspective: Southern Rhodesia, 1890-1953', *Journal of Southern African Studies*, III (1976-7), 187-206.

[5] S.R., *Report of C.N.C. for the Year 1918* (Sess. Paps, A4, 1919), 7.

[6] *Rhodesia Herald*, 27 Dec. 1918.

[7] Van Onselen, *Chibaro*, 222-3.

[8] *Bulawayo Chronicle*, 15, 16, 17 and 18 July 1919; *Rhodesia Herald*, 16 July 1919.

[9] *Bulawayo Chronicle*, 18 July 1919.

[10] *Ibid*. 1 Aug. 1919; D/4/30/5, cases 467-79 of 1919.

[11] *Rhodesia Herald*, 7 Aug. 1919; D/4/7/24, cases 1601-13 of 1919.

[12] N/9/1/22, Report of N.C., Bulawayo, for 1919.

[13] *Rhodesia Herald*, 5 Dec. 1919.

[14] *Ibid. Rhodesia Advertiser*, 2 Dec. 1919; D/4/3/11, case 1137 of 1919; *Bulawayo Chronicle*, 5 Dec. 1919; D/4/17/8, cases 975-86 of 1919.

[15] *Rhodesia Advertiser*, 8 Dec. 1919; *Gwelo Times*, 5 Dec. 1919.

[16] *Bulawayo Chronicle*, 26 Sept. 1919.

[17] Van Onselen, *Chibaro*, 223.

[18] S.R., *Report of C.N.C. for the Year 1919*, 1. See also I. Phimister, 'The Shamva mine strike of 1927: An emerging African proletariat', *Rhod. Hist.*, II (1971), 67-8.

[19] *Bulawayo Chronicle*, 22 May 1920.

[20] *Ibid*. 29 Jan. 1921; D/4/1/39, cases 229-331 of 1921.

[21] Van Onselen, *Chibaro*, 223.

[22] *Rhodesia Herald*, 18 Nov. 1922.

[23] *Ibid*. 21 Jan. and 4 Feb. 1921. For ricksha prosecutions, see the criminal register, D/4/7/28.

[24] D/4/7/24, cases 1985-95, 2169-71 of 1919; D/4/17/8, cases 1033-47, 1083 of 1919.

[25] S.R., *Report of C.N.C. for the Year 1927* (Sess. Paps, C.S.R. 18, 1928), 5.

[26] Phimister, 'The Shamva mine strike', 68-9.

27 N/9/1/22, Report of N.C., Bulawayo, for 1919.
28 *Rhodesia Herald*, 1 Dec. 1919.
29 Lee, 'The trade union movement', 230.
30 For a comprehensive study of the African labour protests on the Rand after World War I, see among others P. Bonner, 'The 1920 Black mineworkers' strike: A preliminary account', in B. Bozzoli (comp.), *Labour, Townships and Protest* (Johannesburg, 1979), 273-97; *Idem*, 'The Transvaal Native Congress, 1917-1920', in S. Marks and R. Rathbone (eds), *Industrialisation and Social Change in South Africa* (New York, 1982), 270-313.
31 *Bulawayo Chronicle*, 15 July 1919.
32 N/9/1/22, Report of N.C., Lomagundi, for 1919.
33 *Ibid*. Report of N.C., Bulawayo, for 1919.
34 N/9/1/23, Report of N.C., Umtali, for 1920
35 A/3/21/52, Medical Dir. to Secr., Dep. of Adm., 7 Oct. 1919.
36 Gov. Notice, No. 487 of 1920.
37 Van Onselen, 'Worker consciousness in Black miners: Southern Rhodesia, 1900-1920', *Jour. Afr. Hist.*, XIV (1973), 254.
38 Stichter, *Migrant Labour in Kenya*, 156.
39 Besides Stichter's work, see especially C. Perrings, 'Consciousness, conflict and proletarianization: An assessment of the 1935 mineworkers' strike on the Northern Rhodesian copperbelt', *Journal of Southern African Studies*, IV (1977-8), 31-51; Goldberg, 'Formulating Worker Consciousness', 32-41; Ranger, *Peasant Consciousness*, 26-7.
40 According to *Bulawayo Chronicle*, 8 Aug. 1919, 'many [of the strikers were] connected with the Sanitary Department'.
41 LG/47/19, Town Clerk, to Secr., Adm.'s Dep., 7 Sept. 1911. The term Tonga or Zambesi is used rather loosely in this study, referring to the peoples living at Monze and its adjacent areas in North-Western Rhodesia. Before around1900, however, the Africans coming from the Zambezi valley in the Portuguese territories were also frequently referred to as Zambesis.
42 M. Dixon-Fyle, 'Agricultural improvement and political protest on the Tonga plateau, Northern Rhodesia', *Journal of African History*, XV111 (1977), 579-82; K. Vickery, *Black and White in Southern Zambia* (Westport, Connecticut, 1986), esp. chapters 2 and 3.
43 Until early 1898 the municipal labour force had been largely drawn from the local Africans and occasionally supplemented by the Shangaans, etc. (LG/47/1, O. H. Ogilvie, Sanitary Insp. to Board of Management, 17 Mar. 1892; *Rhodesia Herald*, 12 Jan. 1894, 16 Feb. and 31 Aug. 1898). By 1903, however, a vast majority of the municipal employees were Tongas (LG/38, Answers to a Comm. appointed by the Chamber of Mines, Transvaal, Aug. 1903).
44 For wage rates for municipal workers, see LG/38, Answers to a Comm. appointed by the Chamber of Mines, Transvaal, Aug. 1903; LG/52/25/2, Town Clerk to Curator, Public Gardens, 9 Sept. 1904; LG/52/6/1, Report by the Compound Manager ..., 6 Oct. 1911; LG/52/6/4, Town Engineer to Town Clerk, 15 June 1922.
45 LG/52/6/1, Compound Manager to Town Clerk, 19 Nov. 1908.
46 LG/52/25/3, Sanitary Insp. to Town Clerk, 6 Oct. 1915.
47 LG/38, Answers to a Comm. appointed by the Chamber of Mines, Transvaal, Aug. 1903.
48 S. Thornton, 'Municipal employment in Bulawayo, 1895-1935: An assessment of differing forms of proletarianisation', in *Southern African Research in Progress*, 4 (Univ. of York, Centre for Southern African Studies, 1979), 131-48. However, Thornton believes that the Tongas of his study were Valley Tongas. An account, similar to that of Thornton, stressing the extremely alienated position of the Tonga municipal workers is given by R. Parry in his 'Murder, Migrants and the Salisbury Municipality, 1907-1912' (Univ. of Zimbabwe, Hist. Dep., Seminar paper, 1983).
49 Thornton bases his argument on an unwarranted assumption that the 1935 Tonga protest was 'the first "major" (recorded) industrial dispute in Bulawayo': *Ibid*., 135.
50 D/4/30/5, cases 467-79 of 1919; D/4/7/24, cases 1601-13 of 1919; D/4/3/12, case 1137 of 1919; D/4/1/39, cases 229-331 of 1921.
51 Cf. Herbert Gutman's thought-provoking words in his *Work, Culture and Society in*

Industrializing America (Oxford, 1977), 16-8: 'Mintz finds in culture "a kind of resource" and in society "a kind of arena," the distinction being "between sets of historically available alternatives or forms on the one hand, and the societal circumstances or settings within which these forms may be employed on the other." "Culture," he writes, "is used, and any analysis of its use immediately brings into view the arrangements of persons in societal groups for whom cultural forms confirm, reinforce, maintain, change, or deny particular arrangements of status, power, and identity."... An analytical model that distinguishes between culture and society reveals that even in periods of radical economic and social change powerful cultural continuities and adaptations continued to shape the historical behaviour of diverse working-class populations.'

52   Vickery, *Black and White in Southern Zambia*, 100.
53   Arrighi, 'Labour supplies in historical perspective'. 189.
54   Vickery, *Black and White in Southern Zambia*, chapter 6. See also Dixon-Fyle, 'Agricultural improvement', 582-3; *idem*, 'The Seventh Day Adventists (S.D.A.) in the protest politics of the Tonga plateau, Northern Rhodesia', *African Social Research*, 26 (1978), 453-67.
55   Quoted in K. Vickery, 'Saving settlers: Maize control in Northern Rhodesia', *Journal of Southern African Studies*, XI (1984-5), 218.
56   *Rhodesia Herald*, 14 Dec. 1910.
57   *Ibid.* 20 May 1909; D/4/7/12, cases 583-94 of 1909.
58   LG/47/19, Town Clerk to Secr., Native Affairs, Livingstone, 9 Sept. 1911.
59   LG/52/6/1, Compound Manager to Town Clerk, 14 Oct. 1910.
60   LG/52/6/2, W. Wardely to Town Clerk, 7 Jan. and 12 Apr. 1920.
61   LG/52/6/2, Town Engineer to Town Clerk, 1 May 1920; *Ibid.*, W. Wardley to Town Clerk, 10 May 1920.
62   *Bulawayo Chronicle*, 16 July 1919.
63   *Ibid.*
64   *Ibid.*
65   *Ibid.*
66   A. Turner, 'The growth of railway unionism in the Rhodesias, 1944-55', in R. Sandbrook and R. Cohen (eds), *The Development of an African Working Class* (London, 1975), 77.
67   *Bulawayo Chronicle*, 17 July 1919.
68   *Ibid.*
69   J. Illife, 'Wage labour and urbanisation' in M. H. Y. Kaniki (ed.), *Tanzania under Colonial Rule* (Harlow, 1980), 287.
70   *Rhodesia Herald*, 24 June 1901.
71   *Bulawayo Chronicle*, 29 Jan. 1921.
72   D/4/17/8, cases of 975-86 of 1919.
73   *Rhodesia Advertiser*, 2 Dec. 1919; *Rhodesia Herald*, 5 Dec. 1919.
74   *Rhodesia Herald*, 5 Dec. 1919.
75   Another example is the 1935 Bulawayo municipal 'strike'. In this case over 300 workers threatened to 'go to gaol' by declaring: 'if one of us is to be dismissed then we all wish to go to prison and be placed under arrest'. 'For fear of further trouble', the employer 'adopted a conciliatory approach to the strikers'. See Thornton, 'Municipal employment in Bulawayo', 134-5. Yet another case of voluntary imprisonment is recorded in *Rhodesia Herald*, 11 Aug. 1923; D/4/7/33, case 2841 of 1923.
76   The major trends of such studies are reviewed in T. O. Ranger, 'Growing from the roots: Reflections on peasant research in Central and Southern Africa', *Journal of Southern African Studies*, V (1978-9), 99-133.
77   Vickery, *Black and White in Southern Zambia*, 149.
78   Arrighi, 'Labour supplies in historical perspective', 191.
79   Vambe, *From Rhodesia to Zimbabwe*, 10-11.
80   S. Stichter, *Migrant Laborers* (Cambridge, 1985), 191. See also *idem, Migrant Labour in Kenya*, 156-7.
81   Stichter, *Migrant Laborers*, 191.
82   Curiously, Stichter tends to ignore this question.

5

Migrant workers' worlds:
the birth of mutual aid associations
after World War I

The way in which migrant workers collectively defended the integrity of their life strategies was not restricted to workplace protest alone. The post-bellum years also witnessed the birth and proliferation of welfare societies as workers intensified their group activities to cope with the hardships of urban/industrial life by creating mutual aid associations. The Tonga munic-ipal workers in Salisbury, whose position we saw in some detail in the previous chapter, were among those who formed such associations. In this chapter we still keep an eye on this group, and try to document the genesis of African mutual aid associations in Salisbury. The records of such corporate bodies, at once authentic expressions of worker creativity and rule-bound organisations, provide the historian with an unusual opportunity to probe into the migrant workers' world. Before delving into this subject, however, it seems appropriate to sketch in some of the new developments occurring in the African life of Salisbury town after World War I.

Background

A peculiarity of the postwar years was a fascinating simultaneity of 'devel-opment'. Important events in urban history followed close on the heels of each other. To begin with, African modern politics made its appearance. In 1919 a group of mission-educated Africans, who were establishing themselves as high-income workers/upper peasants, launched the Rhodesia Native Association. They thereby claimed to be a mouthpiece of 'Native Public Opinion' in relation to the colonial government. Shortly after the establishment of the RNA, there came into being a kind of South African Bantu Congress movement, less biblical and moralistic, and more political than the RNA in outlook. Reacting to the constitutional re-arrangements between the European colonisers and the Imperial government at the time, educated South African blacks held a conference near the Salisbury location in July 1921. They started a Union Bantu Vigilance Association. Unlike the earlier Union Natives Vigilance Organisation (formed in 1914), this body had such an ambitious plan that it aspired 'in time to be representative of all the Bantu peoples in Northern and Southern Rhodesia'.[1]

The postwar years were also the time of grassroots action. We have seen the development of a strike movement, with its peak being around mid-1919 to early 1920. This more or less coincided with the development of community action against beer controls, high rents, and other problems in the Salisbury location, which was then becoming a 'neighbourhood' in which tenants would periodically unite against a common landlord, the town council.

Thirdly, the horizons of popular culture were dramatically extended in these years, and some of the familiar traits of the recreational culture of the latter-day Harare township clearly date back to this period. For example, the tea meeting or party – whose Salisbury style was later on to be 'even spoken of as far away as Cape Town'[2] – was started around the beginning of the War but became very popular after 1918.[3] It no longer meant only a respectable meeting held at chapels and churches but a boisterous all-night dance at the location beer hall or at other places in town. The craze of the tea meeting captured particularly a younger generation and quickly spread into rural areas. It contributed to the creation of a new genre of dance and music, the *Tsaba Tsaba*, and the growth of African performing arts.

Enthusiasm was equally exhibited for open dancing and drumming, held at the southern end of the location, with its particular emphasis on communal values. Innovations were the intensity of its activity (in 1920 the deafening sound of drumming and the noise of songs on Sundays was produced at such a pitch that they wafted to the opposite side of the location and seriously disturbed the religious services at the missions there),[4] as well as the appearance by 1919 of a modernist Beni-type (see below) along with the more familiar traditional forms of dance and music.[5]

Also in these years football ceased to be a sport exclusively played by mission people, South Africans, and African police members, as in the past. It was now regularly played and watched by common workers at vacant plots outside the town. In 1923 the town council set aside a 'recreation ground', the first of its kind within the location, for football clubs.[6] Then, boxing clubs came into being, apparently originating from the Police Camp sometime around 1915,[7] although pugilism became really popular only after 1930.

It can be seen from the above that the modes of popular cultural expression were markedly changing in the years around the war. These modes are of particular interest to us because they were symptomatic of the animated atmosphere of the time. Through group activities and by using old and new cultural resources, workers moulded their lives directly to the urban milieu.

Each of these developments in political and social life had specific, particular meaning and significance, it is true; but it also seems possible to say in general that after the war there was a noticeable move towards Africans grouping together and becoming much more self-assertive in town. The mushrooming of mutual aid associations, yet another new development, must be seen against this background.

The Birth of Mutual Aid Associations

The first person to set up a mutual aid society in Salisbury was, if a 1955 *African Weekly* obituary is to be believed, 'Chief' Zuze Komasho, who came from Tete:

> Mr. Komasho came to Salisbury in 1605 [1905?] and has been residing in the Harare Township ever since that time. In 1918 he influenced his fellowmen to form a burial society which is now known as Tete Burial Society No. 1. As a result of his initiative, many other tribes in the Township followed his example and formed their own burial societies. ... Mr. Komasho was a moving spirit behind his people and all will live to remember his leadership which enabled them to come together and help one another in time of sickness and death.[8]

Yet another association which might have claimed to be 'No. 1' was the Senna Burial Society, also started in 1918. It later split into the Port Herald Burial Society and the Chinde Society Company, Senna Mission.[9] After 1918 the establishment of such societies came into vogue, with the initial energy being concentrated during the several months from about mid-1919 to early 1920. This is attested to by the location superintendent, who first referred to the movement in his annual report for 1919-20: 'Several of the tribes here formed clubs, their subscriptions being devoted to the helping one another in sickness, payment of fines for the less serious offences of members, and indulging in expensive funerals'.[10]

By the middle of the 1920s the Salisbury location was home to, in addition to those already mentioned, such bodies as the Gazaland Burial Society, the Northern Rhodesia Burial Society, the Chikunda Club, the Atonga Society, the Angoni Burial Society and the Chinyao (Nyau) Society. Some of them had branches extending to mines and other industrial centres.[11]

Two examples of the 1920s societies will suffice. The Chinyao society, or societies, enjoyed enthusiastic support from Chewa and Chipeta workers. It was a Malawi secret dance group with long pre-colonial roots. Since it is on record that by 1915 Chinyao was operative on the Shamva mine,[12] it is highly probable that the society was brought into Salisbury in the very early days. But this dance society also functioned as a mutual aid society and gained its strength after the war.[13]

The Tonga or Zambesi workers formed their own society, the Northern

Rhodesia Burial Society. It was started by Simonga, Kawanba and others at the municipal compound on the Municipal Sanitary Farm. Simonga assumed the title of governor of the society. John Simuza was appointed as king. Simuza was one of the Zambesi old-timers at the age of about 40 and was known as 'King of the Zambezi peoples' in Salisbury. He was a cattle-buyer, but he had been a 'police boy' for a number of years. The workers made W. D. Masawi (or Chipwaya), a Sotho messenger for the Native Department, their president, brigadier-general and honourable secretary.

The government and employers were quite uneasy about the growth of these organisations. The former, desiring to bring the societies under supervision, encouraged the placing of their funds in the hands of the Native Department in return for official recognition. In compliance with this policy, the Northern Rhodesia Burial Society opened, as did some other societies, an account at the Native Commissioner's Office. This was on 9 September 1919 – only a few weeks after their August strike, discussed in the previous chapter. On Christmas Day members relished a day of feasting and sports in the location.[14]

One incident which gave a good deal of impetus to the birth of the societies was the influenza epidemic. The societies came into being during the months from 1918 to 1919 when the town, and its African populace particularly, was twice ravaged by influenza (the second epidemic being less severe). The town also had to cope with the onslaught of other infectious diseases which intermittently threatened. The mutual aid activity of migrant communities was, sadly, given a great boost by the epidemic; in the course of the first influenza attack on Salisbury no less than 300 Africans died, and more than 2,000 were confined in an isolation camp.[15] Those who disliked the official camp 'took to the hills around the town for open air treatment of their own'.[16] Many Zambesi workers fell sick, so that the town's sanitary service almost ground to a halt.[17] The influenza scourge brutally accentuated the hardships of town life and drove home to all the Africans of Salisbury the vital importance of mutual help. The trauma which the epidemic inflicted on the people's minds was clearly displayed in the decision to choose the formal names of older burial societies for new associations, whose activities in truth were not simply restricted to funeral-related activities. It thus seems no accident that the Zambesi workers started a mutual aid society in early September of 1919, at the very moment when the people panicked at a recrudescence of the epidemic.

Yet one must not paint the burial society movement totally in tones of darkness and gloom. For example, the Northern Rhodesia Burial Society did possess a colourful and cheerful feature: it was a dance society. It was akin to Beni or, more precisely, to the *après guerre* style of Beni, which staged a dance mocking a military parade.

Beni was then being disseminated from eastern Africa to central and southern Africa apparently through African ex-soldiers and cargo carriers.[18]

Salisbury town must have been quite receptive to such a dance. During the war Salisbury had been a training centre for African soldiers, regularly witnessing the marching of an African military band: 'A large body of the Native Regiment have gone to East Africa during the year [1917], and several more are in training in Salisbury. The Native Regiment band has become quite an institution in Salisbury, and the sight of the Natives marching through the town is an unfailing source of interest.'[19] Significantly, from May 1918 to January 1919 the Rhodesia Native Regiment returned to Salisbury to be demobilised.[20] These returned soldiers, together with the fresh migrants who had served in the war, brought with them the excitement and memories of the campaigns in Tanganyika as well as certain elements of east African popular culture. It is not known whether any Zambesi workers had personally experienced the war, but the society's President W. D. Chipwaya had been a non-commissioned officer of the Second Native Regiment.[21]

Exactly like Beni, the Northern Rhodesia society laid a great deal of stress on hierarchy and status, and modelled itself on a military force and colonial administration. The formal organisational structure was comprised of officers ranging from President at the top, Governor-General, Town Clerk-Business Manager-Interpreter, Solicitor, Brigadier-General, Lieut.-Colonel, Major-in-Charge, down to Warrant Office, and finally to the common soldiers. Like Beni, it possessed a fictitious military band (*beni*) and staged a drill or dance in leisure time. The rules of the society read: 'No soldier to be allowed to be absent from parade at any day, as the parades are to be held at the location ground at 3:30 p.m. every Saturday and at 2:30 p.m. on holidays. R.S.M. is to see that the soldiers are thoroughly trained before they join any platoon. They must know how to salute every now and then. He (R.S.M.) will chose [*sic*] the best of his soldiers which he thinks better for promotion.' Also in a manner typical of Beni, the society very much concerned itself with the smart and clean appearance of members, as another rule stated: 'All soldiers are carefully warned to obtain their uniform which will be of the khaki shirt, 1 knicker (khaki), 1 hat, which will be worn on parade, and puttees (if obtained). Hair to be combed. Feet washed if boots cleaned.'[22]

Thus, these Zambesi workers were among the primary agents who introduced such fashionable modes of dress and the latest dance and music forms into Southern Rhodesia. In participating in such activity, they triumphantly asserted their identities as 'clean dancers' rather than the socially despised 'scavengers' and 'bucket boys'.

Not to be outdone, other societies adopted the Beni mode. Even in mining compounds, employers were noting 'organised drill' in the early 1920s.[23] In Salisbury the Port Herald Burial Society was structured on a Beni-like elaborate hierarchical line,[24] as was the Atonga Society. Interestingly, the latter had a 'women's club' whose members possessed titles of honour like Queen and Deputy Queen.[25] Their military dance, *M'ganda Kapena Malipenga*, was one of the most popular dance modes in early Salisbury: 'The performers were

Returning soldiers of the Rhodesia Native Regiment, Salisbury, 1919
Source: National Archives of Zimbabwe, Harare, Photographic Collection.

Dressed-up 'Queen' and 'Lady-in-Waiting'
(of Atonga society?), Salisbury location, 1927.

Source: Rhodesia Herald, 2 Dec. 1927.

all clad [the *Bantu Mirror* reported in 1937] in white knickers with uniform hats. Some wore spectacles which any way I think were worn for swank rather than as an aid to weak eyesight. The music of this band was typically African, being monotonous, and yet not without some beauty of its own.'[26]

Social Enclaves of Migrants

Such a close juxtaposition of benefit and dance illustrates the multifunctionality of the postwar associations. We will now take a closer look at the ways in which migrants developed mutual aid structures.

Let us see how they travelled to towns. Before embarking upon a long, dangerous journey, African peasants formed a group comprising relatives and friends. They then marched towards an employment centre, often using acquaintances working on their way as stepping stones. One such migrant was David Mwanza, of Northern Rhodesian origin, who recalls his 1936 trans-Zambezi trek to Mashonaland. At that time he was only about twelve years old:

On starting our journey, we were three children and two adults. After three days' journey, we slept at a village in Portuguese territory. There we met others who were going to Southern Rhodesia, and with them formed a single company. On the way we met my brother who was returning from Southern Rhodesia. Since our company was poor and without rations and without blankets, my brother took his blanket and gave it to me, and he gave me sixpence that I might eat on the way.[27]

They crossed the Zambezi by ferry, traversed a long stretch of waterless country, came into southern Rhodesia, and finally reached a pass office:

Next morning we resumed our journey and came to [the farm] of the European where my elder brother, Patisoni, was. On our arrival he was greatly distressed at seeing that I had come. He said, 'Come, let us go home because I have much money and I shall buy all you want'. But I would not agree. And he gave me a half-a-crown that I might eat on the way because [he saw] we really intended to press on. And another acquaintance gave me a shilling: and another, sixpence. We slept the night at that European's farm.

The next day we continued on our way, and, after a long journey, came to where my 'small father', who had married my mother's sister, was. He gave me nine pence. We pressed on. At that time I became very lame: my feet were blistered, and I could not walk properly.[28]

It was then an everyday occurrence in Salisbury for groups of rural migrants to enter the town, celebrating their safe arrival. The following passage in the *Rhodesia Herald* in 1910 portrayed such a scene, which vividly shows how migration itself involved a 'community':

129

A further gang of about 150 native labourers from Nyasaland arrived in town yesterday morning, as usual chanting their ... songs and brandishing sundry sticks and knobkerries. One venerable looking native with a beard caused considerable amusement to an interested number of spectators by halting the gang in Second Street whilst he performed various ... evolutions, punctuated with occasional ejaculations to which the gang gave a deep-toned chorus.[29]

Let us see next how the new migrants moved into employment. A job was frequently handed over from one relative to another, from friend to friend, and from compatriot to compatriot like a prize, not least because, to quote a long-time Hararian, 'it was difficult to find employment in Salisbury at that time. Arrests were the order of the day [owing to a pass system and housing restrictions]'.[30]

One of the many who obtained a job through a kinship connection was Patrick Pazarangu (who was to become a well-known activist of the Reformed I.C.U. after World War II and the first postmaster in Harare township in the 1950s). Born in Mazoe in 1915 and brought up by his aunt at Seke after his mother was killed by the influenza pandemic in 1918, he entered Salisbury's labour market at the age of fourteen. Pazarangu recalls: 'I knew George, son of my aunt who was working for H. G. Moilly, a German gunsmith in First Street. ... He is the only person I knew. I went to him and he sought employment for me. ... My nephew [?] helped in the fixing of the guns while I was employed as a cleaner. If my cousin [*mukoma wangu*] failed to hold the butt properly he was sometimes beaten thoroughly with a gun but. ... I was paid one pound and ten shillings. ... He then left the job to me. He went and worked at the Post Office, leaving me working there.'[31]

This bond between relatives was then used as a lever for procuring a better job. Pazarangu continues: 'I worked here until my nephew called me to work at the Post Office since he was now leaving that employment. My job was simply making tea. My nephew's job was to pass on telegrams at the Telegraph Office.' Before long, Pazarangu managed to take over his cousin George's job: 'I became a messenger, earning two pounds ten shillings per mensum. ... Two pounds ten shillings was a lot of money'.[32]

In addition, relatives and friends were also invariably involved in securing a sleeping space for newcomers and job seekers. Again, Pazarangu's reminiscences are illustrative. To gain housing and shelter, he relied on the hospitality of his brother-in-law, and through this connection he managed to obtain better accommodation: 'I was staying at Creshbam's premises near Charles E. Harris. I had a brother-in-law, Cephas Vhera who married a sister of mine Lilian. ... We lived at those premises sleeping on paper. That in-law of mine liked me very much. From there we went to St. Mary's, Hunyani, that is where we lived and cycled everyday to and from work. ... Sometimes we slept at some backyard in town and used paper for blan-

Patrick Pazarangu and the Reformed ICU, Harare township, c. 1952
Source: *By courtesy of Solomon Davis-Maviyane, Sunningdale, Harare.*

kets until he was allocated a house. ... He managed to get a house in the Old Bricks area of Harare and together with his younger brother Enock Vhera.'[33]

Associations emerged wherever workers met and shared the same experience – at workshops, location, churches, and other places. But at the core of the migrants' associational life lay close-knit kinship and ethnic ties. It was within such a world, grounded in linguistic and cultural affinity, that migrants would 'let their hair down', exchange job information,[34] and discuss the various affairs of their homes. And 'uncles' and 'elder brothers' did not fail to offer assistance whenever workers found themselves in trouble. In return, workers developed a profound sense of loyalty to their own 'communities'.

Like others, the Zambesi workers formed social institutions where a communal spirit was exercised at every turn in the course of their industrial life. They migrated to Salisbury in a group. 'We have always had a constant supply', in the words of their employer, 'one gang coming as soon as the others left, and often boys have been waiting to be taken on.'[35] They worked together and played together. When off work, they would hunt together for small animals like *matapi* (rats) on the commonage.[36] On duty, their group consciousness was exhibited in such a way that gangs of night-soil labourers were in the habit of singing songs to make their night-time routine a little more congenial and pleasant.[37]

Scattered in hidden niches of industrial Salisbury, then, were a diverse set of migrants' social enclaves, which probably dated from the very early days of colonialism. Ethnic clusters at mission churches are one indicator of this trend. Since workers brought their pre-migration patterns of religious affiliation into town with them, early religious congregations in Salisbury were often associated with particular migrant groups (Figure 16). Presbyterianism was almost the national badge for Nyasaland migrants: in 1905 workers 'being mostly from the south-west of Nyassa' (where the influence of the Scottish Church was substantial) started the first congregation of the Presbyterian Church in Salisbury.[38] A few years later their Dutch Reformed Church counterparts followed suit.[39] The core of the Catholic congregation, organised in the town in 1907, 'consisted of young men from the Missions of Chishawasha, St. Triashill and Driefontein, who were at work in or near the town of Salisbury'.[40] In much the same way, the Anglican and Wesleyan Churches had prominent Southern Rhodesian elements, and the earliest supporters of the American Methodist Church were almost exclusively 'Manyika' people who already had contact with that Church in their home areas of the Eastern District.[41]

Occupational concentrations are another useful indicator of the power of the migrant social networks.[42] Partly because the practice of matching job seekers with occupations was constantly operating among friends and relatives, and partly because employers found such an arrangement conducive to a better management of migrant labour,[43] Salisbury's labour market was widely characterised by ethnic clusters at workplaces. My analysis of the 1911 census manuscripts reveals that there were concentrations of Shona and Portuguese workers in domestic employment; ricksha pulling was the preserve of a Shona-speaking group; municipal work was done by the Zambesis; railway workers were mostly men from the Portuguese territory and Nyasaland; Barotse clustered at the Tobacco Warehouse; Angoni and Chikunda predominated at Elcombe & Co.; servants of the Commercial Hotel were almost exclusively Nyasalanders and Portuguese Africans, whereas those at the Empire Hotel were Shona and Chikunda; and drivers of wagons were typically either South Africans or local Africans.[44] Moreover, as in the case of the Zambesi municipal workers, such occupational concentrations frequently continued for years or even decades, gradually resulting in the building up of distinct migrant 'communities'.

Enclaves & Associations

Our hypothesis is that with Salisbury town increasingly becoming a hub of numerous migrants' 'communities' from around the turn of the century, the difficult times around the end of the 1914-18 war cut deeply, and activated the 'communities' on an unprecedented scale. Worker-peasants struggled to defend their life goals, and their instinct in doing so was to resort to what was already familiar. This resulted in the mushrooming of formalised mutual aid associations. Heads of such associations were the key individuals of migrants' social institutions, usually drawn from long-term urban residents and referred to as chiefs, headmen, and kings (as in the cases of Zuze Komasho of the Tete Burial Society, and John Simunza of the Northern Rhodesian Burial Society). This bears testimony to the close link between the kinship- and ethnicity-centred communities and the formalised societies.

Thus it is not surprising that 'it was often difficult', as Ranger writes, 'to draw a meaningful line between dance associations and more formally constituted welfare societies'.[45] As the 'communities' had already done, societies incorporated communal dancing and joy-making into their activities.

The Zambesi workers' association embodied an element of a self-improvement movement and set certain moral standards and etiquette for its members. Just like a family, the migrants' community involved not only mutual aid but also obligations. Its concern with the clean and smart appearance of members may be one example of this. The organised drill, apart from its more pleasurable functions, may be interpreted as a method of moral improvement through discipline. Much stress was placed on seniority: the members were expected 'to salute superior officers whenever they meet them; Lords as well as their wives'. And this rule was extended to other African groups as well: 'Every [sic] soldiers are strictly warned to salute every [sic] seniors, either Chinde, Portuguese, Kings and Governors and Generals. There is no difference.' A corporate action was a virtue, and an egocentric action a vice: 'No member [is] allowed to have interview with Government without proper authority from Brigadier-General [i.e. Chipwaya], who shall always be at their need', and members must not 'leave the township without giving notice to the Association before he proceeds on journey'.[46]

Military metaphors were prevalent. In the words of the Tonga society, 'all soldiers are forbidden to have themselves in bad condition'.[47] Antonio, the Governor for the Port Herald Society, delineated what 'bad condition' meant: 'The people who join the Society must be of good condition not to rough each other. If one of the Society offends you, you can go to the Magistrate, Royal or Judge to appeal, and they will decide you. ... If one of your Lords tells you a thing obey him. If you are not quite satisfied with what he says, you can talk with nicely, until he will have it right.'[48]

Particularly emphasised was fraternity: the ideology of the migrants' community was that of a gigantic kinship group. When proper behaviour was not observed, a general practice was to hold a court to decide the case. The Chikunda Club expelled one member in 1920 on the ground of his involvement in a stabbing incident, and he was forced to leave the town.[49]

The Northern Rhodesia Society was additionally a welfare society to meet the pecuniary and other mundane needs of members. As V. Moller showed in her sociological survey, thrift or pooling societies are more often developed by migrants than by townsmen.[50] As partly shown by the location superintendent's report quoted earlier, societies as a rule offered assistance, through the collection of membership fees, for those member workers in trouble. Benefits were offered when members fell sick, were stranded in town, or were arrested by the police for 'petty crimes', such as offences under the pass laws and the masters and servants laws. Thus, the Port Herald Society had a 'Doctor': 'The duty of "Doctor" is to visit all members daily, and if he finds any of them sick he is to see that such persons condition is brought to the notice of his employer, and if then he does not get proper treatment the Society obtains proper treatment for him with the consent of the employer'.[51]

No thrift function was of more importance than organising a funeral: death in a foreign land was the nightmare of the rural migrant. To allay these fears, the societies sought to socialise urban death in a proper manner. They bought coffins and on occasion hired motor cars, which were a real luxury for the workers in those days. Some societies were so preoccupied by this activity that they squandered funds on funerals to the point of bankruptcy: 'the cost of one or two funerals with motor cars in attendance', wrote the location superintendent in 1920, 'seems to have dampened this movement, and treasurers, etc. are frequently changed'.[52]

To stress the kinship- and ethnicity-centred nature of the migrants' world is not to suggest, of course, that such a world was the result of an automatic extension of a pre-migration culture. On the contrary, it involved an inter-actional process. People used, or created if necessary, cultural forms and social institutions in their efforts to adapt to new realities. This is evident, for example, in the fact that whilst at the functional level all the associations can be regarded as benevolent societies geared towards needs of workers, the styles, symbols, and rituals which they utilised for filling that function were exceedingly colourful and diverse. Many groups, like Beni-type socie-ties, adopted distinctly urban and modern styles, symbolised by a uniform, boots, hats, and combed hair,[53] whereas a few others stubbornly stuck to traditional/country styles. One of the most pre-eminent groups in the latter category was the Chinyao society. 'At the new, the full moon or other chosen time', members of that society secretly met in the bush near the Salisbury location. They would dance in 'grass skirts and masks' and in the effigies of 'elephant, ostrich, giraffe, zebra, buck or some other', depicting the birth of the universe, and the activities of hunting and agriculture.[54]

Such workers' sense of pragmatism can also be found in the manner in which they identified themselves, and with whom they associated. Migrants, while in town, showed a marked tendency to see themselves as members of a large social entity, much larger than that which traditional cultural patterns would engender. The Zambesi group claimed to be representative of the whole of Northern Rhodesia, and its second name was simply the Northern Rhodesia Association.[55] Likewise, other societies stood for large regional or territorial interests. Membership of the Port Herald Society was 'not restricted to any tribe'. And its extensive sphere of influence, with branches in Bulawayo, Umtali, Gatooma, Umsweswe, Gwelo, and Shamva, eloquently testifies to a new quality of coherence and an innovation of its organising principle.[56] The same can be said with the Mozambique Native Association. This society, headquartered in the Midlands, was 'not confined to Portuguese natives', and its operations extended 'to numerous mines', and to Bulawayo.[57]

Contemporaries expressed diametrically opposite views on the grass-roots mutual aid movement. To certain employers it represented a disguised form of trade unionism. The Secretary for the Rhodesia Chamber of Mines, for instance, informed the Chief Native Commissioner in 1922: 'It is now stated to be the basis of labour movements, strike committees paying the fines of natives convicted of crime with the option of a fine. Natives of all tribes... are beginning to join the movement.'[58] The location superintend-ent of Salisbury, however, held a different view. Noticing that the societies were exerting a considerable influence in moralising location residents, he came to view them as an agency of social control: 'up to the present [benefit societies] are doing more good than harm. Most of the officers chosen are quite intelligent and have frequently assisted the Location Police and myself in our work', he reported in 1921.[59]

In the same sort of way, but at the other end of the spectrum, African public opinion later on was divided over the subject. In some instances, the narrow horizons of unity as well as the inward-looking nature of the ethnic enclaves were frowned upon, or openly condemned. Such criticism was not totally unfounded, to be sure. Occasionally ethnic enclaves clashed violently when quarrelling parties failed to find a peaceful means to solve problems of 'anti-social conduct', such as the seduction of a wife.[60]

In other instances, however, the benefit societies were remembered as the precursor of trade union movement. T. C. Shato Nyakauru (who started the African Waiters Association in Salisbury in 1941) recalls: 'Our association in those days was just like a burial society; we helped each other.' And we know that one of the major attractions of later trade unions was their burial and other mutual aid schemes.[61] Nor was this all. Some of the so-called tribal societies were to act for nationalist politics. By the 1930s the Northern Rhodesian community in Salisbury had a Northern Rhodesia Bantu Burial Society, with its membership chiefly drawn from the ranks of Bemba rather than from Tonga workers. One of the promoters of this movement, D. L. Yamba, was a teacher based in Salisbury, who was instrumental in initiating a Bantu Congress movement in central Africa. Members of the Congress were generally ardent supporters of nationalist politics.[62] No less political were the Nyasaland 'tribal' societies. The first public meeting of the Nyasaland African Congress, Salisbury Branch, held in the Harare township in 1946, was attended by the Achewa Society, the Angoni Society, the Mang'anja Society, the Msasa Welfare Association, and others.[63]

All these seemingly incongruous views and facts more or less mirrored the complexities and ambiguities of the migrant workers' world. They pointed to the fact that enclaves and associations were located at the inmost recesses of popular daily life. At such fundamental levels of life migrants could be found, at different times and different places, working, relaxing, helping each other, quarrelling, imitating, resisting, submitting, and protesting.

Conclusion

Running through the fabric of industrial life in Southern Rhodesia were the threads of a complex set of kinship- and ethnicity-centred communities which migrant workers made. Denied adequate services and protective regulations, migrant workers were forced to rely on their own resources. Separated from their rural homes, they sought security and survival through their own urban communities. Difficult times around the end of World War I seriously undermined and threatened the life goals of Africans employed in industrial areas and sparked new forms of popular response. One was the establishment of mutual aid societies. By forging formalised associations migrants pooled their financial resources for the common weal and strove to solidify a moral order within their communities.

While their character was considerably marked by the particular circumstances of the late 1910s and the early 1920s, the societies were, nevertheless, firmly embedded in an already well-established migrants' tradition. In other words, much of the ethos of the societies lay in an African worker-peasant culture – the values of 'patriotism', fraternity, reciprocity, obligation, thrift, seniority, and many others. Such a culture or values cannot simply be reduced to external stimuli alone.[64] So intense was the affinity of the mutual aid movement with a worker-peasants' culture that once the movement made its debut, it was easily imitated, quickly disseminated and, as time went on, developed in all sorts of ways.

A few African workers, however, also dared to try to impose a moral order upon the wider world. They bravely raised a voice of protest against 'unjust' wages and rations, 'unjust' work procedures, and 'unjust' prices of commodities, although the system wielded an almost absolute economic and disciplinary power over them. When industries felt a keen shortage of labour after the war, migrants became more inclined to act collectively at workplaces. Particularly after the Bulawayo railway workers had managed to make a break-through in July 1919, workers' consciousness rose to a new level. This manifested itself in a wave-like occurrence of industrial action at least from mid-1919 to early 1920. Strikers sought to negotiate with their employers by resorting to unusual tactics, including those peculiar to workers who were 'not fully proletarianised' or were subject to the repressive regime of the master and servant regulations – threats of going back home, demands to be discharged before completing work contracts, attempts to make the leadership anonymous, and the act of going to gaol together.

It is obvious that the directions of these two post-bellum phenomena, the mutual aid societies and the industrial protests, were far from contiguous. The thrust of the protests was characterised by determination, commitment, self-sacrifice, and a workplace/workmate-centred solidarity, whereas that of the societies nurtured a sense of pragmatism, an ability to adapt to realities, and a loyalty towards the culture of a homeland. Nonetheless, these two phenomena grew from one and the same root: a struggle to defend the integrity of the migrant workers' world. Indeed, these apparently very different themes unfolded side by side. They even converged at the municipal compound in Salisbury. The Zambesi workers, together with other workmates, shocked their employer by attempting a work stoppage in August 1919, and only a month later they officially registered their Northern Rhodesia Burial Society. This means that these men began to talk about industrial protest and mutual aid practically at the same time.

We now pick up the thread of discussion left off at the end of the previous chapter. It was noted there that migrant labour was markedly institutionalised in the early 1920s. A large number of Africans came to lead a life underscored by regular involvement in two different modes of production, i.e., the indigenous, peasant and the colonial, capitalist modes of production. Migrants thus formed, to quote Stichter's words, 'a class, in the minimal sense of occupying a definable place in the structure of production'.[65] It was then suggested that the beauties of this notion lie particularly in that it prompts us to look for distinctive class-related behaviour and consciousness of migrants.

Chapters 4 and 5 have proceeded to show that a dramatic intensification of group activities occurred amongst migrants in the post-World War I years – to defend or promote their interests at workplaces and in the broader spheres of their lives. If social class can be conceptualised as a category that is intrinsically variegated – as discussed in the Preface – this analysis of migrant workers must then most surely conclude that they emerged as a social class in this period.

Notes

[1] *Rhodesia Herald*, 25 July 1921. For the politics of South African Blacks in Southern Rhodesia, see also N/3/7/2, W. S. Taberer, Supt. of Natives, Salisbury, to C.N.C., 30 Mar. 1914; *Rhodesia Herald*, 6 Dec. 1922; correspondence in N/3/21/6; Ranger, *African Voice*, 88-109.

[2] R. R. Willcox, *Report on a Venereal Diseases Survey of the African in Southern Rhodesia* (Salisbury, 1949), 41.

[3] LG/52/6/1, Location Supt. to Town Clerk, 3 Mar. 1914; LG/47/44, Town Clerk, Salisbury, to Town Clerk, Umtali, 15 Feb. 1927; correspondence in S235/392.

[4] LG/52/6/2, Location Supt. to Town Clerk, 7 June 1920; *Rhodesia Herald*, 28 June 1920.

[5] See note 22 below.

[6] *Rhodesia Herald*, 14 July 1923.

[7] S1542/S12, 'A Study of Recreation for Urban Natives, with special reference to Boxing among Natives in Salisbury', in R. Howman, N.C., Salisbury, to Secr. for Native Affairs, 29 June 1939.

[8] *African Weekly*, 19 Oct. 1955.

[9] See correspondence in N/3/21/2 and S138/10.

[10] Location Supt.'s Report, in *Mayor's Minutes*, 1919-20.

[11] In addition to notes 8 and 9 above, see *Rhodesia Herald*, 12, 17, 27, 31 Jan. 1920; 28, 29 Aug. 1923; LG/52/6/2, Location Supt. to Town Clerk, 31 Dec. 1920; correspondence and reports in S715/1; D/3/5/78, case 3281 of 1927.

[12] S7/15/1, R. Moorhead, Detective Sgt, to A.D.S., C.I.D., Salisbury, 1 July 1917.

[13] By 1922 the superintendent had expelled the Chinyao society from the location following their fights with non-members: LG/52/6/3, Location Supt. to Town Clerk, 30 May 1922.

[14] This paragraph is based on D/3/5/49, case 2624 of 1919.

[15] LG/47/29, Town Clerk to C.N.C., Salisbury, 6 Nov. 1918; *ibid.*, Town Clerk to Medical Dir., 9 Nov. 1918.

[16] *Rhodesia Herald*, 25 Oct, 1918.

[17] *Bulawayo Chronicle*, 25 Oct. 1918.

[18] Perhaps the most comprehensive and detailed examination of Beni history is T. O. Ranger, *Dance and Society in Eastern Africa 1890-1970* (London, 1975). For a sociological analysis of Beni-Kalela dance on the Copperbelt, see J. C. Mitchell, *The Kalela Dance* (Manchester, 1956).

[19] A/8/1/7, Civil Comm.'s Report, Salisbury, for 1917.

[20] *Rhodesia* Herald, 25 May 1918 and 8 Jan. 1919. For African war experience, see P.

McLaughlin, 'Collaborators, Mercenaries or Patriots? The "Problems" of African Soldiers in Southern Rhodesia during the First and Second World Wars' (Univ. of Rhodesia, Hist. Dep., Henderson Seminar Paper No. 47, 1979).

21 N/3/20/3, H. J. Taylor, C.N.C., to Staff Officer, Salisbury, 27 Jan. 1922.
22 *Rhodesia Herald*, 12 Jan. 1920.
23 N/3/21/4, Secr., Rhodesia Chamber of Mines, to H. J. Taylor, C.N.C., 7 Aug. 1922.
24 See correspondence in S138/10
25 D/3/5/78, case 3281 of 1927.
26 *Bantu Mirror*, 5 June 1937.
27 D. Mwanza's story collected by M. G. Marwich, in Heisler, *Government of Migration*, 147.
28 *Ibid.* 148.
29 *Rhodesia Herald*, 27 Aug. 1910.
30 AOH/47, H. Dzvairo, Interview by D. Munjeri, 30 Jan. 1979. Schwab's survey in the 1950s revealed that 'over 50 per cent of the men came to work in Gwelo because a kinsman was already there': W. B. Schwab, 'Social stratification in Gwelo', in A. Southall (ed.), *Social Change in Modern Africa* (London, 1961), 130. See also A.P. Cheater, *The Politics of Factory Organisation: A Case Study in Independent Zimbabwe* (Gweru, 1986), 43-9.
31 AOH/56, P.G. Pazarangu, Interview by D. Munjeri, 24, 29, May, 12 June 1979.
32 *Ibid.*
33 *Ibid.*
34 According to Mwanza's story (in Heisler, *Government of Migration*, 148-9): 'We slept the night on the way, but in the bush. Next morning we reached the farm of a European where we found many Tumbuka people. We asked them about the character of their European [master]. They gave a good account of him; and we went to ask him for employment. He took us on civilly, and immediately gave us maize-meal. He told us to go and build ourselves huts.'
35 LG/47/19, Town Clerk to Secr., Adm.'s Dep., 7 Sept. 1911.
36 LG/38, I. Smith to Sub-Insp., S. R. Constabulary, Salisbury, 18 July 1909.
37 LG/38, M. Thompson to Town Clerk, 16 Oct. 1912.
38 *Rhodesia Herald*, 1 May 1906.
39 LG/38, Rev. W. Adshade to Town Clerk, 18 Oct. 1910; LG/47/18, Town Clerk to Rev. Adshade, 28 Oct. 1910. See also H. M. L. du Toit, 'The Church of Central Africa-Presbyterian', in P. S. King (comp.), *Missions in Southern Rhodesia* (n.p., [1959]), 70.
40 *Zambesi Mission Record*, IV (1910-13), 554.
41 My interview with Rev. S. Machingura (c. 1907-1985), Mbare, Harare, 29 Mar. 1983.
42 My analysis here is much inspired by the works of a group of American labour historians who have systematically examined such clustering in industrial America: for example, Stephan Thernstrom, *The Other Bostonians: Poverty and Progress in the American Metropolis, 1880-1970* (Cambridge, Mass., 1973).
43 In some cases employers' preference was the major determinant in creating occupational clusters: for example, many of the African members of the B.S.A. police were Angoni and Yaos, especially Muslim ones, because the colonial government deliberately recruited complete outsiders for the police force, which was in fact a semi-military organisation.
44 My analysis of the Salisbury householders' returns of the 1911 census (C/5/2/12-16).
45 Ranger, *Dance and Society*, 136.
46 All the quotations in this paragraph are from *Rhodesia Herald*, 12 Jan. 1920.
47 *Ibid.*
48 S138/10, Memo., 'The Condition of Salisbury Association' by Governor Antonio, 10 Dec. 1923.
49 LG/52/6/2, Location Supt. to Town Clerk, 31 Dec. 1920. Of the arbitration functions of postwar societies, see also N/3/23/2, F. Stephens, Major, Chief Comm. of Police, Zomba, [to C.N.C.?], 27 July 1921.
50 V. Moller, *Urban Commitment and Involvement among Black Rhodesians* (Durban, 1978), 275-6.
51 S138/10, Asst. N.C., Shamva, to N.C., Mazoe, 2 Jan. 1924; quoted in Phimister, 'The

Shamva mine strike', 83.
52 Location Supt.'s Report, in *Mayor's Minutes*, 1919-20.
53 Mitchell noted that one 'modernist' dance society reaffirmed and upheld the 'traditional' culture of their homelands in their dance performance: Mitchell, *The Kalela Dance*, 8.
54 *Rhodesia Herald*, 7 Feb. 1928: S715/1, Statement by T.A Wright, 20 Sept. 1926. However, even this rigorously traditional group had undergone important changes when transplanted in town. Originally Chinyao performed two major functions, viz. conducting initiation and funeral rites, in a rural society. But for obvious reasons, according to a Ngoni detective: 'There is no initiation ceremony in Salisbury'. And 'a native who joins has to pay money to the man who organises the first dance which he attends', which meant that Salisbury Chinyao was to all intents and purposes a voluntary association: S715/1, Statement by D. Saidi, 13 May 1926.
55 *Rhodesia Herald*, 12 Jan. 1920.
56 S138/10, Asst. N. C., Shamva, to N. C., Mazoe, 2 Jan. 1924.
57 N/3/21/4, Supt. of Natives, Gwelo, to C.N.C., 16 Aug. 1922.
58 *Ibid*. Secr., Rhodesia Chamber of Mines, to C.N.C., 7 Aug. 1922; quoted in Phimister, 'The Shamva mine strike', 81.
59 Location Supt. 's Report, in *Mayor's Minutes*, 1920-1.
60 For example, see a 'faction fight' between Chipeta and Angoni groups in 1922, which resulted in the death of a worker: D/3/5/57, cases 1398, 1596 of 1922; LG/52/6/4, Location Supt. to Town Clerk, 30 May 1922.
61 My interview with T. C. Shato Nyakauru, Mbare, Harare, 18 Apr. 1985; R. Riddell, 'The Salisbury Municipal Workers' Union: A case study', *Rhodesian Journal of Economics*, VII (1973), 1, 27-9.
62 *Bantu Mirror*, 15 Apr. 1939; My interview with S. Chidyamatamba, Highfield, Harare, 13 June 1985.
63 *African Weekly*, 23 Oct. 1946.
64 Here I am paraphrasing, of course, E. P. Thompson's argument: Thompson, 'The moral economy of the English crowd in the eighteenth century', *Past and Present*, 50 (Feb. 1971), 76-136.
65 Stichter, *Migrant Laborers*, 191.

Figures

Figure 1 – European population by birthplace, Salisbury, 1897, 1911

	1897			1911		
	Male	Female	Total	Male	Female	Total
Africa						
S. Rhodesia	4	7	11	155	142	
South Africa	94	65	169	442	343	
Other	3	5	8	32	69	
Sub-Total	111	77	188 (26%)	629	554	1183 (34%)
UK	375	39	414 (58%)	1167	449	1616 (46%)
European Continent						
Aust. Hungary	23	3				
Germany	13	9	22 47	60		
Russia	9	1	10 64	24		
Poland				10	5	
Italy				19	4	
Greece				108	8	
Other	17	1	18	65	18	
Sub-Total	39	11	50 (7%)	336	122	458 (13%)
Asia	11	1	12 (2%)	52	14	66 (2%)
America	13	2	15 (2%)	41	16	57 (2%)
Oceania	21	1	22 (3%)	65	26	91 (3%)
Other/Unspec.	15	3	18 (2%)	6	2	8
Total	585	134	719 (100%)	2296	1183	3479 (100%)

Many of the UK-born immigrants were formerly South African residents.

Source: B. A. Kosmin, 'On the Imperial frontier', Rhodesian History (1971) II, 29-30; C/5/7/2, 1911 Census, Birthplaces.

Figure 2 – Plan of Salisbury location, 1940

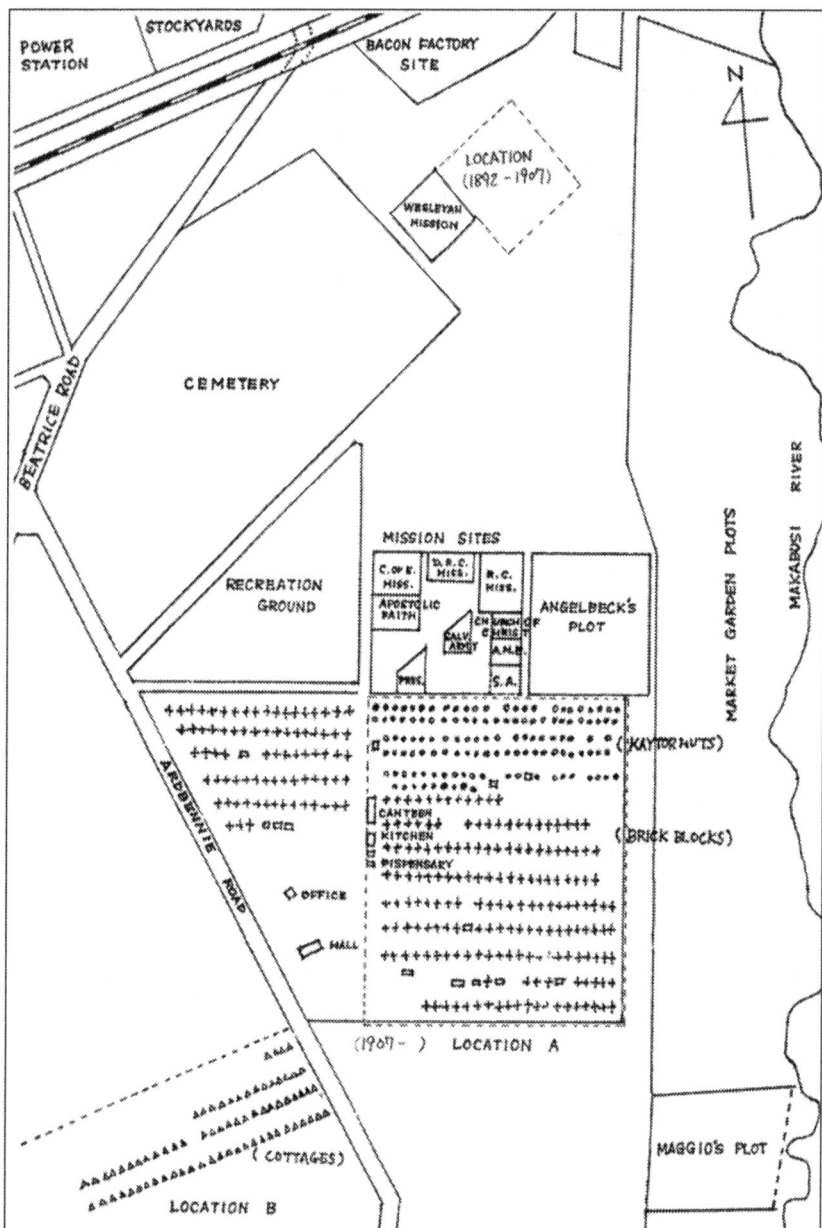

Figure 3 – Ratio of location population to total African population, Salisbury, 1904-1940

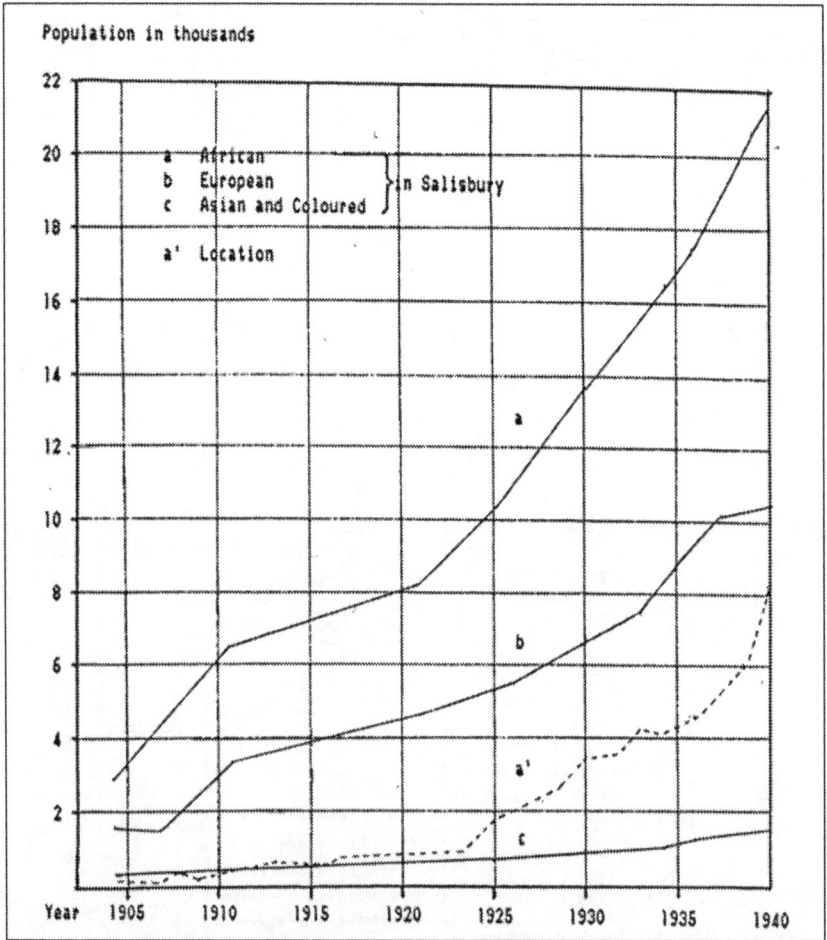

Source: *S.R., Reports of Census, 1904, 1907, 1926, 1936; C/5/7/1-3; Mayor's Minutes, 1904-5 to 1939-40; LG/52/6/1-4, Location Supt.'s reports; LG/47/21, Town Clerk to Medical Dir., 4 Sept. 1913.*

Figure 4 – Employer-rented housing units* in Salisbury

	No. of Employer-rented units (a)	Total no. of units in location (b)	a/b x 100(%)
July 1913	25	156	16
Feb 1916	39	180	22
Feb 1919	35	205	17
Aug 1920	35	247	14
Nov 1922	58	252	23
? 1939	357	1903	19
May 1942	687	2538	27

* Huts, rooms, and cottages.

Sources: LG/52/6/1, Ranger's Report for July 1913; Reilly to Town Clerk, 1 Mar. 1916; LG/52/12, Mason to Town Clerk, 28 Feb. 1919; LG/52/6/2, Mason to Town Clerk, 31 Aug. 1920; G/52/6/3, Mason to Town Clerk, 30 Nov. 1922; City of Harare, Town Clerk Department Files, 26/7/10R, F. 12/7, 6, Memo. by Stodart, [1939]; Ibid., 24/11/10R, F. 12/7/64, J. 1, M.O.H. to Mayor and Councillors, 14 May 1942.

Figure 5 – African population pyramids, Salisbury, 1911, 1969

A. *Salisbury township, 1911*

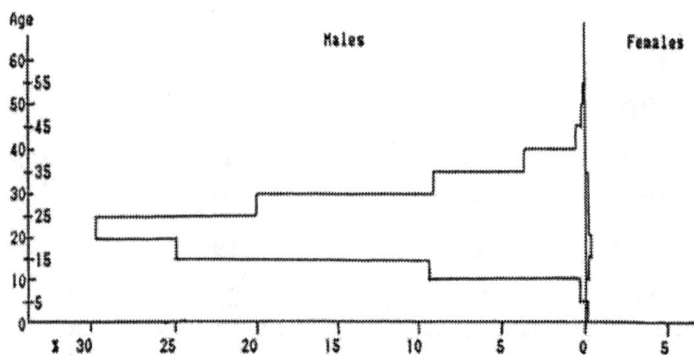

B. *Greater Salisbury, 1969*

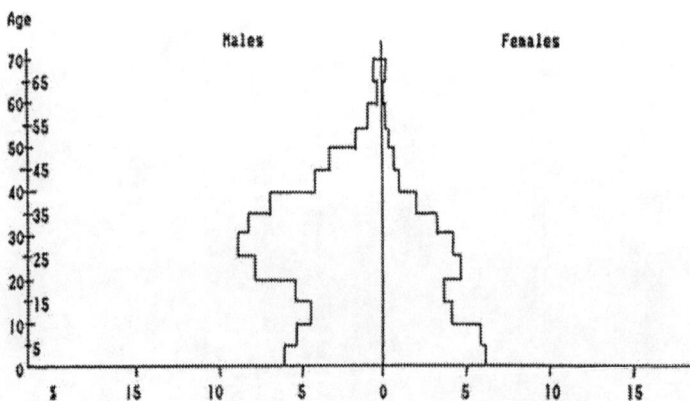

Figure 6 – Ethnic/regional composition of Africans, Salisbury, 1897, 1911

1897			1911			
Mashona	481		Mashona	1887		
Umtassa	89	46%	Rhodesia	36		
Victoria	7		S. Rhodesia	89	2052	50%
Matebele	75	6%	Matabele	40		
Blantyre	16	1%	Blantyre	355		
			Nyasa	247		
			B.C. Africa	54		
			Achewa	12		
			Yao	37		
			Angoni	342	1155	28%
			Tonga	8		
			Zambesi	55		
			N.E. Rhodesia	20		
			Awemba	9		
			Barotse	33		
			N.W. Rhodesia	1		
			N. Rhodesia	2		
Portuguese	335	26%	P.E. Africa	193		
Zambesi	121	9%	Chinde	32		
			Nyungwe	62		
			Sena	130	879	20%
			Manganja	6		
			Chikunda	121		
			Tete	217		
Shangaan	121	9%	Shangaan	109		
Cape Boy	41	3%	S. Africa	41	1%	
			Other	29	1%	
			Unspecified	66	-	
Total	284	100%	Total	4222*	100%	

* A sample from C/5/2/12-16.
The term 'Zambesi' in 1897 seems to have refrred to the Africans from the Tete region.

Sources: DS/1/1/4, Actg O.C. Mashonaland Police to Actg Magistrate, Salisbury, 12 Nov. 1987; C/5/2/12-16.

Figure 7 – Prosecutions under the Kaffir Beer Ordinance,
Salisbury and Bulawayo, 1912-36

	Salisbury			Bulawayo		
	male	female	total	male	female	total
1912	2	0	2	18	23	41
1919	21	11	32	15	15	30
1921	72	49	121	30	9	39
1922	43	38	81	53	21	74
1923	32	20	52	62	44	106
1924	61	43	104	65	18	83
1925	71	24	95	158	15	173
1926	55	37	92	82	31	113
1927	35	39	74	101	23	124
1929	54	27	81	115	19	134
1930	60	33	93	317	22	339
1931	49	21	70	167	36	203
1932	42	20	62	143	28	171
1933	34	16	50	127	51	178
1934	24	11	35	114	72	186
1935	13	20	33	115	65	180
1936	41	13	54	167	66	233

In Salisbury, beer regulations were most rigorously enforced in the early 1920s, and in Bulawayo from the mid-1920s to the early 1930s.

Source: J/5/1/1-8, Dep. of Justice, Form No. 1, Criminal Cases, 1912-36.

Figure 8 – Annual profits of canteen, Salisbury location, 1913-1930

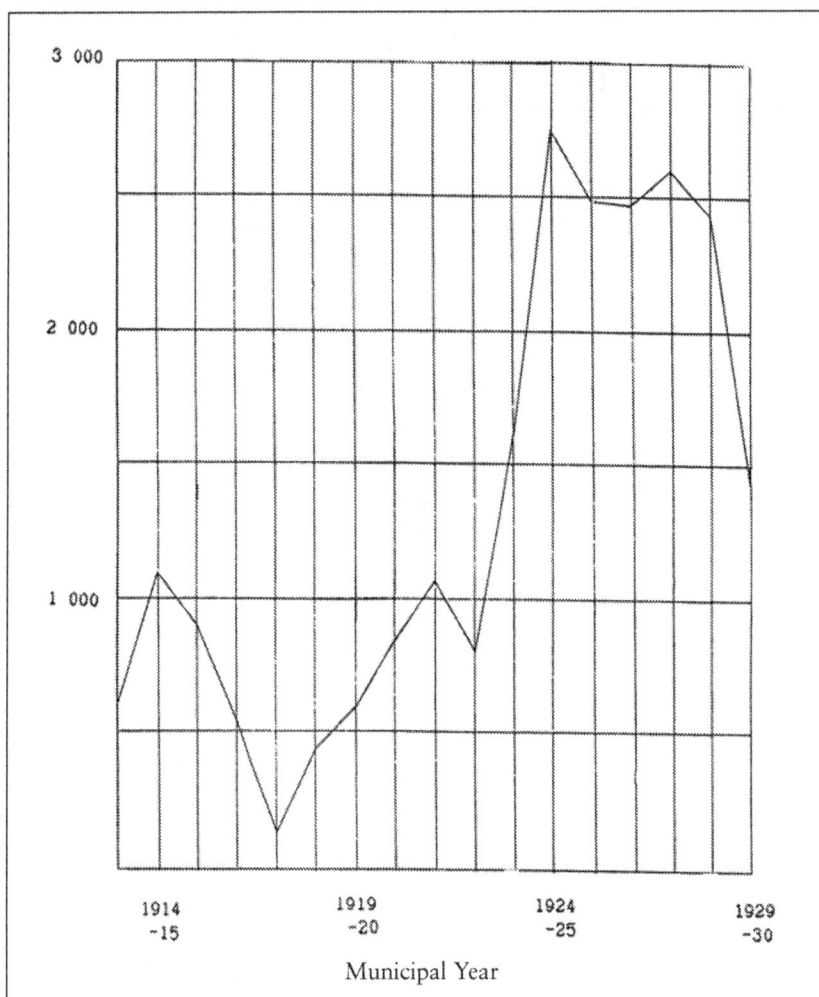

The consolidation of the municipal beer monopoly in the early 1920s contributed to the use of *'hop beer'* and, after the Great Depression, the use oif *'skokiaan'*.

Source: Revenue and Expenditure Accounts (General), in Mayor's minutes, 1913-15 to 1929-30: S85, Annexure E.

Figure 9 – Men, women and children in Salisbury location, 1914-47

Year	Men (M)	Women (W)	Children Male	Children Female	Total*	Ratio M/W	Ratio C/W
1914	420			60	480		
1920					763		
1924	888	282		250	1420	3.1	0.9
1925	1065	352	191	130	1738	3.0	0.9
1926	1200	370	140	160	1870	3.2	0.8
1927	1470	454	135	116	2175	3.2	0.6
1928	1633	471	204	168	2475	3.5	0.8
1929	2174	651	203	204	3232	3.3	0.6
1930	2352	679	233	224	3488	3.5	0.7
1931	2371	691		478	3540	3.4	0.7
1932	2380	700		480	3560	3.4	0.7
1933	2766	803		720	4289	3.4	0.9
1934	2578	806		748	4132	3.2	0.9
1935	2692		1672	4364			
1936	2900	800		875	4575	3.6	1.1
1937					5600		
1938					6200		
1939					7150		
1940					8130		
1943	6000	1500		2500	10000	4.0	1.7
1945	7571	2276		3520	13367	3.0	1.5
1947	8392	2535		4579	15511	3.3	1.8

*The 'floating' people, numbering about 500 in the 1920s, are not included.

Sources: LG/52/6/1, Reilly to Town Clerk, 3 Mar. 1914; LG/52/6/2, Mason to Town Clerk, 30 June 1920; City of Harare, Town Clerk's Dep. Files, 28.10.6R, 1/9/, J. 1, Location Supt.'s Report for May 1924; ibid, 26.7.9F, 12/7, J.4, Report by A. Wilkins, 7 Mar. 1935; Mayor's Minutes, 1924-5 to 1946-7; Rhod. Her., 12 Nov. 1943.

Figure 10 – Sketch of Salisbury location, by superintendent, 1920

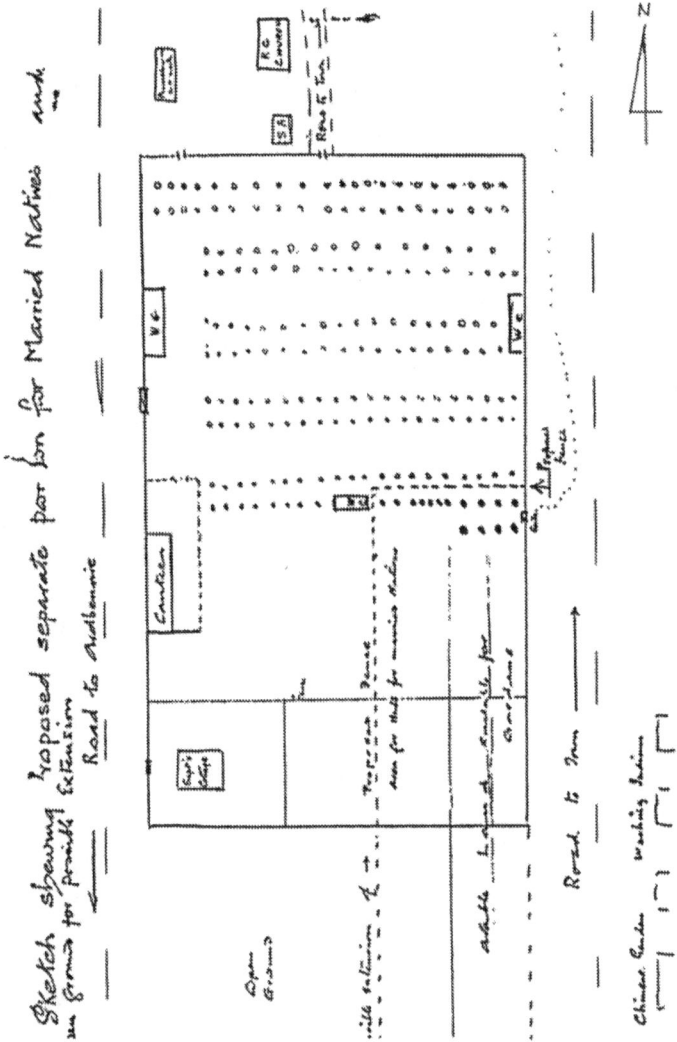

Lines of Kaytor huts (Matank), the canteen (beer hall), three communal latrines, and barbed-wire entanglements dominated the location's landscape in 1920. The European superintendent lived in the cottage at the south-western corner of the premises. The road west of the canteen is the present Chaminuka Street. There were Chinese market gardens and Indian laundries to the east, near the Mukuvisi river.

Source: LG/52/6/2, Mason to Town Clerk, 31 Aug. 1920.

Figure 11 – Ethnic/regional composition of Africans in Salisbury and Bulawayo, 1921

	SALISBURY			BULAWAYO (TOWN)		
	Male	Female	Total	Male	Female	Total
S. Rhodesia	95	10	105	86	22	108
Mashona	1577	170	1747	332	23	355
Matabele	52	50	102	1735	488	2223
Bakorekore	263	9	272	12	-	12
Manyika	390	13	403	130	1	131
Bazezuru	277	17	294	18	-	18
Babudya	101	-	101	1	-	1
Bahera	7	-	7	-	-	-
Vahungwe	178	3	211	54	-	54
Banjanja	20	1	21	3	-	3
Shangaan	12	1	13	9	1	10
Karanga	25	-	25	1048	27	1075
Basuto	22	16	38	211	28	239
Banyai	4	-	4	161	1	162
Batonka	3	-	3	249	1	250
Zansi	-	-	-	22	-	22
Enhla	-	-	-	13	-	13
Unspecified	-	-	-	27	-	27
Subtotal	3026	320	3346 (41%)	4111	592	4703 (50%)
Nyasa	3179	40	3219 (40%)	781	27	808 (9%)
P. E. Africa	1022	127	1149 (14%)	702	28	730 (8%)
N. Rhodesia	355	11	366 (4%)	2601	67	2668 (29%)
S. Africa	27	25	52	189	151	340
Kenya/Tanganyika	6	1	7	21	-	21
Other	-	-	-	11	2	13
Total	7615	524	8139 (100%)	8416	867	9283 (100%)

Source: C/6/4/5, Tables re. Salisbury and Bulawayo.

Figure 12 – Population in Salisbury location, 1930

	Birthplace	Male	Female	Total	%
Adults	Southern Rhodesia	1024	426	1450	(48)
	Nyasaland	750	72	822	(27)
	Northern Rhodesia	146	58	204	(7)
	Portuguese Territory	432	119	551	(18)
	Union of S. Africa	–	4	4	
Sub-total (100)		2352	679	3031	
Children	School-going	79	68	147	
	Under school age	154	156	310	
Total		2585	903	3488	

Source: Location Supt.'s Report, in Mayor's Minutes, 1929-30.

Figure 13 – Major private locations outside Salisbury commonage, 1914-29

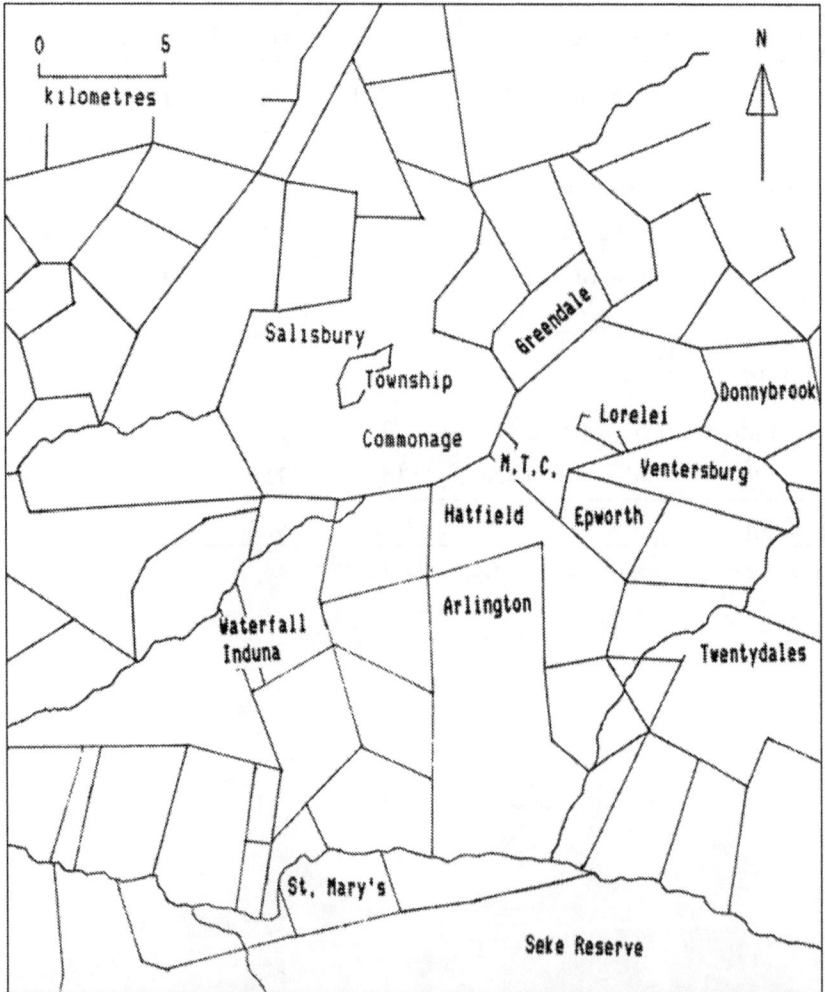

Greendale: 11 tenants, 1914; 21 huts or rooms, 1915; 29 tenants, 1918. Lorelei (Williams's farm): 9 tenants, 1914; 39 huts or rooms, 1915; 39 tenants, 1924. M.T.C.: 77 huts or rooms, 1915. Hatfield: 51 huts or rooms, 1915. Arlington: 69 tenants, 1918. Ventersburg: 10 tenants, 1917. Epworth: About 50 tenants employed in town, 1920. St. Mary's: c. 25 tenants employed in town, 1925. Waterfall Induna: 2 tenants, 1913, 14 tenants, 1925. Twentydales: 26 tenants, 1929. Donnybrook: 14 tenants, 1929.

Source: LG/52/6/1, Ranger to Town Clerk, 17 May 1915; N/5/1/4, N/5/1/12-16, S235/447-449, Private location agreements; Rhod. Her., 28 June 1920; S96, Memo. by W.G. Webster, Evidence by F. Sixubu.

Figure 14 – Rental structure of Salisbury location, 1930

	Kaytor hut	Brick room	Cottage
	12 ft in diameter	Room (12 ft x12 ft) & outside kitchenette (6 ft x 6 ft)	2 rooms (2x 12 ft x 12 ft) (10 ft x 6 ft)
Original Building Cost	£12	£54	£130
Monthly Rent	10s.	12s.	15s.
Annual Return	50%	13%	7%

'*Witnesses both European and Native were unanimous in pointing out the extreme disparity between this rent [of cottages] and that of the Kaytor huts. ... The poorest type of dwelling tends naturally to be occupied by the poorest tenant, which implies that the tenants in the Kaytor huts are helping to bear the burden' (S86, Report by Native Affairs Comm. of 1930, 22).*

Source: *S86, Report on Native Affairs Comm. of 1930, 11, 21.*

Figure 15 – African industrial protest (and criminal cases of 'refusing to obey'), November 1918 to December 1921

	TOWNS (AND MAGISTERIAL DISTRICTS)						MINES
	Bulawayo	Gwelo	Que Que	Gatooma	Salisbury	Umtali	
1918							Nov. Strike Globe & Phoenix
1919	(Mar. 4 Accused)						Mar. Strike Sanitary Workers Wankie
				(May 3 Accused)	(May 3 Accused) (June 3 Accused)		
	July Strike Railway			July Strike Railway 13 Arrests 13 Arrests			(July 5 Accused)
					(Aug. 3 Accused)	Aug. Strike Municipal 13 Arrests (Oct. 11 Accused) (Oct. 3 Accused)	
	? Strike Municipal ? (Dec. 4 Accused)	(Nov. 3 Accused) Dec. Unrest Municipal			(Nov. 3 Accused) Dec. Strike Municipal 11 Arrests (Dec. 3 Accused) (Dec. 15 Accused)		Dec. Strike Municipal 34 Arrests
1920	(Jan. 12 Accused)						Jan. Unrest Bushtick Jan. Store Boycott Shamva
		(Mar. 5 Accused) (Mar. 4 Accused)					
	(Apr. 3 Accused) (May. 13 Accused)						
			(June 3 Accused)		(June 3 Accused)	(June 6 Accused)	
		(Aug. 22 Accused) (Sep. 3 Accused)					
					(Oct. 3 Accused) (Oct. 3 Accused)		
			(Dec. 3 Accused)		(Dec. 12 Accused)		

	TOWNS (AND MAGISTERIAL DISTRICTS)						MINES
	Bulawayo	Gwelo	Que Que	Gatooma	Salisbury	Umtali	
1921	Jan. Strike Municipal 103 Arrests (Feb. 5 Accused)				Feb. Strike Ricksha Pullers (Mar. 3 Accused) (Mar. 3 Accused)		
			(Apr. 7 Accused)	(Apr. 8 Accused)	(Apr. 3 Accused)		
	(May 3 Accused) (June 4 Accused) (July 4 Accused) (July 3 Accused) (Aug. 3 Accused) (Sep. 3 Accused)				(Sep. 3 Accused)		Sep. Strike Wankie
		(Nov. 10 Accused)		(Nov. 6 Accused)			
			(Dec. 5 Accused)	(Dec. 11 Accused)	(Dec. 7 Accused)		

(1) The cases of 'refusing to obey' – the contravention of (6), 1, Chap. IV, the Masters and Servants Ordinance (No. 5 of 1901) as amended – as indicated by ( ), are taken from criminal registers, when more than three persons were brought up at the magistrate's court at one time. They are arranged according to magisterial districts. Thus, not all the prisoners shown under magisterial districts were the persons employed in towns. For example, the five accused at the Bulawayo district court in February 1921 and the fifteen at the Gatooma court in December 1919 were farm labourers and woodcutters respectively.

(2) The precise date of the Bulawayo municipal strike that took place after the railway strike of July 1919 is not known. The incident could be the one shown as the case of December 1919 or the case of January 1920 in the above list.

Source: (1) Bul. Chron., 15, 16, 17 and 18 July, 1 and 8 Aug., 5 Dec. 1919; 29 Jan. 1921. Rhod. Her., 16 July, 7 Aug. and 5 Dec. 1919; 4 Feb. 1921. Rhodesia Advertiser, 2 and 8 Dec. 1919. Gwelo Times, 5 Dec. 1919.

(2) D/4/1/34, case 3796, 1919; case 257, 1920; D/4/1/35, cases 1217-19, 1487-99, 1920; D/4/1/39, cases 229-331, 630-4, 1921; D/4/1/40, cases 1484-6, 2034-5, 2034-5, 2065-8, 2096-8, 2152-4, 2725-7, 1921; D/4/20/8, cases 168-71, 633-5, 1919; D/4/20/9, cases 158-62, 187-90, 483-504, 585-7, 1920; D/4/230/7, cases 809-13, 1921; D/4/17/7, cases 552-4, 656-8, 1919;d/4/17/8, cases 955-7, 975-86, 1016-18, 1033-47, 1919; cases 702-4, 743-5, 1920; D/4/17/9, cases 333-40, 967-72, 1112-22, 1921; D/4/7/23, cases 1097-9, 1919; D/4/7/24, cases 1601-13, 1985-95, 2169-71, 1919; D/4/7/24, cases 1601-13, 1985-95, 2169-71, 1919; D/4/7/26, cases 1498-1500, 1920; D/4/7/28, cases 3125-36, 1920; cases 763-5, 795-7, 1048-50, 2194-6, 3268-74, 1921; D/4/3/12, cases 677, 1137, 1919, case 546A, 1920.

(3) N/9/1/22, Annual Report of N.C., Bulawayo for 1919.

(4) Phimister, 'The Shamva mine strike of 1927', Rhod. Hist., II (1971), 67-8; van Onselen, Chibaro, 222-3.

Figure 16 – African Christians* by ethnicity, Salisbury, 1911

	Angl	Wesl	Cath	Lms	Amec	Sa	Pres	Drc
Mashona	220	86	39	6	3	8	7	
Umtali, Manyika	27	2	8	1	3			
Maungwe, Makoni	5		1		1			
Marandellas	2	6						
Mrewa, Mtoko	2	1		2				
Makorekore, Lomagundi	19	1						
Mazezuru	6							
Seke, Chiremba	2	2						
Goromonzi	2							
Chilimanzi	1							
Melsetter	1							
Matabele	4	6	1	2				
S. Rhodesia, Rhodesia	13	5	1		1			
Atonga, Kotakota	1	1					7	
Bandawe							3	
Nyasa	4	5	1	1			26	3
British Central Africa	1		1				20	18
Blantyre, Port Herald	20	6	1	3			39	6
Yao	3						12	
Angoni	19	7	2				34	27
Awemba	3	3					3	
N.E. Rhodesia			1	1				
Zambesi		5						
Shangaan	7	2	1				1	
Chikunda	5	2	14				1	
Nyungwe	6	1	5			1		
Tete	8	3	6				1	
Sena	8	2	7				1	
Portuguese East Africa	11	3	2				3	3
Chinde	1	5					1	
South Africa	7	6	2		1		6	4
Other, Unspecified	12		3					
Total	420	158	99	15	9	9	165	61
%	45	17	10	2	1	1	18	6

Angl: Anglican, Wesl: Wesleyan, Cath: Catholic, LMS: London Missionary, AMEC: American Methodist, SA: Salvation Army, Pres: Presbyterian, DRC: Dutch Reformed.

*A 'sample survey' based on the Salisbury householders' returns of the 1911 census.

Source: C/5/2/12-16, 1911 Census.

Figure 17 – Salisbury population by race, 1897-1969

	European	Asian	Coloured	African	Total	Ratio of Eur. to Afr.
1897	719	49	3	1284	2055	1:1.8
1901	1395	89	91	n.a	n.a	n.a
1904	1726		260	2823	4809	1:1.6
1907	1684	n.a		n.a	n.a	n.a
1911	3479	165	174	6400	10218	1:1.8
1921	4579	246	253	8143	13221	1:1.8
1926	7324	326	337	(12096)	20083*	n.a
1931	9619	450	413	(15112)	25594*	n.a
1934	8039	599	384	16526	25548	1:2.1
1936	1386		1273	22126	34785	1:1.9
1941	14630	734	810	28119	44293	1:1.9
1946	15475		1680	44592	61747	1:2.9
1948	19000		1980	53962	74942	1:2.8
1956	34740		3140	91560	129440	1:2.6
1961-2	88710	2580	3260	215810	310360	1:2.4
1969	96764	4055	5136	280090	386045	1:2.9

* *Including suburbs*   *() Africans in employment*

Source: S.R, Reports of Census, 1901, 1907, 1961, 1962, 1969; S.R., Official Year Books, No. 2, No. 3; Salisbury Mayor's Minuets, 1929-30, 1933-4, 1935-6, 1943-4, 1945-6, 1947-8, 1955-6; C/3/2/7, 1904; C/5/11/1, 1911; C/6/4/1, 1921; Kosmin, 'On the Imperial Frontier', Rhod. Hist., II (1971), 25-37.

Figure 18 – African population by nationality, Salisbury, 1911-1969

	1911	1921	1931	1936	1941	1946	1951	1962	1969
Southern Rhodesia	2052 (49%)	3346 (41%)	6406 (49%)	9550 (55%)	12935 (49%)	15810 (44%)	30958 (41%)	154870 (72%)	231980 (83%)
Nyasaland		3219 (40%)	4637 (36%)	5406 (31%)	7665 (29%)	9509 (26%)	16399 (22%)	41530 (19%)	28830 (10%)
Northern Rhodesia	1155 (28%)	366 (4%)	791 (6%)	774 (4%)	935 (4%)	1355 (4%)	2339 (3%)	4800 (2%)	2770 (1%)
Portuguese East Africa	879 (21%)	1149 (14%)	1008 (8%)	1612 (9%)	4665 (18%)	9486 (26%)	25367 (34%)	13350 (6%)	13460 (5%)
South Africa & Others	70 (2%)	59 (1%)	161 (1%)	119 (1%)	161	198	425	1260 (1%)	1870 (1%)
Unspecified	66								1180
Total	4222(a) (100%)	8139 (100%)	13003(b) (100%)	17461(b) (100%)	26361(b) (100%)	36358(b) (100%)	75488(c) (100%)	215810 (100%)	280090 (100%)

(a) A sample from C/5/2/12-16
(b) African males in employment
(c) Africans in employment

Source: C/5/2/12-16, 1911; C/6/4/5, Tables re Salisbury, 1921; S.R., Reports of Census, 1931, 1936, 1941, 1946, 1962, 1969; Salisbury Mayor's Minute, 1946-7.

Figure 19 – African employees by occupation, Salisbury, 1904, 1911

1904			1911	
	M	F		
Persons engaged in			Domestic Servants	1667
Domestic duties	1569	19	General Servants	203
General Labourers	278	-	Labourers	326
Persons engaged in			'Store Boys'	401
Banks, Offices, Shops,			'Office Boys'	42
Stores, etc.	248	-	Messengers	42
BSA Police, Constables,			Police	101
Goal Warders	71	-	Gaol Warders	13
			'Post Office Boys'	8
			Labourers at Public	
			Gardens	13
			Drivers	81
			'Stable Boys'	117
Persons engaged in			Ricksha-Pullers	112
Railways	106	-	Railway Labourers	222
			'Railway Goods	
Persons working for			Delivery Boys'	64
Carpenters, Brick-layers,			Employees at	
Blacksmiths,			Builders'	246
Builders, etc.	75	-	Timberyards	63
			Brickyards	35
			Hotels	165
Farm & Market Garden			Restaurants, etc.	51
Labourers	132	-	Printer's	11
			Mills	55
			Tobacco Warehouses	50
			Brewery	38
			Cold Storage	26
			'Mine Boys'	11
			'Farm Boys'	54
			Carpenter	1
			Teachers	2
Unspecified	17	-	Unspecified	6
Total	2496	19	Total	4226*

*A sample from C/5/12-16

Source: C/3/2/5, [18]; C/5/2/12-16.

Figure 20 – African employees by industrial sector,
Salisbury and its suburbs, 1936-69

	1936	1941	1946	1951	1969
Domestic Service	6365 (32%)	10370 (33%)	14324 (32%)	19653 (26%)	43304 (31%)
Commerce, Finance & Services	4065 (21%)	9529 (30%)	13401 (30%)	16029 (21%)	37450 (27%)
Manufacturing (15%)	3058 (15%)	4779 (19%)	8596 (25%)	19039 (24%)	32747
Construction (10%)	1924 (9%)	2802 (7%)	3165 (18%)	13451 (9%)	12668
Transport & Communications	1603 (8%)	1458 (5%)	2241 (5%)	3448 (5%)	5542 (4%)
Electricity & Water	300 (1%)	680 (2%)	218 (2%)	1400 (1%)	1593
Agriculture	1871 (9%)	1482 (5%)	2467 (5%)	1473 (2%)	4091 (1%)
Mining & Quarrying	348 (2%)	366 (1%)	321 (1%)	995 (1%)	957 (1%)
Other	476 (2%)	192	283 (1%)		
Total (100%)	20010* (100%)	31658* (100%)	45016* (100%)	75488 (100%)	138352

*African male employees

Source: S.R., Reports of Census, 1936, 1941, 1946, 1951, 1969.

www.ingramcontent.com/pod-product-compliance
Lightning Source LLC
Chambersburg PA
CBHW021819270326
41932CB00007B/253